THE PROJECT COOL® GUIDE TO ENHANCING YOUR WEBSITE

TERESA A. MARTIN *and* GLENN DAVIS

WILEY COMPUTER PUBLISHING

John Wiley Sons, Inc.

New York • Chichester • Weinheim • Brisbane • Singapore • Toronto

Publisher: Robert Ipsen
Editor: Cary Sullivan
Assistant Editor: Pam Sobotka
Managing Editor: Erin Singletary
Electronic Products, Associate Editor: Mike Sosa
Text Design & Composition: Ampersand Graphics

This book is printed on acid-free paper. ♾

Published by John Wiley & Sons, Inc.
Published simultaneously in Canada.

Library of Congress Cataloging in Publication Data:

Martin, Teresa A., 1961–
The project cool guide to enhancing your website / Teresa A. Martin, Glenn Davis.
p. cm.
ISBN 0-471-19457-3 (alk. paper)
1. Web sites—Design. I. Davis, Glenn, 1961– . II. Title.
TK5105.888.M365 1997
006.7'776—dc21 97-31836
CIP

Printed in the United States of America

10 9 8 7 6 5 4 3 2 1

CONTENTS

DEDICATION

Around the time I really needed to be delivering chapter drafts, a small but persistent being decided to make her presence felt. Through the magic of hormone power and few sharp kicks to the ribs (not to mention various other internal organs—ow!) my daughter Allegra Elizabeth kept me acutely awake —and in front of my computer —through many a working night. So to Allie, my love, thanks (¿) for keeping me awake, alert, and watching the sun rise.

—-Teresa A. Martin

ACKNOWLEDGMENTS

No book is ever written by an author (or even authors) in a vacuum. This book is no exception. We'd like the thank all the people who offered input on its contents, a patient smile as the writing process moved forward, and the occasional (sometimes painful) jab of web reality.

We'd especially like to thank programmer/artist Frances Killam for sharing her multi-media knowledge, and Lyn Bishop for her thoughts on animated GIFs and her wonderful "walking bears" example. A round of applause should also go to editor Pam Sobotka, whose patience finally helped deliver a complete manuscript.

Of course, there's always a special thanks to the staff at Project Cool and to Project Cool's readers—all of whom help to keep us honest and reminded that the web is really about people, their ideas, and a changing medium that keeps us all on our toes.

FOREWORD

Who would web developers have been before the web?

Architects? Auditors? Artists?. . . Run through the alphabet of careers, and you'll find a lot of hints but no exact matches.

In the newspaper industry where I hung out for 45 years they would have been editors or printers or photographers or ham radio column writers or designers or those early data-processing systems experts.

The process of putting pages together in a newspaper prior to 1960—and later for some newspapers—might best be described as scattershot. The uncharitable might call it scatterbrained. In hindsight, it was one of the primitive precursors to web-page publishing.

What's mind-boggling today is that anyone with basic intelligence and relatively inexpensive resources can become a publisher. And further bending the mind is the fact that the audience is worldwide. Television networks can't even make that claim.

No wonder web developers are in such demand today in just about every industry and every field of endeavor.

Indeed, we have only seen the beginning, because—as this book clearly demonstrates—the creative possibilities are bottomless, the tools are becoming more sophisticated and yet easier to use—and the need is there, be it on the internet, the intranet, extranet or whatever comes after; be it on watchbands or on marquees.

"People in other professions can bemoan corporate cutbacks," Claudia H. Deutsch wrote in the New York Times (Sept. 29, 1997). "But when it comes to people with technological skills, the supply never seems to approach demand."

Then, too, there are the amateurs, who develop web pages for the fun of it, or to test their talents, or to support a personal philosophy or a volunteer organization or a community of interest. They are the hobbyists, the activists, and the dreamers.

As someone whose home page was voted the world's ugliest by a group of computer-science students, I am nevertheless excited by the prospects, because the dimensions are so vast compared with the basic forms of publishing I have been exposed to all my life. It's more than multimedia, because it's interactive. It's one-on-one publishing. It's more than what appears on a web page, because there is so much rich description possible underneath what is seen on the surface. It's more than a new form of art, because the audience is an active player in the process. The "couch potato" syndrome is out—we're talking push and pull, we're talking hot, we're talking cool.

I don't want to be charged with being anti-couch potato. Hey, whatever works. Indeed, you could read this book while sunk in the cushions. But it won't be as intimate, it won't be as much fun and you won't learn as much if you don't have a laptop or PC nearby. The authors invite you to play by expounding on a technique, then prompting you to "TRY IT." Like right then and there.

This is an aside, but we haven't exhausted the possibilities of complementing book-reading yet. William J. Mitchell, Dean of the School of Architecture and Planning at MIT, wrote "City of Bits," which has a World Wide Web counterpart with hundreds of links to other sites, but more importantly the web version enables readers to jump into the text, add your own comments and read those of others, including Mitchell who weighs into the discussion himself pretty frequently. Call it an evolving debate, call it a living book . . . whatever.

TRY IT: http://mitpress.mit.edu/e-books/City_of_Bits/wjm_welcome.html

Back to the business at hand. In all candor, I am more than a fan of Glenn Davis and Teresa Martin (after all, they re-ran a story I wrote for their site seven times in this book!). They are proven summa cum laude web developers, but they also have stretched themselves to teach others through the vehicle of a website (http://www.projectcool.com) and through the publication of two guidebooks, this being the second in two years. They've done it with a whole lot of expertise and humor mixed in, as you soon will discover as you read on. I am convinced that the fact one of the authors was pregnant when this was written had something to do with some of examples, such as the oft-used "Eat at Joe's" or the line, "You might think of a web page as being a little like a pizza." When examples are cited, the text frequently is seasoned with food references.

I could tell you they started out in a garage, but the fact is that their beginnings were much more ostentatious in Palo Alto, the heart of Silicon Valley. OK, so you have to wander down a back alley to get to their office. And you have to climb some narrow, creaky stairs. And, sure, their digs are a couple of cubbyholes off a stairwell. But from that little bit of heaven they have become standard-setters for web development. In addition, their daily selections are made with thoughtful care. It's no accident that family-oriented sites often pop up on Saturdays or entertainment-oriented sites late in the week or that smut simply doesn't make it.

In a word, Davis and Martin have experienced the joys and agonies of web-page development. They are not pontificators; they are doers. They know that making a pizza is a lot harder than eating one, and assure you of such in Chapter 2 when discussing the difficulty of making style and tone consistent, adding: "We know. We've had struggles with it."

Web developers and those interested in learning how will soon discern that good web creation requires good thinking with a heavy complement of judgment and restraint mixed in with feistiness and mischievousness when appropriate. Speaking of Dynamic HTML, they state in this dynamic book: "Use it in a way that is appropriate for your readers and your content (Chapter 7)." 'Nuf said.

Two messages that weave through these pages are: (1) Focus on the user, providing what is useful and what adds value to their experience; (2) be aware that your site is never done.

I can't think of two more compelling reasons to be a web creator.

Part of the attraction of being a journalist is that each day's edition is like a version. You are constantly trying to improve subsequent versions. Now I realize we've had it easy. Eric Meyer, a visiting journalism professor at the University of Illinois, summed up the shift in an interview with MediaINFO.com (September 13, 1997):

"For newspapers to truly prepare to exit a century in which they wrongly assumed that text was king (it ruled only because there were few challenges to its authority), they must begin to see the journalistic, not merely technical, challenges in presenting information in non-textual ways."

So too the web developer must not only master a new medium but also the new tools that are described in this guidebook. The magic of the tools is not in their ability to adorn but in their ability to enhance, a word carefully chosen by the authors for use in their title. Enhance. I'll dance to that.

Jack Driscoll
October 1997

Jack Driscoll is Editor-in-Residence at the MIT Media Lab and former Editor of the Boston Globe.

1 INTRODUCTION

So, you've created a website. Your pages are up and running and you're feeling pretty good about it . . . except that you want it to do more. Welcome to the addictive world of website development!

That's right. Building your own page or site is just the first step. Once you've been bitten by the bug, there always seems to be some way you can improve your site. And with technology moving at its current pace, you're probably smart to be thinking about how to enhance your site—what was cutting edge six months ago will be the expected standard minimum next month. Your readers expect more. You expect more. And the web is constantly improving, changing, adapting, and growing. It only makes sense to grow with it.

That's why this book came to be. *The Project Cool Guide to Enhancing Your Website* is a natural follow-up to *The Project Cool Guide to HTML,* and is about the "next steps" you can take to enhance your site.

ENHANCING YOUR SITE

"Enhancing" can be a tricky word. What enhances something to one person might be viewed as detracting from it by another. Look at frames—for every person who loves them there seems to be someone else who hates them.

When we talk about enhancing, we don't mean to imply that more is better or that incorporating the latest in HTML or add-in technologies is the right answer and automatically makes your site better. Enhancing is the natural evolution of seeing your site grow, watching how people use and respond to it, and tweaking the contents, the presentation, and the technology to continually make it a better reader experience that expresses your goals as well.

One of the most important things to remember when creating for the web is that you are building a flexible, every-changing environment in which your readers and your content meet and interact. Enhancement is simply keeping that environment as effective, useful, and fun as it can be.

This book addresses a number of technology areas that have been emerging as tools through which people can add value to their site. Not all these tools are appropriate for every site, every web builder, and every reader. Your decisions about what to use are best based on understanding your audience, your content, and the interaction between the two. And you don't need any special technology for that—that understanding is largely based on good old-fashioned listening and feedback.

In the end, websites are really about people. They reflect the people who create them and the people who use them. And no technology is a magic bullet to making that part work.

USING THIS BOOK

This book addresses nine areas or technologies that you can use to add value to your website. Some, like Dynamic HTML, require that you first understand others, like Cascading Styles Sheets and JavaScript. Others are standalone additions.

This book is divided into six basic segments.

1. Chapter 2 shows you how to enhance your existing website by improving its performance, without adding additional features.
2. Chapter 3 helps you leverage the power of the meta tag to make your site findable by search engines and add some all-browser effects.
3. Chapter 4 focuses on helping your readers find things within your site by offering site searching.
4. Chapters 5–7 show how to add interaction, feedback, and dynamism with JavaScript, Style Sheets, and Dynamic HTML.
5. Chapters 8 and 9 explore motion and sound.
6. The remainder of the book offers a reality check for building pages that work in the real world.

This book also comes with its own website (http://www.projectcool.com/guide/enhancing). Many of the examples and samples can be downloaded from the site, including several complete JavaScript scripts that—with just a little tweaking—can immediately make your site more interactive. It includes links to all of the resources mentioned in this book, as well as other updated information.

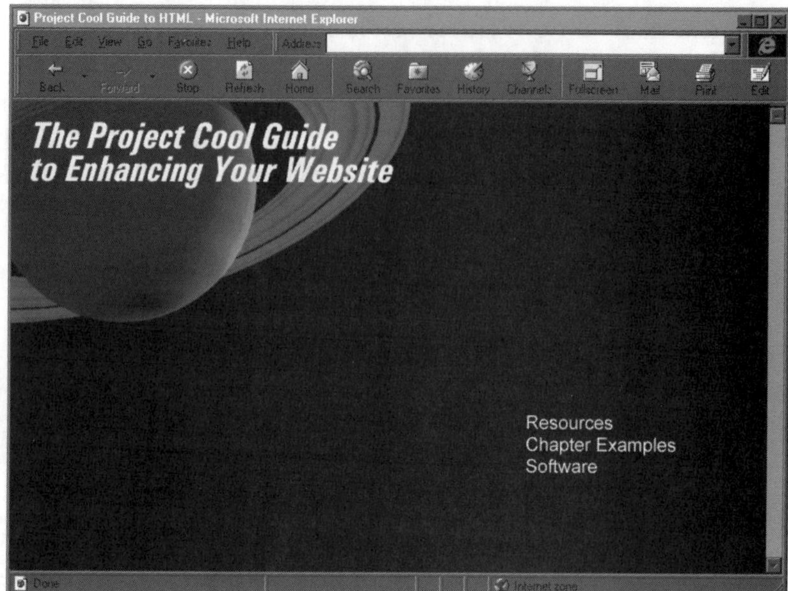

Figure 1.1
The companion website is an online resource section for this book.

Figure 1.1 shows the website.

Part of the website is a TRY IT section. Throughout the book you will see sections that are noted with a TRY IT icon, like this:

TRY IT
This is a TRY IT section in the book.

Every time you see the TRY IT section, it will include something that you may want to look at in the companion website or an exercise that you may want to complete in the TRY IT section of the website.

The TRY IT section is a page into which you type code, click on a button, and see the result. All you need to use it is a web browser and Internet connection.

Sometimes the TRY IT exercises will include calls to image, sound, or other supporting files. When you enter the example text and code in the TRY IT window, it will access these supporting files. This way you can, for ex-

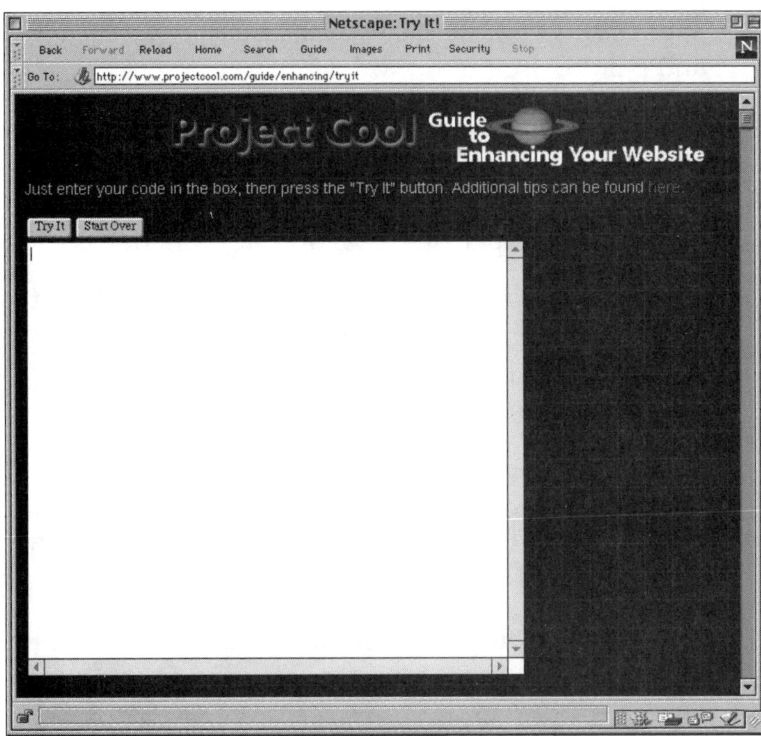

Figure 1.2
TRY IT lets you test your HTML skills.

ample, see the effect of adding a sound file without actually having to create one yourself.

Figure 1.2 shows the website's TRY IT section.

INSIDE THIS BOOK

This book has ten chapters:

Chapter 1: Introduction. You're reading the Introduction right now. It introduces the reasons for and concepts behind enhancing your site.

Chapter 2: Enhancing Graphics. One the easiest ways to enhance your site is to make it perform faster and smoother. Optimizing both your individual graphics and the way you use graphics is a logical first step for taking your site to that next level.

This chapter also introduces the ideas of color space and palette use on the web.

Chapter 3: Using Meta Tags. Meta tags are general data-holding HTML tags that can be employed to do many different things. In current common use, however, they perform two primary functions.

1. First, they can enable you to add some automated effects to your site, such as sounds that play automatically and pages that reload automatically.
2. Second, they can make your site more "findable" by the search spiders used by the major directory services. If you want your site listed, it is worth your time to add search meta tags to your pages.

Chapter 4: Adding Search Features. If you have more than a few pages of information in your site and your information is of the type that people use when they are looking for something specific rather than browsing for enjoyment, you'll probably want to consider adding search features to your site. A search component lets your readers quickly and easily find a topic, section, or reference within your site. A good search interface can mean the difference between a frustrated and a satisfied reader.

Chapter 5: Adding Interactivity with JavaScript. JavaScript is an increasingly popular way of adding reader-page interaction to a site. JavaScript is a scripting language; the scripts you create with it reside within your HTML file and can be programmed to do many different things. You don't have to be a programmer to learn how to write scripts. JavaScript works with the most recent versions of both Netscape Navigator and Microsoft Internet Explorer.

This book includes several scripts that add often-requested types of interactivity, along with detailed directions for customizing them to work with your site. These scripts will let you add functionality to your site immediately, by just changing a few sections.

Chapter 6: Cascading Style Sheets. Cascading Style Sheets (CSSs) are among the newest set of tags to be endorsed by the web standards committee. They give you additional control over layout and element placement, and provide a way to create a look once and apply it to many different pages. CSS features are supported by the 4.0 release of Netscape Navigator and the 3.0 and later releases of Microsoft's Internet Explorer.

Chapter 7: Dynamic HTML. Dynamic HTML combines the power of Cascading Style Sheets with the programming control of JavaScript to let you create pages that not only respond to user actions, but can also re-create themselves on-the-fly. Dynamic HTML is supported by Microsoft's Internet Explorer 4.0 and Netscape's 4.0 and later browsers. It offers great potential for creating active pages.

Chapter 8: Adding Animation. Animation can be overused and is one of those "enhancements" that has the potential to become an annoying detraction—but it can also be a wonderful eye-catcher or a powerful way to explain a concept or idea. This chapter looks at the various methods of creating animated effects, from HTML techniques through plug-ins such as Macromedia's Flash and Shockwave. It also explores some of the design decisions behind choosing to add animation as a component of your site.

Chapter 9: Adding Sound and Video. For some sites, sound or video are important enhancements that might be critical to the site's content. When you visit a band's site, don't you expect to hear the band's music? There are a variety of methods for incorporating sound and video; each has tradeoffs. This chapter explores some of the basic methods and techniques.

Chapter 10: Cross-Platform Issues. With "browser wars" still underway, all of us who are building for the web find ourselves caught in the crossfire between two popular browsers that support slightly different "standards." This chapter suggests some paths to follow through the battlefield while Microsoft and Netscape slug it out.

This book is set up to give you a sense of the different ways you can enhance your site. By reading this book, you'll be able to make intelligent choices about which enhancements make sense for you and your site, and you'll be able to begin building your site in new directions.

This book isn't designed to be a complete reference guide to each and every topic. After all, each of the areas the book covers is worthy of multiple volumes itself! This book does give you enough detail to understand what is involved and to learn the basics of the "next step" techniques. It won't make you an audio expert, for example, but it will teach you what you need to add simple audio to your website and to see if audio is the type of enhancement that works for your content and audience. It won't turn you into an ace JavaScript programmer either, but it will show you the potential of incorporating scripted interactivity into your site, help you explore the first steps toward adding it, and provide several script templates that let you incorporate some basic JavaScript interactivity right away.

Playing with the different technologies is fun. The

best way to learn what your website can do and become is to poke around, test things, and try things. You probably won't add everything in this book . . . but after you try the different possibilities, one or two areas might turn out to be just what you were looking for.

So welcome! We hope you have as much fun building your website and exploring its potential as we do building ours.

2 ENHANCING GRAPHICS

When you were first putting together your site, it was easy (and often necessary) to focus primarily on pulling all the pieces together. You probably had some ideas about what would and wouldn't work, but you needed to try them, to get the site up and running, to see what did and didn't work in reality.

Now that you're happy with the basic site, it's time to look at how you can enhance it, to make it perform better, meet your reader's needs, and adapt to the every-changing web technology.

One of the first ways that you can enhance your website is to do a sanity check on all your graphics, to make sure they are inserted with clean code, used well, and that the graphics themselves are as tight as possible. You don't need to learn new technology for this . . . you just need to step back and play consultant with your own site.

Well-oiled graphics make for a faster performing, smoother feeling, and more fluid site. A site that responds quickly is one of the enhancements your readers are mostly likely to notice—and appreciate.

When we are asked to do a "web tuning" on a client site, graphics are the first element we examine. Just about every website has some area of its graphics that can be tweaked to make the site perform better and feel faster.

THINGS TO EXAMINE

There are a number of factors you should keep in mind when using graphics within your websites. Here are a few questions to ask yourself about your site's graphics.

- Do the graphics make sense?
- Does each graphic add meaning or comprehension?
- Does text need to be a graphic?
- Is the style and tone of the graphic consistent with the site's overall style?
- Can larger graphics be split up?
- Is the site making use of cache?
- Can the site make use of preloading?
- Does the background image work as intended? Does it add or distract from the page's readability?
- Is the image tag fully employed?
- Are the image formats the best match for the image content?

Do the Graphics Make Sense?

Among the first questions we ask when we visit a site is: Do the graphics make sense? Do they add value to the site? This might sound obvious, but it's amazing how many graphical elements on the web add more bandwidth than value.

Many sites have lots of graphics. Lots and lots of graphics: photos, icons, buttons, text treated as a graphic. Sometimes the graphics are wonderful, well thought out, and their very existence enhances both the site and the reader's ability to use the site. Everyone should applaud these designs.

More often, some of the graphics are great, some are okay, and some do very little to make the site a better place to visit. This last group of graphics should be removed, replaced, or rethought. Maybe these no-value graphics are remainders from an earlier draft and get used because: "Heck, we've got these buttons—we may as well use them." Maybe the page creator believes that everything needs a graphical icon to be understandable. Or maybe the person who built the page just likes creating graphics.

It is often very difficult to step back and look at your hours of hard work and ask "Do I really need this? What does it offer my readers?" But that's the first step in critiquing your own site and being your own toughest critic.

By no means are we suggesting that you eliminate graphics—not at all! Just use them wisely and well, and try to be honest with yourself about what value they bring.

TIP: *Use only graphics that add value to your site. Simplicity can actually enhance the end result.*

Here are few common places you might want to look for extraneous graphic elements.

Not all choices need a graphical button. Some sites seem consumed with "button mania." Links and options, especially at a secondary level, often work just fine as text links and don't require a button cluttering up screen space. Use buttons where they add navigational clarity.

Icons don't explain it all. For the past decade or so, graphic design seems to have gone a little icon-crazy. Not all functions require a pictogram to explain what they do. In fact, we've seen sites where it takes longer to figure out what the cute little icon means than to actually do the task the icon indicates. Text is sometimes more direct and words can be very good communication tools. Some icons are a great boon that help readers understand your site—keep using those!—but others just confuse and fill bandwith. Look at your use of icons and use them when and where they make sense.

A picture has the bandwidth of many thousands of words. Let's be honest. There's a certain ego involved in creating a website. Maybe it's a business's ego. Maybe it's an individual's ego. In either case, these egos often lead to big photos, beloved primarily by the site's founders, their spouses, and parents. Do you really need a half-screen photo of the leasing office? Do readers feel better because they can see your building has a full parking lot?

Does the Text Need to Be a Graphic?

Until recently, the only way to use real typography on the web was to create the type elements separately, save them as graphics, and insert the graphics into the HTML page. Many of us are in the habit of doing this and just automatically create type elements this way. But the web is changing.

If your readers are using newer browsers, you may be able to streamline your site by using the <font> tag or Cascading Style Sheet elements to display text in different sizes, faces, and color—without the overhead of multiple GIF files.

The Font Tag

```
<font face="name,name" size=+/-X color=
         "value">text</font>
```

With Navigator 3.0 and IE 3.0 or higher, you can use the font tag to control some basic typographical parameters through HTML. These parameters are still limited, but they show the future direction of the web.

The Face switch lets you specify a typeface for displaying the text that follows it. The browser reads the face values in the font tag, then looks at the fonts installed on the reader's computer, trying to match the specified face. If the font you want to use is a common system font, such as Times, Courier, or Helvetica/Arial, this is a bandwidth-wise way of using the typeface.

To use the Face switch in the font tag:

1. Start the font tag.

   ```
   <font
   ```

2. Type the word *face* followed by the equal sign.

   ```
   <font face=
   ```

3. Inside double quotation marks, type the name(s) of the face or faces you want to use. Type the one

you want first, followed by backup options. Separate each option with a comma. In this example, the browser will try to find and display Futura first. If it can't find Futura, it will look for Helvetica. If it can't find Helvetica, it will look for Arial. And if it can't find Arial, it will use the default typeface. The capitalization of the face names doesn't matter.

```
<font face="futura,helvetica,arial"
```

Remember to specify both Macintosh and PC system fonts, such as Helvetica and Arial, where necessary.

4. End the tag as usual.

```
<font face="futura,helvetica,arial">
```

The Color switch lets you specify a color for displaying the text that follows it. You can use the hexadecimal color values or common browser color names to specify the color. (See Appendix B or the companion website for color lists and samples.)

For example, this tag creates green Helvetica text:

```
<font face="helvetica,arial" color="forestgreen">
```

The Size switch lets you specify a size for displaying the text that follows it. Typically, you'll use a relative size value. You specify relative size by typing a plus or minus sign and a unit number.

For example, this tag creates a purple Helvetica line of type that is two units larger than the line that precedes it. Figure 2.1 shows how this tag appears in a browser window.

```
<p>Fred was hungry.
<p><font face="helvetica,arial" color="purple"
size=+2>Fred was a hungry monster!</font>
<p>Fred licked his monster chops loudly and looked
longingly at the bowl of oatmeal with fresh cream
```

Figure 2.1
The <font> tags let you add face, size, and color to type, all within HTML and without separate graphic files.

```
that was sitting on the wooden table across the
room.
```

TRY IT

If you are using a newer browser, go to the TRY IT section (http://www.projectcool.com/guide/enhancing) and type the Fred example:

```
<p>Fred was hungry.
<p><font face="helvetica,arial" color="pur-
ple" size=+2>Fred was a hungry
monster!</font>
<p>Fred licked his monster chops loudly and
looked longingly at the bowl of oatmeal
with fresh cream that was sitting on the
wooden table across the room.
```

Then click on TRY IT to see what happens.

Try changing the color name, size value, and typeface name. For exampe, try changing the color value to "darkred." Try changing the face value to "times." Try changing the size value to -1. Click on the TRY IT button to see the results of each of your changes.

Style Sheets

If your readers are using Navigator 4.0 or IE 4.0 or later, you may want to explore Cascading Style Sheets. These let you add additional style and placement control directly within HTML, without inserting separate image files. Style sheets have their own chapter in this book, Chapter 6.

Are the Style and Tone Consistent?

Another set of questions we ask are design questions: Do the graphics meet the style and tone of the rest of the site? Are their style and tone consistent with each other?

The site is a coherent user environment, with a series of moods and messages. If a visual doesn't fit—no matter how nicely it may be executed—removing it will enhance the overall flow of the site. It's really easy to fall in love with a graphic . . . but when you cast a cool appraising eye on it a few months later it becomes clear that it just doesn't mesh with the rest of the site.

Also, the graphics themselves should feel like they are part of the same package. A visual bump feels jarring. Getting rid of those bumps is an easy way to enhance the overall effect of the site.

It can be tough to decide a graphic that you like just doesn't fit. We know we've had struggles with it. But being tough with your decisions really does make for a better reader experience in the long run.

TIP: *Use graphics whose style, tone, and mood are consistent with the style, tone, and mood of the site, and dump those that aren't.*

Can Large Graphics Be Split Up?

Big graphics covering large amounts of screen space can feel really, really slow. That's because the browser needs to download the entire graphic before the reader can see anything useful on the screen. The reader sits there and watches (and probably twitches impatiently) as a large graphic draws one line at a time.

That's what happens on the opening page of the fictitious Happy Craters website, as shown in Figure 2.2. That large graphic is nice, but it is 95K in size. That means a reader on a 14.4 modem will be waiting at least 96 seconds —over a minute and a half—to see it. Even the faster dial-in connections are still looking at about a minute of waiting time. Remember, given the realities of the telecommunication environment, actual connection speed is often less than the given modem speed. Will readers be willing to wait for this graphic however nice it might be?

One way to deal with this is to divide large single graphics into several smaller pieces. Each piece displays as it loads. Although the total download time is seldom any faster, the perceived download time is quite different. The reader feels that something is happening and believes that the site is performing quickly.

Figure 2.2
This is a nice, effective image but large.

> **Perceived Speed:** The speed at which a reader thinks the page downloads, rather than the literal number of seconds the download takes.

Using techniques that add to perceived speed is a great way to enhance a site without much extra work. If readers think the site is fast, then it is fast—no matter what a ticking second hand reports. Perception creates reality.

Conversely, if readers think a site is slow because they have to wait for one large graphic early on, then the site is slow to them, no matter how much you may be able to "prove" otherwise.

Dividing up large graphics into smaller slices is one of the techniques that can greatly increase the perceived speed of a site and enhance its perceived performance. You can also analyze the smaller pieces to see if each of them can be saved in a format that makes them more size-efficient.

TIP: ***Take advantage of techniques that increase perceived speed, the speed at which a reader feels that a page downloads.***

TRY IT

To see how the use of graphics can effect perceived speed, go to the companion website to this book, http://www.projectcool.com/guide/enhancing.

1. Click on Happy Craters, V1. Notice how the page feels as it loads.
2. Now click on Happy Craters, V2. Unless you're on a very speedy T1 or T3 connection, you'll experience firsthand the difference a graphic can make.

Treat splitting up graphics as a step-by-step process. To split up large graphics:

1. First look at the original and see where you can make logical divisions.

   Look again at the page in Figure 2.2. It is one large image, but it divides into logical subsections, as shown in Figure 2.3. Some of the subsection pieces can be more economically stored as GIFs; others as JPEGs. By breaking the file into these pieces, we've reduced the combined graphic size to 65K—or about 30 seconds less.
2. Create the small graphic files.
3. Insert the small graphic files into your web page using standard HTML code, like this. *Notice that there are no spaces or returns between the individual image tags and the border of the image is set to zero.* These

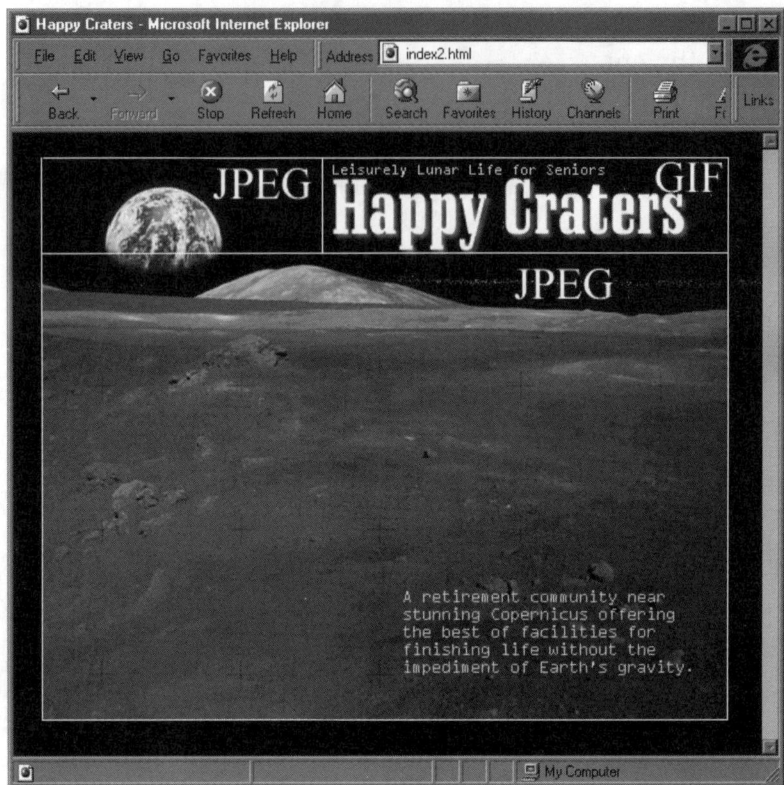

Figure 2.3
One large image divided into logical subsections for faster loading.

are important items to remember when combining smaller individual graphics into one larger graphic.

If you add a space or return between the tags, you may see a little white space between sections of the image on some browsers. If your border isn't set to zero, you might see a border between the segments where links exist. You can, however, put a return in the middle of an image tag to make it break nicely in your HTML text file; this will not affect the display of the page.

If you have divided the page into both horizontal and vertical slices, you may want to use a table to align all the pieces properly.

The HTML code for the revised Happy Craters first page looks like this. It uses the <div> tag and a table to center the image on the page, and it has a comment line to note what is happening:

```
<html>
<head>
<title>Happy Craters</title>
</head>

<body bgcolor=black>

<!--These graphics make the earth&moon. DO NOT ALTER
SPACING.-->

<div align=center>
<table><tr
><td><a href="home2.html"><img src="images/earth-
cut.jpg" width=228 height=82
border=0 alt=""><img src="images/logo.gif" width=343
height=82 border=0
alt="Happy Craters"><br
><img src="images/surface.jpg" width=565 height=368
border=0 alt=""></a
></td></tr></table>
</div>

</body>
</html>
```

When the page displays, the end result will be exactly the same as if the image were one large file, but the process of getting there will feel faster to your readers. It's a little extra work up front, but well worth the effort in the end.

TIP: *Divide large graphics into small slices to give your readers the illusion of a faster-loading page.*

Another nice side effect of splitting up large graphics, especially if you are using them as imagemaps, is that you can create pseudo imagemaps and apply links to individual sections.

Pseudo-Imagemaps: A way of creating multiple links within a graphic without using client- or server-side map tags or a server-side map script.

On the mythical Happy Craters site, there is a lot map that links to information about individual lots. It uses a large graphic, and the graphic has multiple links. If we divide it up as shown in Figure 2.4, we can add links to the appropriate sections and create the effect of an imagemap, with a page that works on all browsers, seems to load faster, and requires no additional server processing time.

Here's the HTML code that builds the pseudo-imagemap for the lot-map page. Notice again that *there are no spaces or returns between the individual image tags or between image tags and anchor tags. Additionally, the border of the image is set to zero.*

You'll note that there are several small, individual graphics, each in its own table cell with its own link to lot information. The pieces of the image and their links

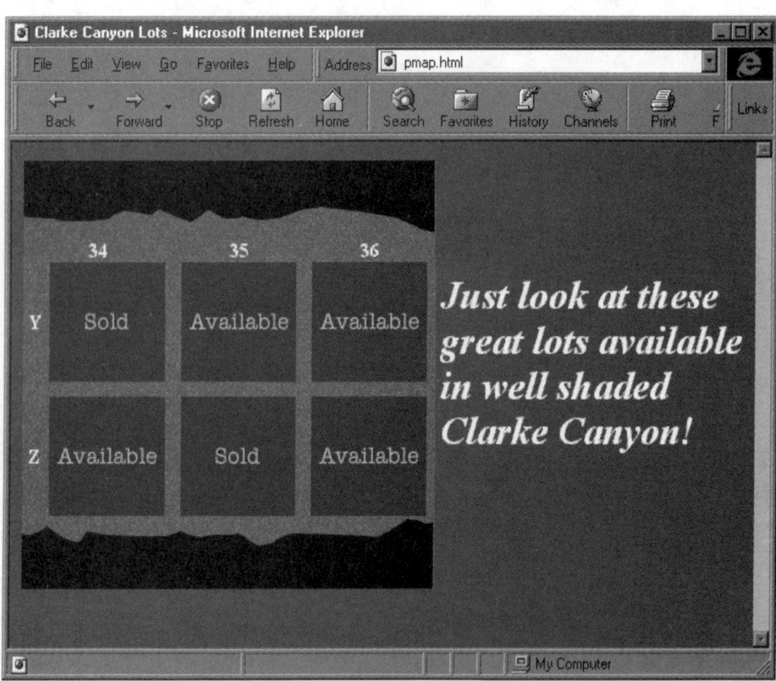

Figure 2.4
A large imagemap divided into logical subsections, each with its own link.

are positioned using a table. This lets us control the placement of each more accurately.

We also used background colors for the table cells, and the "sold" and "available" graphics are reused, again minimizing download time.

```
<html>
<head>
<title>Clarke Canyon Lots</title>
</head>

<body bgcolor=666666 text=white link=gold
vlink=gold>

<div align=center>
<table border=0 cellpadding=0 cellspacing=0
background="images/ground.gif"><tr
><td colspan=4><img src="images/top.gif" width=339
height=58>
</td
><td rowspan=6 bgcolor=666666> </td
><td rowspan=6 bgcolor=666666><h1><i>Just look at
these great lots
available in well shaded Clarke Canyon!</i></h1>
</td
></tr
><tr align=center
><td colspan=2><b>34</b></td
><td><b>35</b></td
><td><b>36</b></td
></tr
><tr align=center valign=middle
><td> <b>Y</b></td
><td><a href="sold.html"><img src="images/sold.gif"
width=95 height=95 border=0></a></td
><td><a href="avail.html"><img
src="images/avail.gif"
width=95 height=95 border=0></a></td
><td><a href="avail.html"><img
src="images/avail.gif"
width=95 height=95 border=0></a></td
></tr
><tr><td colspan=4><font
size=1> </font></td></tr
```

```
><tr align=center valign=middle
><td> <b>Z</b></td
><td><a href="avail.html"><img
src="images/avail.gif"
width=95 height=95 border=0></a></td
><td><a href="sold.html"><img src="images/sold.gif"
width=95 height=95 border=0></a></td
><td><a href="avail.html"><img
src="images/avail.gif"
width=95 height=95 border=0></a></td
></tr
><tr><td colspan=4
><img src="images/bottom.gif" width=339
height=58></td
></tr
></table>

</body>
</html>
```

The page seems to use a large imagemap, but its perceived speed has been increased and a reader can take action immediately, without waiting for all the graphic pieces to download.

TIP: *Consider using pseudo-imagemaps as appropriate.*

Is the Site Making Use of Cache?

Cache: A method of computer data storage.

Cache is a temporary storage area in which web browsers keep frequently used graphics so they don't need to be downloaded again and again. As a web builder, well-used cache can be your friend.

The browser typically uses two types of cache: *disk cache* and *memory cache*.

1. The disk cache stores frequently loaded graphics from one browser session to the next. When the browser accesses a page for which it has cached

images, it simply pulls them from the disk cache and doesn't need to download them.

2. Memory cache stores graphics during a single browser session. It stores the most recently used images and can redisplay them almost instantly. Memory cache can be very useful if you know how to take advantage of it.

Disk Cache: A way of storing frequently loaded graphics across several browser sessions.

On the mythical Happy Craters site, the logo gets used over and over again, but sometimes it has a different subtopic below it: Happy Craters Lots, Happy Craters Lifestyle, and so on. You could make a separate logo file for each of these subtopics, or you could take advantage of cache.

Memory Cache: A way of storing graphics during a single browser session.

By splitting the logo and the subtitle into two different components, you can save download time and increase the site's perceived speed. After the files have downloaded once, you can reuse each of them in different combinations on subsequent pages. Because they are stored in memory cache, you can use them without the download time penalty.

Figures 2.5 and 2.6 show two different logos. Each could be created as its own graphic file.

You could create each of these logos as a stand-alone graphic and use that single graphic on the page. However, the Happy Craters text is reused in all logos—why reload it over and over again? Instead, we split it out into its own file. It loads once and is stored in cache. The individual section names are very small. We can get many "different" logos with only minimal overhead. Figures 2.7, 2.8, and 2.9 show the different, reusable components.

This is the HTML code for the different Happy Craters buttons. Each button is created from two elements, one of which ("hc.gif") is used over and over, as the first part of the graphic. As with splicing together any group of images, be sure that there are no spaces or returns between the image tags. Figure 2.10 shows the full result.

```
<html>
<head>
<title>Happy Craters: Retirement Without
Gravity</title>
</head>

<body bgcolor= text= link= vlink=>

<a href="URL"><img src="images/hc.gif" width=300
height=60 border=0 alt=happy craters"><br
><img src="images/lifestyle.gif"
width=300 height=45 border=0 alt=lifestyle">
<p>
```

Figure 2.5
This element has two parts: Happy Craters and the section name.

Happy Craters
*Lifestyle

Figure 2.6
This is another variation on Happy Craters and the section name.

Happy Craters
*Home Lots

Figure 2.7
The Happy Craters element.

Happy Craters

Figure 2.8
One section name.

*Home Lots

Figure 2.9
Another section name.

```
<a href="URL"><img src="images/hc.gif" width=300
height=60 border=0 alt=happy craters"><br
><img src="images/lots.gif"
width=300 height=45 border=0 alt=home lots">

</body>
</html>
```

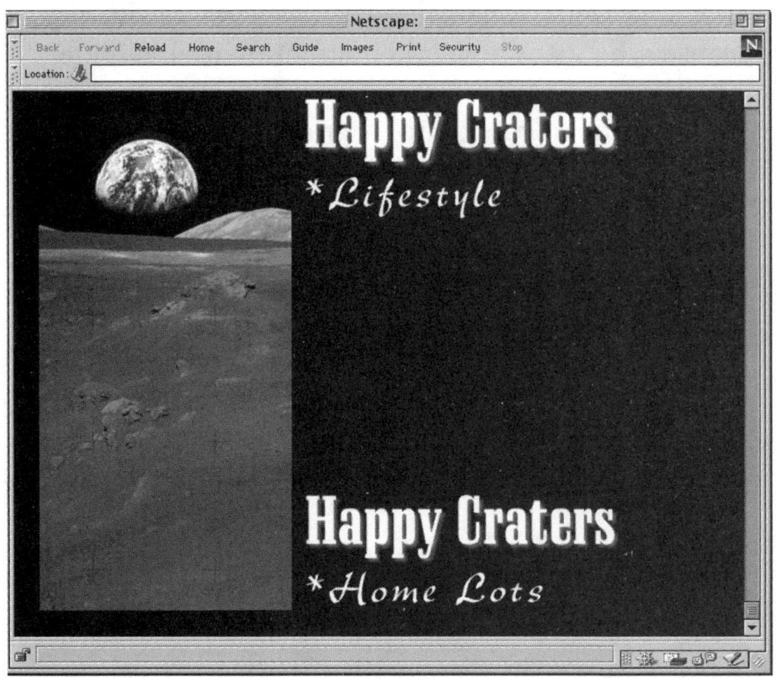

Figure 2.10
The same elements can be reused to save bandwidth.

Reusing graphics and taking advantage of the cache allows to you build graphically rich pages without your site grinding to a halt. With careful planning, your site can have graphic-intensive pages that remain low-bandwidth, because most of the images are pre-cached.

TIP: *Cache is your friend. Resuse graphic components where possible to make your site perform faster.*

Can the Site Make Use of Preloading?

Another way to increase perceived speed is to use graphic preloading techniques where possible. This technique is a little like what happens when the magician redirects your focus on his right hand, while his left hand pulls the ribbon from his sleeve; or the way a theme park makes long waiting lines bearable by distracting you with some pre-ride show. Likewise, with preloading, your readers don't notice a graphic loading because it happens while their attention is elsewhere.

In the Happy Craters site, we might preload graphics for the photos on the navigational page while the reader is reading the welcome message on the first page.

To use this technique, you'd put image tags for the graphics you want to preload into the first-page HTML file, but you'd set their width and height to one pixel. They'll be downloaded but won't display on the screen, effectively making the process invisible. They will, however, be saved in cache.

When the reader clicks to go to the main navigational pages, the preloaded photos get pulled from cache and pop right into place. You've just enhanced the speed of the page by a clever use of basic HTML.

Don't force preloading into pages and sites where it makes no sense, but if you have the opportunity, give the technique a try.

TIP: *If the site is structured to allow for it, preload graphics as one-pixel images.*

Does the Background Image Work?

It's very easy to go wrong with background images, and it's very easy to enhance the appearance of a site by using an effective background.

Here are a few things that can cause problems with background images.

A busy image obscures the text. With an overactive background, unless you know what the text says, it is very difficult to read because the image is so busy.

The background image is a very large file, a very slow file. When the background image is huge, readers wait and wait for it. Does the image have so much value that it is worth the wait? If not, make the image smaller, tile a subset of the image, or pick something else entirely.

The background color is unspecified, but the background image has a strong color. Often, you'll use a contrasting color for the text you place over an image. Maybe you used white text on a dark image. But if you don't specify a background color as well, readers who turned off graphics or received a broken image can't read the text, because your sharp white text is virtually unreadable against the default gray browser background.

As a rule of thumb, any background image should have wide areas of like colors and be subtle enough that it doesn't interfere with the text. Unless you're using one-pixel GIFs and tables of fixed width, there's no guarantee how the strong image and the text on the page will line up in any reader's browser.

Replacing the busy background image with a smaller, simpler file is certainly an enhancement for the eyes of the mythical Happy Craters readers. And adding a complementary background color to the body tag ensures that all readers will be able to see the text, whether they have images turned on or turned off. Compare the readability of the two sides of Figure 2.11.

TIP: *Use background images that allow for easy reading of text.*

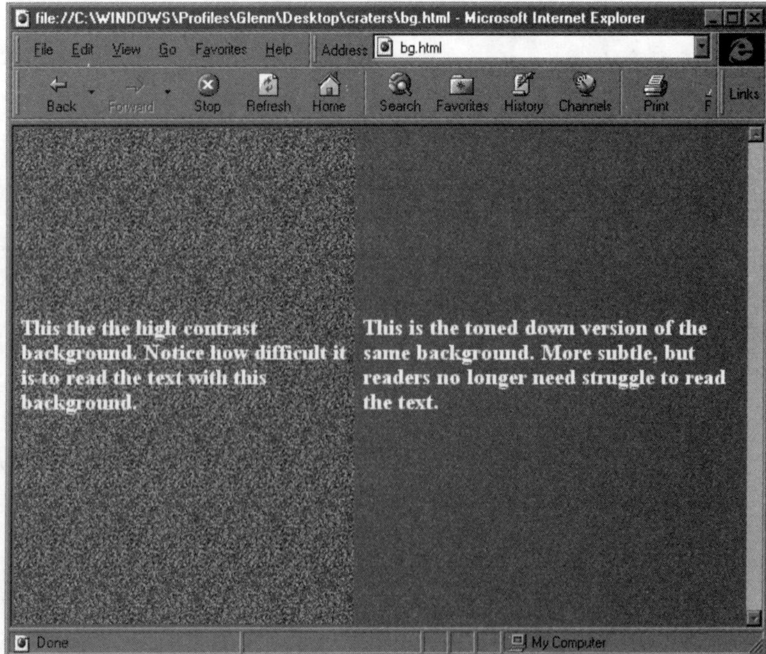

Figure 2.11
The image shows the result of different background textures.

Is the Image Tag Fully Employed?

There are two switches in the image tag that can make a difference in site performance: the Height switch and the Width switch.

When we're tuning a site, we check to be sure that the page creator included these switches in the <img> tag. More and more HTML editing programs automatically insert these switches and so it is more common to find them in place than it was a year ago It is still surprising, however, how many times these switches have been omitted. They are a small addition that creates a large enhancement.

If you *don't* use the Height and Width switches, the load process works like this:

1. Browser encounters an image tag.
2. Browser stops and pulls in the entire image. Nothing appears in the window.
3. User's computer calculates the size of the image (grind, grind, grind) and eventually displays it in the browser window.

But, if you *do* use the Height and Width switches, the load process works like this:

1. Browser encounters an image tag and immediately knows how much space on the page to hold for the image.
2. A placeholder for the image appears and the rest of the page continues to be displayed while the image downloads.

3. The image pops into place. The user's computer doesn't have to calculate the image size because the Height and Width switches have already done that work.

Needless to say, the second scenario is much more pleasant and less painful to watch.

In most cases, it is a good idea for the pixel size in the Height and Width switches to match the pixel size of the image that is being downloaded. If the switches specify a size different from the image's real size, the browser will recalculate the image and try to display it at the size specified in the image tag.

The exceptions to this are, of course, when you are using the one-pixel preloading technique or a one-pixel GIF placement trick—or when you want to intentionally distort the image to create a special effect.

In addition to the Height and Width switches, it is also a matter of good style to always include an Alt Text switch in the <img> tag. This ensures that your readers have some sort of description of the image, even if they have images turned off, if they are working in an environment that doesn't support graphics, or if something happens to prevent the image from downloading fully.

TIP: *Remember to use Height and Width switches and always include alt text.*

Are the Image Formats the Best Match?

Once upon a time, in the early days of the web browser, all images were GIF images. The JPEG format was supported only through a helper application.

Those days are long gone.

All browsers now support both GIF and JPEG graphic formats, but from habit or perhaps because they aren't sure what the difference between the two is, some people still insist on using GIFs and only GIFs. GIFs are great for certain types of graphics; however, for other types of graphics the GIF format creates an unnecessarily large file with lower-quality results.

As a general rule of thumb:

- Use a GIF format if the image has large areas of solid color or is an illustration or artwork with minimal gradation changes. For example, the Happy Craters logo is saved as a GIF file.
- Use a JPEG format if the image is photorealistic and has a wide tonal range. JPEG usually produces smaller file size and better end quality for these types of images than the GIF format does. For example, the earth and moon image is saved as a JPEG file.

To better understand the two formats, let's look for a moment at how their respective compression techniques work.

GIF uses the LZW compression algorithm. This algorithm looks at the pixels in a row and counts how many are the same color. Instead of mapping each individual pixel, the algorithm notes how many pixels are the same in a row and saves that information as a mathematical notation. So, a 5-pixel-deep by 50-pixel-long yellow line would be reduced from 250 mapped pixels to a tiny five-line note that says "50 yellow pixels, 50 yellow pixels, 50 yellow pixels, 50 yellow pixels, 50 yellow pixels." No data is lost; the image is compressed mathematically. You can see how this approach is an ideal match for images with blocks of color. Conversely, you can see how this approach is *not* an ideal match when every pixel is a different color—the algorithm can't do much compressing.

In addition, the GIF format saves colors in an 8-bit mode. That means it can identify only 256 different colors. The GIF formatting tool will ask you which palette it should use when mapping those colors; your choice can make a difference in how the graphic appears to your readers. (You can learn a bit more about palettes later in this chapter.)

JPEG, on the other hand, was originally designed to compress photographic images. The technique it uses for compression analyzes the pixels and drops out some of them, to simplify the image and make its file size smaller. With JPEG there is always a tradeoff between file size and final quality. You can test the image and select the tradeoff that works for your specific image and reader base.

JPEG images are all 24-bit color. You don't have to choose between palettes. The format automatically tries to display the image with as many colors as the reader's computer will support based on the image data in the file.

TIP: *Use JPEG for photorealisitic images. Use GIF for images with large areas of solid color.*

TRY IT

Go to the companion website and click on MOON AS GIF/MOON AS JPEG. Look at the difference between the two methods of saving the same graphic.

OPTIMIZING ORIGINAL GRAPHICS

You can use graphics well and cleanly in the website design, but if the original images were saved in odd format combinations, you'll have a site that could still use some work in the file size area. Since speed is a very desirable enhancement, it's worth a few minutes to look at how you are creating your graphics and be sure you are optimizing them for publishing on the web.

Resolved: 72 dpi

For people who are accustomed to working in print, the idea of rendering a final graphic at 72 dpi (dots per inch) feels, well, not quite right. But rest assured. The computer screen can't display greater than 72 dpi, so why create extra overhead that no one will see by saving your graphics at 1200 dpi?

You'll save download time without sacrificing quality by keeping image resolution at a web-appropriate level.

TIP: *A 72-dpi resolution is high enough for graphics that will be viewed on a computer monitor.*

Painter's Palettes

Palette decisions are one of the toughest and most subjective decisions in creating web graphics. Entire books and websites have been devoted to the issue. This is just a brief discussion. The best way to learn about which palette choices work for you and your site is to save the same graphic in different ways and see how the decisions create a balance between file size and viewing quality.

TIP: *The best way to understand palettes is to try saving the same file in GIF format, using different palette choices in your image editing program, then look at the differing results.*

The palette decisions you make won't impact the size of the file, but they will make a difference in how the image appears to the reader. Palette decisions, combined with file format and bit depth, create the best balance between size and quality.

TRY IT

As you read through this section, go to the companion website. There, you can see the same image from the Happy Craters site saved as both GIF and JPEG, and with different palette choices.

Color Spaces

Computer monitors display graphics by projecting red, green, and blue lights. When all the lights are on 100 percent, you'll see a white pixel. When all the lights are on 0 percent, you'll see a black pixel. By combining all the different percent variations of these three lights, the RGB color space can, in theory, produce something in the neighborhood of 16,777,216 different color values.

In reality, however, many computer monitors work with an 8-bit color structure that can produce a scant 256 distinct hues. An increasing number work with a 16-bit color scheme that produces thousands of color. A few work with a feature called TrueColor that offers a 24-bit color scheme supporting millions of colors. Your readers will likely be viewing your graphics under all three situations, and on both Macintosh and Windows machines, with an assortment of color boards and other monitor support. In other words, you can't count on anything.

You can, however, use different combinations of palettes, file formats, and bit depth to create a graphic that will look reasonable on most computers and be contained in a file size that is modem friendly.

System Palette and Web Palette

Much has been written about the *system palettes* of the Macintosh and Windows machines. The standard system palette on each uses 256 colors, 216 of which are the same on both platforms. Because so many people are designing for the web, these 216 colors are now identified as the *web palette*.

System Palette: The standard 256 colors supported by a computer operating system.

One school of design says that if you want to be sure that your readers see the color you want them to see, you should create art using only these 216 colors. For example, if you are creating a logo or a color scheme and you want your readers to see it as close as possible to your original intent, you may want to consider using the web palette. You can find a copy of the web palette on the companion website to this book at http://www.projectcool.com/guide/enhancing, as well as at many other locations across the web.

Web Palette: The 216 colors that the Macintosh and Windows machines have in common.

When you save a GIF file, you are asked which palette you want to use. If you want to map the colors in your image to those in the web palette, select the web palette option. (Before the advent of the web palette, you would have chosen system palette as your option; you should use system palette if your image formatting program doesn't yet support the web palette as an option.)

When the reader's browser displays your GIF file on

his or her screen, it will attempt to display each color in your GIF as one of these 216 colors.

TIP: *Use the web palette when you want to map your graphic's colors to the cross-platform 216 colors.*

Exact Palette

The *exact palette* maps exact colors in your original image and then tries to display them on your reader's monitor. If your graphic uses only black and white or only the colors in the web palette, you may want to save your GIF file using the exact palette option.

TIP: *Use the exact palette when your graphic is only two colors, or when it uses only the 216 colors in the web palette.*

Adaptive Palettes

The *adaptive palette* is a shifting palette that uses the 256 available colors to create a palette that best matches the color range of your image. If your image has lots of reds and oranges, the adaptive palette will map toward the red and orange side of the scale. If you image has mostly purples and reds, the adaptive palette will map toward the red/blue/purple side.

It is often suggested that using the adaptive palette in conjunction with the smallest possible bit depth will produce the best balance between file size and quality.

However, if you have several GIFs on your page and each has a very different color slant, the adaptive palette is not a good choice; the adaptive palette will adjust itself to the first image that downloads and the others will be skewed to that range. This could create some odd color effects.

TIP: *Use the adaptive palette at low bit depths to achieve the best color quality.*

Bit Depth

The standard GIF maps 256 colors. Each bit in the image can have one of eight different values. You can reduce the size of a GIF file by reducing the *bit depth* at which the file is saved.

Bit depth is one of the areas that you can play with to find a balance between file size and image quality. Some images, when combined with the adaptive palette, look fine at 4-bit depth. You'll need to test your specific image to see how the color holds at different bit depths. In general, the fewer colors in the image, the lower the bit depth can go without a noticeable loss of quality.

TIP: *Play with bit depth and your specific image to see where the balance is between file size and image color quality.*

Dithering

Dithering is a technique that lets the 8-bit color mapping of a GIF simulate 24-bit color mapping.

When the GIF format encounters a color beyond the 256 it can map directly, you can have it dither the color. That is, the color gets analyzed and displayed as two different color pixels. When the two colors sit side by side and are viewed simultaneously, they approximate the original, out-of-range color.

With dithering, you can simulate a higher color depth than the GIF can normally support. However, this comes at the expense of file size. If you are dithering a GIF to get best results, you may want to save the same image in JPEG format and compare the resulting file sizes and quality to determine which format is most appropriate for this particular image.

If your image has lots of gradients and you are saving it as a GIF file without dithering, you may end up with blotchy colors and banding.

TIP: *Use dithering when the image has many gradients and you need to simulate more than 256 colors.*

TRY IT
Go to the companion website. Click on MOON DITHERED/NOT DITHERED to see the difference dithering makes in the same image.

Interlacing

Interlacing defines the way in which the image gets painted on the screen by the web browser. Normally—that is, without interlacing—the image paints line by line, from top to bottom. With interlacing, the image paints every other pixel in every other line, then backs up and fills in the space. Some people like interlacing because they believe it gives a general sketch of the image more quickly. Others dislike interlacing because they find it annoying and think it makes the image paint in a jerky, blotchy, slow manner.

We generally recommend against using interlacing. A noninterlaced display pattern feels sharper and cleaner.

TIP: *Avoid interlaced GIFs; noninterlaced GIFs paint cleaner and sharper on the screen.*

As you can see, there are many ways you can enhance your site by working on your graphics—both the way you use them and the way you create them.

There is no single formula for graphics. The more you try different approaches, the more you'll come to understand what works for your site.

It is worth the time and effort to tweak your graphics; they are the single area in which simple adaptations can create a dramatic change in the response time of your site and the way it is perceived by your readers.

3
WORKING WITH META TAGS

> "The <META> element is an extensible container for use in identifying specialized document meta-information."
>
> —HyperText Markup Language, RFC 1866 (The HTML 2.0 spec, introducing meta tags)

The official definition of *meta tags* is pretty vague, which is why meta tags have been interpreted in many different ways and have given rise to all sorts of hopeful misunderstandings—like the idea that adding meta tags magically makes your site findable by every search engine, or that the best use of meta tags is to fill them with the same word over and over again because your site will index better. Wrong on both counts!

Meta tags are not magic, not a cure-all for the search-engine blues, not a secret solution for pulling in data and, despite being part of the HTML specs, not at all standard.

The original idea of meta tags was to create a way to identify information about a page. The definition basically said that the meta tag has two parts, one that names the tag and one that contains the information associated with the name. The basic outline remains, but the interpretations have been many, and the meta tag has been adapted for many different types of information.

TIP: *Meta tags aren't magic! Meta tags do some useful things, but they won't solve all your search-engine blues. They can help some search services index your site better, but only if you define the tags carefully.*

DEFINING A META TAG

At their core, meta tags are simply placeholders for storing information that may or may not be processed by an HTTP server or indexed by a *search spider*. In practice, however, people do three basic things with meta tags:

Store information about the document, such as author or expiration date, and pass that information on to their HTTP web server. The web server then processes the information and performs an action, such as automatically generating header data based on the page's creation date and department author.

Intranets are the most common environment in which meta tags are used in this way. Within an intranet, the IS department and webmasters can configure a server to expect certain types of meta tag data and require that everyone building a web page for the intranet include the specific meta tags and their data. For this process to work correctly, the server must be set up to accept the meta tag names and a certain set of possible values for each—and the page builders must actually insert the correct names and values.

Make something happen to the page automatically. The two most common examples of this meta tag application are using the meta tag to play a sound or to automatically refresh a splash screen with another page. These applications work because most server and browser software have agreed to handle a meta tag named "refresh."

Improve the way search spiders index a site. Perhaps the most common—and most misunderstood—use of meta tags is using the tags to help define the way automated web search spiders index the site. Search spiders are tools used by some indexing/directory services (like AltaVista) to identify the contents of sites on the web.

One frequent misconception is that you must include meta tags in order to have your site indexed. This is not true—the automatic crawlers will index all sites, meta tags or no. What meta tags *can* do is provide information about your site so that it will be indexed more cleanly and in a more focused manner.

Not all spiders support meta tags. For example, neither Yahoo! nor Excite, two of the leading search/directory companies, pay any attention to meta tags when they compile their lists of sites. But others, including AltaVista, Infoseek, and HotBot, do use meta tag data. Using meta tags can help the placement of your site within these search indices, but—and this in an important caveat—using meta tags doesn't guarantee that your site will be indexed "correctly" either.

This chapter will look at each of these uses and explain them in more detail.

There really aren't any disadvantages to using meta

HTTP Server: A server that "speaks" HyperText Transfer Protocol (HTTP). Another way of describing a web server.

Search Spider: A program that searches the web to build an index of all accessible pages. Sometimes called a crawler.

tags, except the time they take you to create them. They won't break a browser or create odd problems. At worst, they'll just be ignored.

Like most other web creation elements, use meta tags when they add value to your page.

- Think about meta tags when you want to automatically play a sound file or automatically refresh the contents of a page or a frame.
- Consider using a well-thought-out meta tag structure when working within an environment that allows meta tags to be useful information markers.
- Add meta tags when you want to improve your chances of being indexed under certain words or phrases by some of the search spiders.

UNDERSTANDING BASIC META TAGS

The basic rules for using meta tags are quite straightforward.

1. In general, meta tags belong within the header section of your HTML file, between the <head> and </head> tags. (There's one exception to this, but we'll deal with that later.)
2. You can use multiple meta tags in the same HTML document.
3. There is no guarantee that meta tag data will actually be used, but if the browser doesn't know what to do with the tags, it will just ignore them.

Meta tags have two switches:

- The first switch describes the meta tag by assigning it an action or name.
- The second switch defines the data or content the tag contains.

This is what a couple of typical meta tags look like. The first tag would be used to automatically refresh a page with another page. It is sending a particular action to the server.

```
<META HTTP-EQUIV="refresh" CONTENT="30;
URL=index2.html">
```

The second would be used to help identify keywords for a search index, which is why it carries the name of "keywords."

```
<META NAME="keywords" CONTENT="music, polka, dance,
polish, festival, August events, bands">
```

Like other HTML tags, it doesn't matter if you use all uppercase or all lowercase characters. For these examples, we are putting the switch in uppercase and the value of the switch in lowercase, just to make it easier to see the difference between the two.

The Http-Equiv and Name Switches

In every meta tag, the first switch assigns the meta tag an action or a name. It describes what this meta tag's role is.

This switch can be either Http-Equiv or Name. You'll use either one or the other; you won't use both in the same tag.

- Use Http-Equiv if you are creating data that you

want a server to process. The value you enter after Http-Equiv is an action that the server will perform.

For example, if you have your server set up to automatically generate a header that lists the page's expiration date and reply to information, you'd use the Http-Equiv switch, like this:

```
<META HTTP-EQUIV="expires" CONTENT="31 Jan 99">
<META HTTP-EQUIV="reply-to" CONTENT="fred@ad-
dress.com">
```

The Http-Equiv switch tells the server: "Hey! This data is for you to use!"

If you want to start a server action, such as playing a sound file or displaying another page automatically, you'd also use Http-Equiv. For example, to play a sound file, you'd use a meta tag like this:

```
<META HTTP-EQUIV="refresh" CONTENT="30;
URL=http:/www.fred/sounds/oompah.au">
```

Again, the Http-Equiv switch tells the server: "Hey! This data is for you to use!"

- Use the Name switch if you're using the meta tag as a container for storing information about the page. For example, if you are using a meta tag to create a description you hope will be indexed by a search spider, you'd use the Name switch in a meta tag like this:

```
<META NAME="description" CONTENT="Jake & the Tubas
is the Northeast's most exciting polka band,
available for dances, festivals, and gigs of all
sorts.">
```

The Name switch won't communicate with the server. It will just let the meta tag serve as a holding bucket for information. That information will be used only when a search spider encounters the meta tag and understands the tag's name.

TIP: *Use Http-Equiv when you are communicating with a server. Use Name when the tag is an information container.*

The CONTENT Switch

The second switch in the meta tag is called Content, and it describes the data or information stored in the meta tag.

If the meta tag is about playing a sound file, the Content switch would contain the elapsed time before the file should play and the name of the file.

```
<META HTTP-EQUIV="refresh" CONTENT="30;
URL=http:/www.fred/sounds/oompah.au">
```

If the meta tag is listing keywords, the value of Content would be a list of the keywords you want associated with the page.

```
<META NAME="keywords" CONTENT="music, polka, dance,
polish, festival, August events, bands">
```

USING META TAGS WITH AN HTTP SERVER

If you are working with a specific HTTP server you may want to configure it to collect and process data about the web pages it serves. For example, some intranets generate automatic page headers based on content creation date, expiration date, author, and department.

Different server software requires different configuration settings. If you are interested in using meta tags in this way, consult your server documentation and the system person who sets up and runs the web server. You'll need to coordinate the server configuration with the meta tags that users enter when they build a page.

You'll want to sketch out a plan detailing the tag Http-Equiv values, the acceptable Content values for the tags, and how the information will be processed.

USING META TAGS TO REFRESH A PAGE

This section shows you how to use meta tags to automatically refresh a page. For example, you can use this technique to make your splash page automatically change to display your homepage.

You've probably encountered pages that appear in your browser window and, a few seconds later, disappear only to be replaced by another page. This effect is produced using a meta tag.

Splash Screen: Or splash page. A page that appears to introduce a site. It typically helps set the mood or tone of the site or is designed to entice readers to enter the site.

Figures 3.1 and 3.2 show how this two-stage effect might work. When you enter the site, you see Figure 3.1. You can click on the picture right away to enter the site, but if you don't click, after 30 seconds that first splash screen disappears and the front page of the site appears in your browser window (see Figure 3.2). A meta tag tells the browser to change the file it displays.

TRY IT

If you want to see how this effect works "live," go to http://www.projectcool.com/guide/enhancing. You'll see the automatically loading splash screen in action.

Design Considerations

Automatically loading pages can be a powerful and attention-grabbing feature that surprises and delights peo-

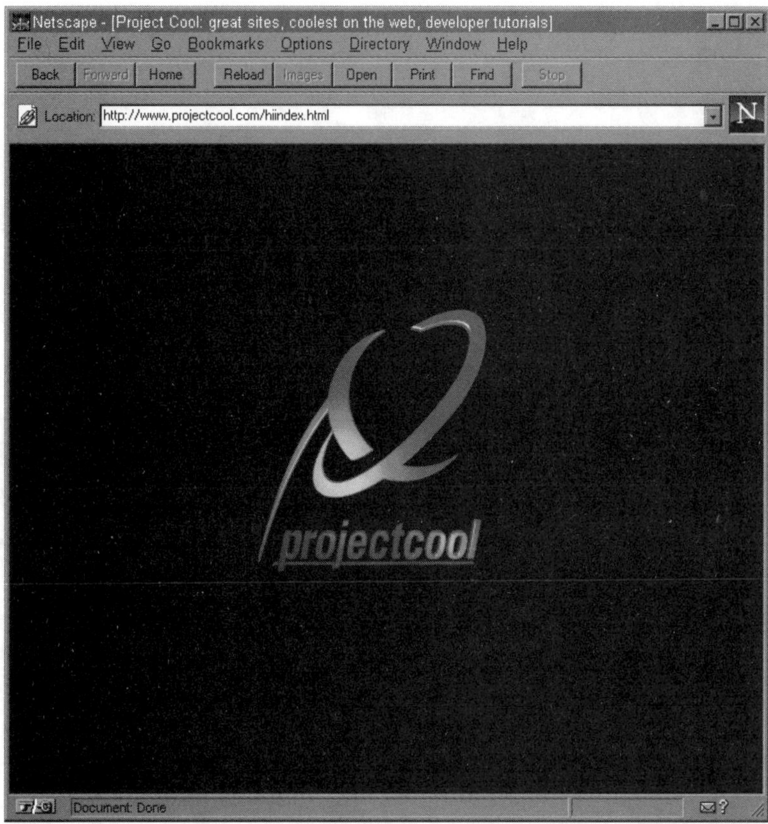

Figure 3.1
The page that appears on the screen when you first enter the site stays on the screen for 30 seconds or until the reader clicks on the picture.

ple. It can also be used to create a simple "slideshow" effect that can effectively present certain types of information. That's the good part.

But it's easy to overuse this effect. Readers can become frustrated if they feel that their computer is "acting on its own" without reason. If you're going to use a splash screen, make sure it adds something—besides one more page—to your site.

Typically, a splash screen is used as an introduction to a site. It stays on the screen 30 seconds or so, then automatically disappears and is replaced by the site's main navigational screen. The reader also has the option of

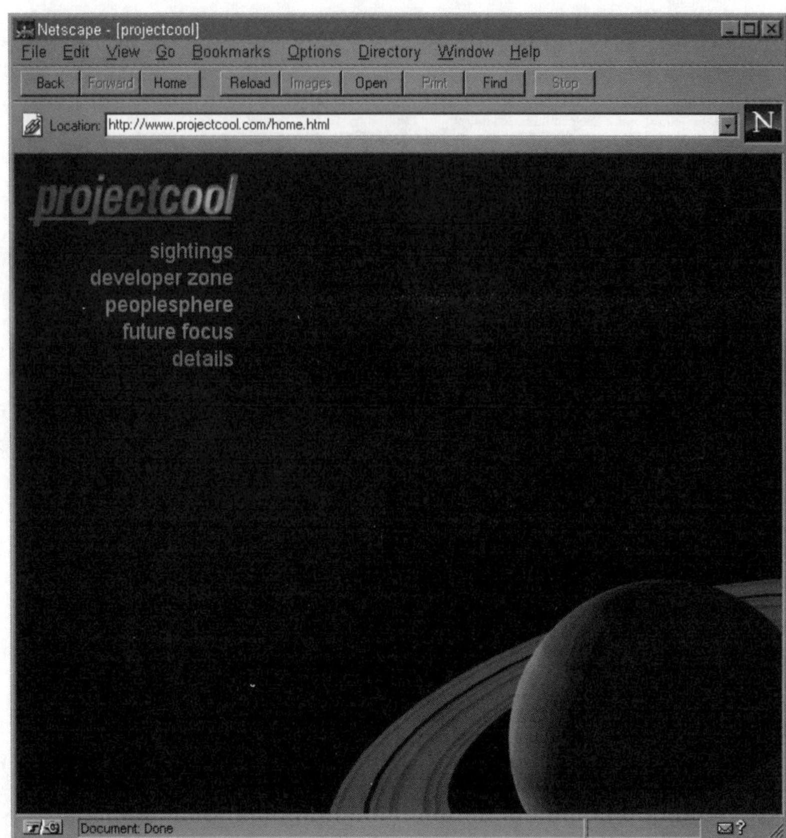

Figure 3.2
An automatically refreshed homepage.

clicking on the splash screen to enter the site automatically, which means the entire page or some obvious section of the page should be a link to navigational page.

The splash screen might display a greeting, information about the site, an artistic expression or presentation, or a changing message. Some designers think of splash screens as being a little like a mini opening scene for a movie or TV show.

However you choose to use it, remember that when you incorporate a splash screen, that screen takes time to download into your reader's browser. So, when you are setting up this effect, make sure you specify enough seconds of delay time between the display of the two pages. If you don't leave enough time, a partially loaded page will just disappear to be replaced with another—and you'll have a reader shaking his or her head in frustration. A good rule of thumb is that on a 14.4 modem it takes one second for every 1K of information transferred. So, add up the size of all your graphics and the size of your page and use that as the minimum number of delay seconds.

Even in an environment where people are using 28.8 modems, the 1K/1 second rule works. In the real connect world, one seldom achieves a nice steady 28.8 connection to the Net, and the 1K/1 second rule ensures a good margin of safety.

Creating the Effect

It's quite simple to create an automatically loading page. You create this effect by using a meta tag to force the browser to pull in something else automatically from the server. In this case, that something is an HTML page that overwrites the first page.

You do this by adding one simple line of code to the HTML file.

```
<META HTTP-EQUIV=refresh CONTENT="#seconds; URLof
the page">
```

The tag's name is META.

The first switch is Http-Equiv. You use this switch and not the Name switch because the meta tag needs to communicate with the server.

The value for the switch is refresh, a standard action value understood by most recent browsers and servers. The word refresh does not need to be in quotes.

The second switch is Content. It tells the browser how to go about performing the refresh action.

The value for the Content switch is the number of seconds to wait before beginning the refresh action, followed by a semicolon and the URL of the file with which to refresh the page. The entire value of the Content switch must be surrounded by quotation marks, because this information is getting passed along to the server.

For example, this code:

```
<META HTTP-EQUIV=refresh CONTENT="30;
http://www.fred/fredhome.html">
```

tells the browser that after 30 seconds, it should refresh the browser window and display the file named "fredhome.html." What the reader sees is a first page appear in the browser window, and then, after a small amount of time passes, the screen repaints and a different HTML page appears.

There's one very important item to note when using a meta tag to refresh a page. Remember that earlier in this chapter we said that there was one exception to placing the meta tag within the header. Well this is it. *To automatically refresh a page, the meta tag must be the very first item in the file, even before the opening <html> or <header> tags*. If it is not the first item, some server/browser combinations will not display the correct page after the refresh. If you are trying to create this effect and it just won't work right, make sure the meta tag is the absolute, first line in the HTML text file.

TIP: *To work correctly, the refresh meta tag must be the very first line in your HTML text file.*

This is how the source file for a page that includes a refresh meta tag looks:

```
<META HTTP-EQUIV="refresh" CONTENT="20;
http://www.projectcool.com/developer/alchemy/05B-au-
topage.html">

<html>

<head>

<title>Refreshing a Page</title>

</head>

<body>
Body of the HTML page
</body>
</html>
```

Notice that the meta tag precedes everything; it is even before the <html> and <header> tags.

Making a Framed Slideshow

The most common use of the refresh meta tag is to replace a splash page with a homepage, but you can also use it to create slide shows—and the replaced content can be within a frame, not necessarily the entire page.

Figures 3.3 through 3.5 show how a series of images can be linked together to create an effect. When you enter the site, you see Figure 3.3. After a few moments, the illustration in the frame changes, as you see in Figure 3.4. A few seconds later it changes again, as you see in Figure 3.5. These figures can cycle through in a loop or can end with the last image as a static part of the page.

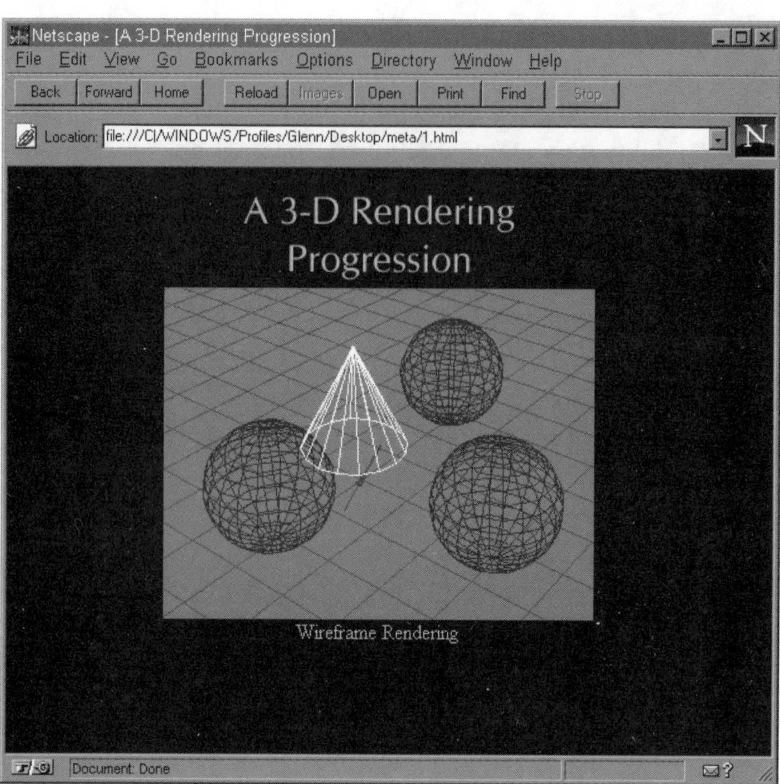

Figure 3.3 *The page that appears on the screen when you first enter the site.*

TRY IT

If you want to see how this effect works "live," go to http://www.projectcool.com/guide/enhancing. You'll see the framed slide show in action.

The code that created this effect is quite simple. The first HTML file began with a refresh meta tag that told the page to refresh after 30 seconds. The page was within a frame, so only the frame changed. The rest of the page remained the same.

The second page also started with a refresh meta tag. This tag also specified a 30-second pause, and then called for the third HTML page. Again, the page was within a frame, so only the frame changed.

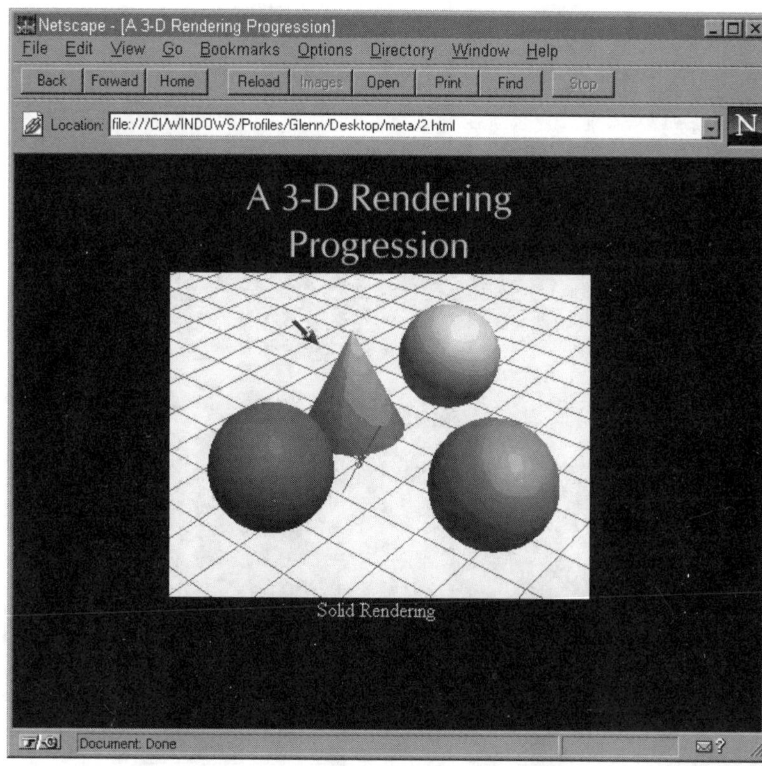

Figure 3.4
After a 30-second pause, this second illustration appears in the frame.

The third page started with a refresh meta tag. This tag specified a longer pause, 60 seconds, then called for the first HTML file again, thus creating a loop that refreshes the series of three images one after the other.

There are lots of creative ways you can use this tag. For example, picture a small frame along the edge of the screen that displays a series of images about a social problem on a nonprofit page designed to help solve that problem. Another use might be a series of sketches of an architectural project, showing the project from various angles in various stages of creation on a page about the building.

The applications for using automatic page replacement go on and on, and let you add a sense of motion and interactivity with one simple meta tag.

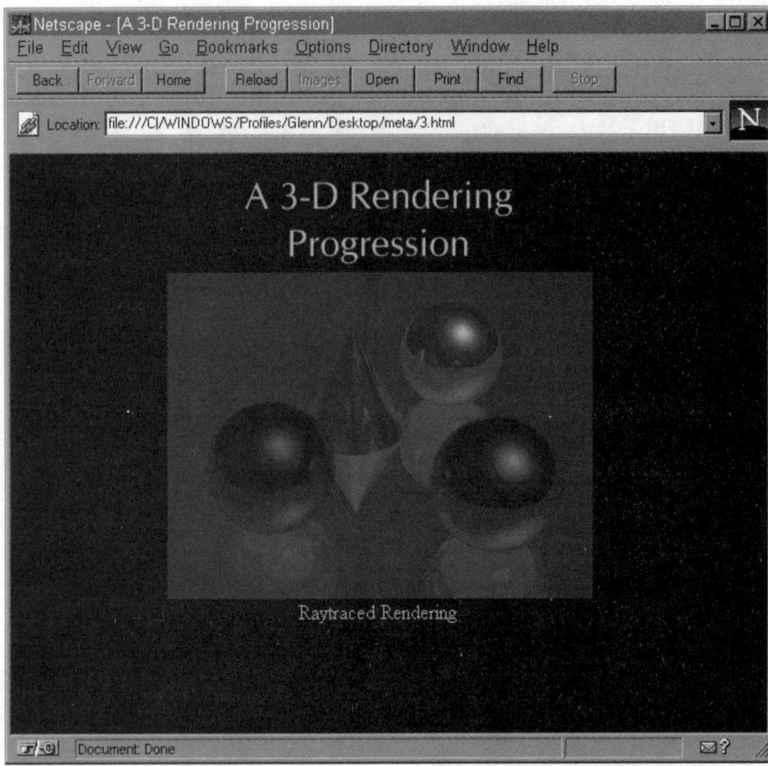

Figure 3.5
After another 30 seconds, this third image appears in the frame. Then, 60 seconds elapse and the entire cycle starts again.

USING META TAGS TO PLAY SOUND FILES

This section shows you how to use meta tags to automatically play a sound when someone uses your page.

There are a number of different ways to tell the browser to play a sound file. Both Netscape Navigator and Microsoft Internet Explorer have their own unique tags for making this happen, but you can also create this effect with a meta tag—and the meta tag will work across both platforms.

To create automatic-playing sound files you need a sound-recording tool for your particular type of computer or a preexisting sound file. To hear the sound on the web you need to have a sound-playing tool installed as a helper application in your browser. If you have a PC, you'll also need a sound card to play the sound.

Design Considerations

Sound is a very noticeable effect. It can either enhance your site experience or annoy the heck out of your readers. It also requires an extra amount of download time.

When you are putting automatic-playing sound files on your page, give some thought to your audience and the environment in which they are likely to be viewing your site.

- Are they in a work setting? If so, are you sure you want your page to shout "YO! VISITOR! WELCOME TO GREG'S GALAXY!" 20 seconds after it loads?
- Will the sound help set the mood or tone of the page?
- Will the sound further the message of the page?
- Will the sound play on the most common platforms that your audience is using?
- Will the sound take so long to download that your reader will be long gone before the first chirp arrives?
- Is the quality of the sound file suitable for your audience? Is it a grainy home-computer recording or a carefully created snippet of sound?

Creating the Effect

It's quite simple to create a page that loads a sound file automatically. The process is virtually identical to creating a page that loads automatically. You create the sound-playing effect by using a meta tag to force the browser to pull in something else automatically from the server. In this case, that something is a prerecorded sound file.

You do this by adding one simple line of code to the HTML file.

```
<META HTTP-EQUIV=refresh CONTENT="#seconds; URLof
the sound file">
```

The tag's name is META.

The first switch is Http-Equiv. You use this switch and not the Name switch because the meta tag needs to communicate with the server.

The value for the switch is refresh, a standard action value understood by most recent browsers and servers. The word refresh does not need to be in quotes.

The second switch is Content. It tells the browser how to go about performing the refresh action.

The value for the Content switch is the number of seconds to wait before starting the sound, followed by a semicolon and the URL of the sound. The entire value of the Content switch must be surrounded by quotation marks, because this information is getting passed along to the server.

For example, this code:

```
<META HTTP-EQUIV=refresh CONTENT="15;
http://www.fred/sounds/oompah.au">
```

tells the browser that after 15 seconds, it should play the sound file called oompah.au. What your reader experiences is that a file starts loading and 15 seconds later, the helper application launches, and he or she hears the merry sounds of six bars of an oompah-pah polka.

When you use a meta tag to play a sound, remember that the tag must be located within the header section of your HTML page. Ideally, it would be the first line after the <head> tag. If you put the tag elsewhere in your file, the browser may simply ignore it.

TIP: ***To work correctly, the refresh meta tag that calls a sound file must be within the header section of the HTML page. If it is in the body, the browser may just ignore it.***

This is how the source file begins for a page that automatically plays a sound.

```
<html>

<head>

<META HTTP-EQUIV="refresh" CONTENT="15;
http://www.fred/sounds/oompah.au ">

<title>Refreshing a Page</title>

</head>
```

TRY IT

1. Go to the TRY IT section.
2. Type this code:

```
<html>

<head>

<META HTTP-EQUIV="refresh" CONTENT="15;
http://www.projectcool.com/guide/sounds/oom
pah.au ">

<title>Refreshing a Page</title>

</head>
```

```
<body>
<h1>Here Comes the Band!</h1>
<p>It's festival time again in Mountain
Edge. And as they have for the past 17
years, Fred and his amazing Ommpas will
lauch the events.
<p align=center>Join us for a free concert
at the gazebo near Lake Wallaponit!
<p align=center>Friday --- 8 pm
<p>Bring blankets and lawn chairs and join
us under the stars.
</body>
</html>
```

3. Click on TRY IT and watch (and listen) to the results.

USING META TAGS TO HELP INDEX YOUR SITE

This section shows you how to use meta tags to help some search spiders index your site better.

First, let's clear up a couple of common misconceptions about meta tags and indexing.

Rumor #1. Your page must have meta tags in order for the spiders to find and index it. Not true! Spiders find your page whether or not it has meta tags. The tags do, however, help some of the spiders index it in the way you want it indexed.

Rumor #2. You can control the exact way your site is indexed by using some magic formula of meta tags. Wrong again. For some spiders, the meta tags provide guidelines, but the content of meta tags is weighed with other factors, and each spider uses meta tag information a little differently.

Rumor #3. You can "trick" a search directory into listing your site high in someone's search results if you pack the page with certain words within meta tags. Three strikes! Not only is doing this in bad taste and style, but it can actually work against you. Some spiders have been trained to ignore repetitions or to toss out any pages that it feels are trying to spam it.

Oh, and don't include words like "hot babes" in your indexing meta tags just because you think a lot of people search for those types of phrases. It's tacky. And besides, do you think someone looking for "hot babes" is really going to be interested in your site about polka bands? Use meta tags intelligently to increase your odds of having readers who are truly interested in your content find your site.

TIP: *If you include inappropriate words, pack your files with the same phrase, or try any other alleged "trick" to get your site a higher search result, your efforts won't work. At best, you'll end up with a disinterested, mismatched reader; at worst, you'll be excluded from the index.*

That said, there are ways to use meta tags to enhance your chances of being indexed in a way that helps your site be found by potential readers. But even then, indexing tags may not be for everyone.

In general, if you don't care how your site is indexed, if your audience already knows where to find you, and you don't plan on indexing your own site, don't worry about adding meta tags for search spiders. For example, if your site is a report on last month's Smith Family Reunion, you've probably already told all interested parties that you exist. But, if you are trying to reach people who don't know you are out there and they are likely to be using search services, take a little time and think about the meta tags that will best describe your site and its content. It is worth the effort.

Also, if your site makes a heavy use of frames, then using meta tags is a particularly important consideration. If you don't use meta tags, spiders index a page based on the first few hundred characters in the HTML file's body. In framed documents, those first few hundred characters are usually a frameset—from which a spider can't find any text and therefore has no idea how to index the page.

TIP: *If you are making heavy use of frames, it is a good idea to add meta tags so that the search spiders have some text—besides your frameset—to index.*

Understanding Spiders, Engines, and Directories

Before detailing how to use meta tags to enhance the search process, it is helpful to understand a little more about how searches on the web work. There are five components you should be aware of when you are thinking about how to make your site "findable." These components interact with each other to make your site stand out to the searcher.

Search Spider: A program that automatically traverses the web, creating an index of all accessible pages in cyberspace.

First is the search spider. Some of the search/directory services employ spiders; others don't. The spider is an automatic agent that goes out and searches the web for anything new. It turns its results into an index.

The index is a listing of all the content the search service knows about. Some services, like AltaVista and WebCrawler, use primarily spider-generated indices. Others, like Yahoo!, are primarily directory-based indices.

Directories are compiled, organized sets of sites. There is typically some human intervention that says "polka bands belong in the music, bands category." Directories don't include every single page on the web, but by limiting themselves they can often be more useful, if less comprehensive. Directories, too, generate indices but these indices are guides to the contents of the directories rather than maps of the entire Web. Yahoo! is probably the best-known directory service.

A search engine is the tool that translates a reader's search request into a query that searches through the indices and returns a search response. Search engines use all sorts of technologies including items like keywords, weighting, proximity, and full-text search. Don't drive yourself crazy trying to understand how each works; just know that no two engines work exactly the same, and there is no silver bullet for making your site hop to the top of every list.

Finally, the search interface is the way in which a reader enters his or her question. Don't underestimate the human factor in searches—if you know people refer to your content area by a particular name or description, use that in a meta tag and in the description of any directory submissions you make for your site. By thinking like your readers, your readers are more likely to find you.

Search Index: A compilation of a set of searchable data.

Directory: A compilation of some subset of all websites, created with human input and through human decision making.

Search Engine: The program that translates a reader's search request into a query that searches an index or database and returns a list of matching results.

Search Interface: The way a human "talks" to a search engine.

Understanding Search Sites

There are eight major search services; this list is subject to change at any time, but at the moment they are, in alphabetical order:

AltaVista (http://www.altavista.digital.com)

Excite (http://www.excite.com)

HotBot (http://www.hotbot.com)

Infoseek (http://www.infoseek.com)

Lycos (http://www.lycos.com)

Open Text (http://index.opentext.net)

WebCrawler (http://www.webcrawler.com)

Yahoo! (http://www.Yahoo.com)

And, naturally, none of them index pages—and use meta tags—in the same way.

As you prepare to create your indexing meta tags, it is helpful to understand a little about how the different search services use the tags. It is also helpful to know about your audience's habits. Do most people you want to reach prefer one service over the others? If so, then optimize your use of meta tags for that service.

The best way to get a feel for the way a particular search site works is to visit it, and read its FAQs and hints for how to prepare your site for it. Run some test searches on phrases that relate to your site. View the source on the top matching URLs to see how they employ meta tags or use key phrases in the body text.

AltaVista

Digital's AltaVista is popular and huge. It claims to have the largest web index of over 31 million pages on 627,000 servers—and growing. If it's out there, it is likely that AltaVista will have it indexed. It's also likely that your site will be lost in the deluge of responses that many people get when they submit a search query.

Fortunately, the AltaVista spiders index both keywords and description meta tags. If you've included a description meta tag, it will be displayed as the summary for your URL in the search results.

If you don't include meta tags, AltaVista will index all the words in the document and use the first few as the summary text. That means if you don't include a description meta tag, you could find your site described as something vague, like this:

"If you were using a Java-enabled browser, you would see an animated, scrolling text sign that looks like this: We want to welcome you to the lovely Central . . ."

rather than something useful, like this:

"A travel guide to New York's Hudson Valley Region including places to eat, sleep, and shop, points of interest, attractions, activities, recreation, sports."

Both the examples are real summaries from an Alta Vista search on the same word. With the sheer volume in AltaVista, it makes sense to use every tool you can to clarify what your site is about and to make it easier to find.

Figure 3.6 shows a screenshot from AltaVista.

Excite

Excite is a combination directory/search service. Its offerings include the City Net guides and other editorial content. It claims it lists 50 million URLs and completely updates its index every two weeks.

The company does not support meta tags for indexing. On its site it says, "We believe our decision protects our users from unreliable information." Its reasoning is that by using meta tags, people create little ads for their sites, rather than describing what the site is actually about.

Figure 3.6
AltaVista is popular, and huge; thousands of search results are common.

Instead of relying on the site's author, the Excite software automatically generates a description of the page, based on the words in the HTML file. It indexes full text, but cannot handle framed pages unless the page also includes a no-frames section.

Figure 3.7 shows a screenshot from Excite.

HotBot

Wired's HotBot is a full-web index and search service. It claims that its search spiders and indexing processes are the only ones that can keep up with the ever-changing web. Its crawlers constantly search the web for new items and its index is updated once a week.

HotBot relies on technology for its indexing intelligence and supports more meta tag names than any other

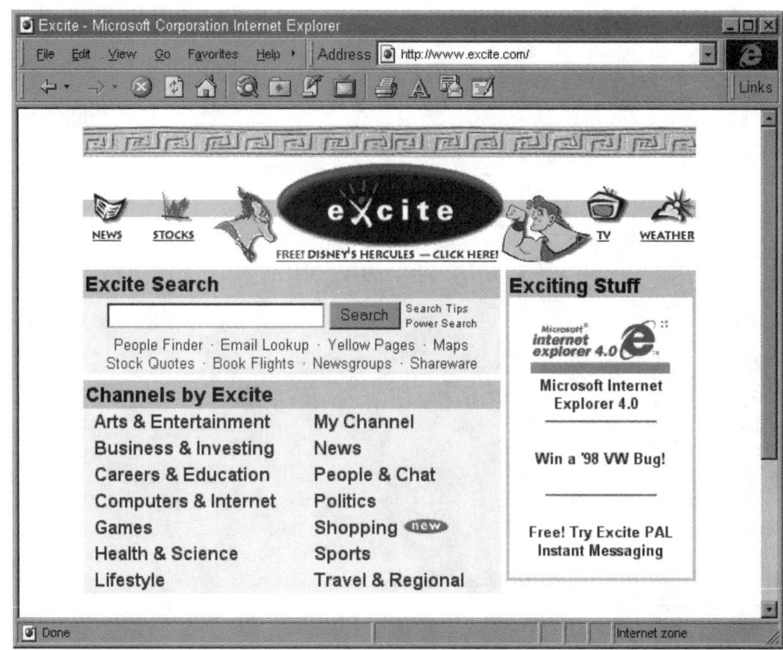

Figure 3.7
Excite doesn't use meta tags, preferring to rely on its own software to extract meaning from pages.

service, including description, keywords, author, and robots.

Like its parent, Wired, it has the most visually stimulating user interface with the most vivid colors. It also has a loyal core of followers.

Figure 3.8 shows a screenshot from HotBot.

Infoseek

Infoseek is part directory, part search service. Ultraseek is its search component, through which it claims an index of over 50 million URLs. The Ultraseek index supports keywords and description meta tags. On graphics-only pages it will use the "alt text" value in the image tag as indexing text.

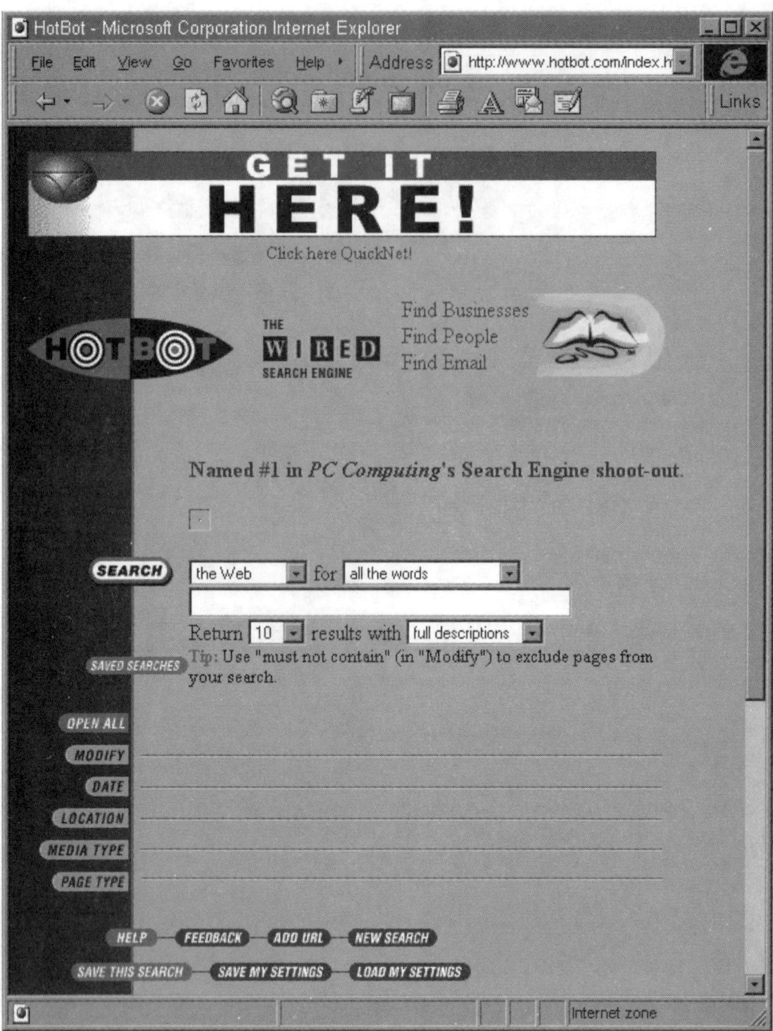

Figure 3.8
HotBot relies on technology for its indexing, supporting more meta tags than most.

Ultrasmart is the directory component. Directory sites are chosen manually, culled from the automatically compiled index based on "editorial value, traffic, and the number of links to the site."

If you want to be well indexed in the Infoseek service, it is worth your time to include a keywords and description meta tag in your HTML pages.

Figure 3.9 shows a screenshot from Infoseek.

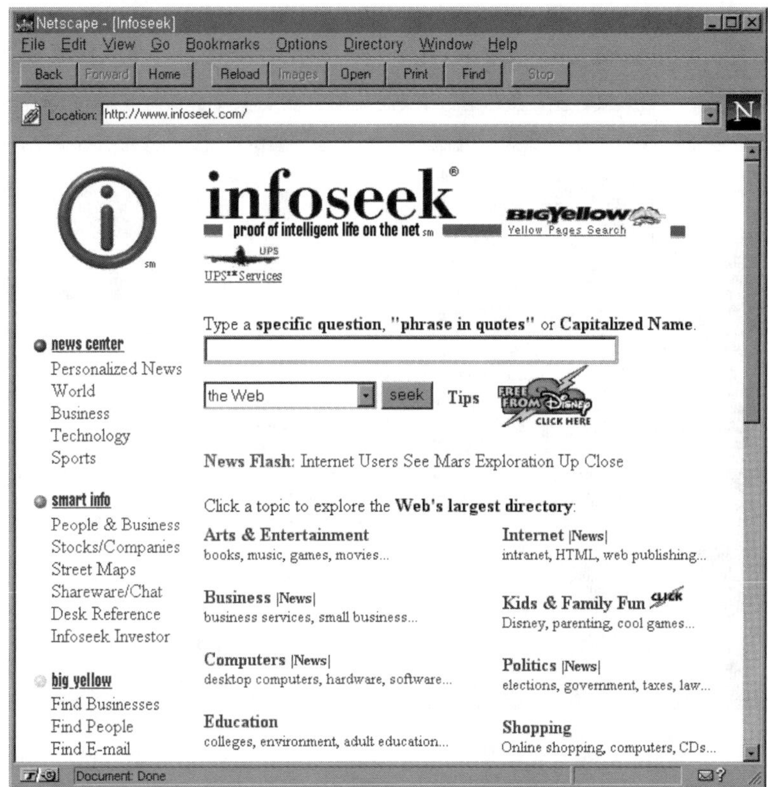

Figure 3.9
The Infoseek spider uses both keywords and description meta tag data as it builds its index.

Lycos

Lycos was one of the first group of search services, originally based on technology developed at Carnegie Mellon. It acquired Point and uses the "Point Top 5%" as part of its directory component.

Figure 3.10 shows a screenshot from Lycos.

Open Text

Before there was "The Web," Open Text Corporation was making full-text search engines for other applica-

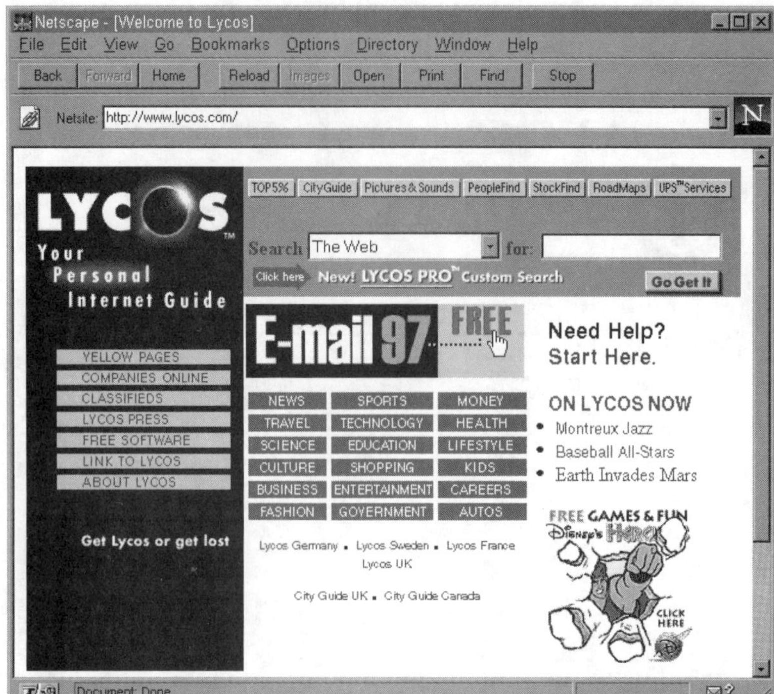

Figure 3.10
Lycos includes the Point directory as part of its search service.

tions. It applied its approach to the web and created the Open Text Index, which bills itself as "The Internet's Home Page."

Open Text relies on full-text indexing and automatically creates search summary text based on the first 200 words on the page. Its index is continually updated, and Open Text claims it has the fastest search engine and more comprehensive index of web pages.

The Open Text technology makes no use of meta tags, relying instead on its own search technology to build the index and provide URL summaries.

Figure 3.11 shows a screenshot from Open Texts.

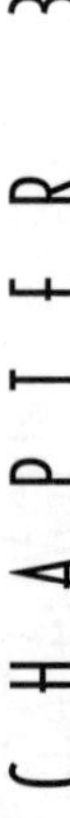

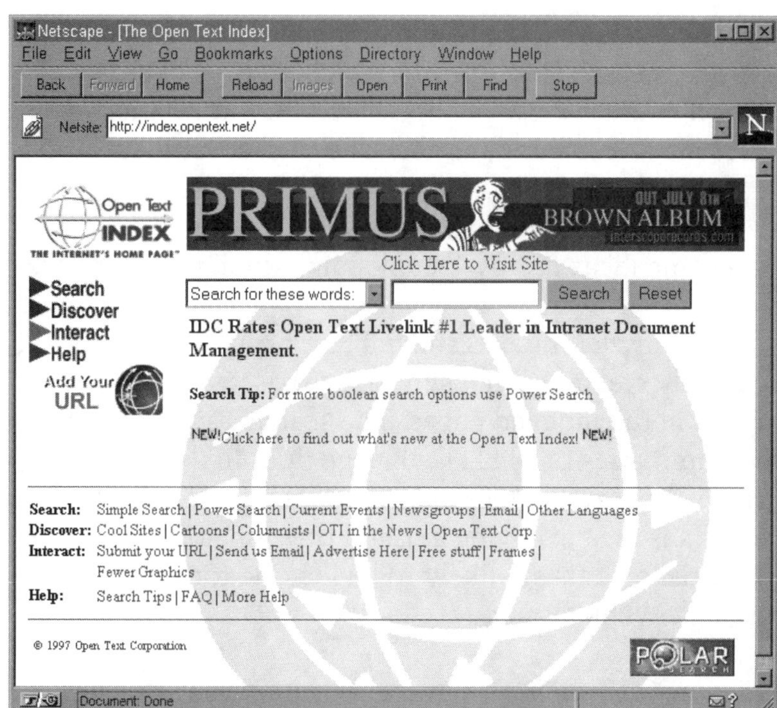

Figure 3.11
Open Text is a search company that applied its technology to the web.

WebCrawler

WebCrawler was the first full-text search engine on the Internet. It began as a research project by student Brian Pinkerton in 1994 at the Department of Computer Science and Engineering at the University of Washington in Seattle. It was initially a small single-user application to find information on the web; by the fall of 1994 it had a web interface and was receiving 15,000 search requests a day. It continued to grow and in 1997 was purchased by Excite. Today WebCrawler claims it receives 3 million queries a day.

Its early "just because" academic spirit lives on, though, and the service contains links that help people develop their own web crawlers. It also runs a Java applet that shows a scrolling ticker of real searching being run on WebCrawler. If you have a Java-enabled browser, it's worth a look (http://www.webcrawler.com/WebCrawler/SearchTicker.html). Watching the ticker is also a good study in how people search for information—there are an amazing number of typos, specific scientific terms, and requests for actress/models du jour. It is a little snapshot into the minds of web users and can give you some ideas of how people might look for your site.

WebCrawler indexes the full text of sites and automatically creates search summaries based on the first words in the indexed pages. The searcher can see either the summaries or the HTML page titles in the search display. WebCrawler does not support the indexing meta tags. This means having a useful title is helpful if your potential readers are likely to be looking for your topic through WebCrawler.

Figure 3.12 shows a screenshot from WebCrawler.

Yahoo!

Yahoo! is the web's best-known directory, and being a directory is a key to its success. Unlike HotBot or AltaVista, it does not employ spiders to crawl throughout the web routinely, indexing all content. It is a compilation of sites, organized by humans.

To be included in Yahoo!, you must submit your site, along with a 20-word description of its content. You can recommend the category to which it should belong, but final decisions on both inclusion and placement are in the hands of Yahoo!.

Yahoo! doesn't care about any meta tags you may have included. Its search index is created from its directory contents.

Figure 3.13 shows a screenshot from Yahoo!.

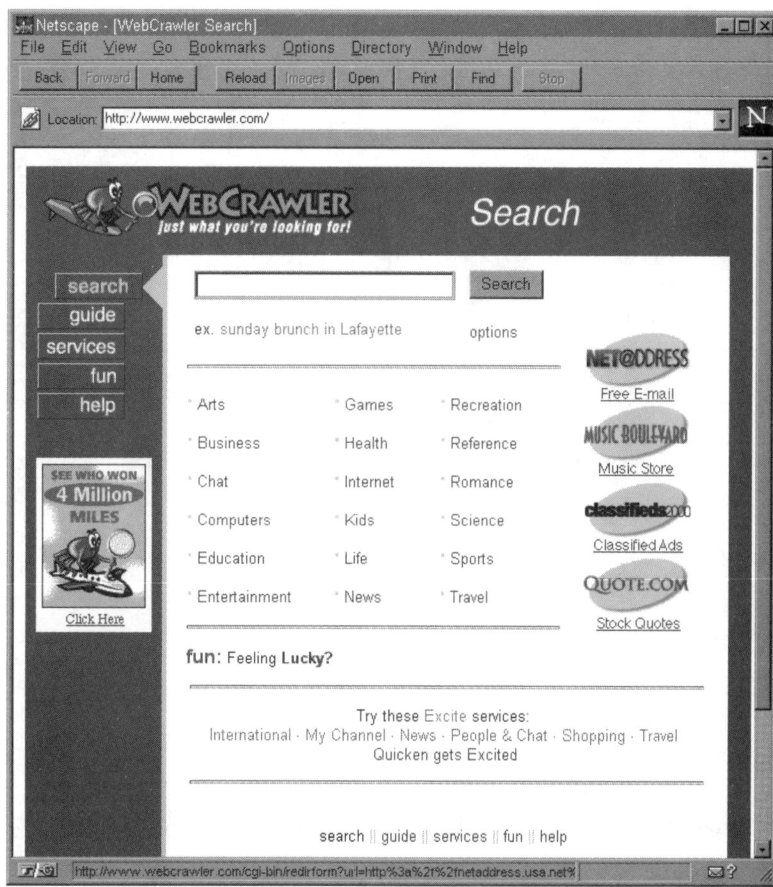

Figure 3.12
WebCrawler still shows its academic roots in its use of inhouse technology for its indexing—but its search ticker is fun to watch.

TRY IT

To see a list of links to the search sites and their submission requirements, go to http://www.projectcool.com/guide/enhancing.

You might also want to type a couple of sample searches for your site in each of the services and compare the results.

Or, test a very simple search. For example, just try typing the word "horse" into each service and compare the first 10 results.

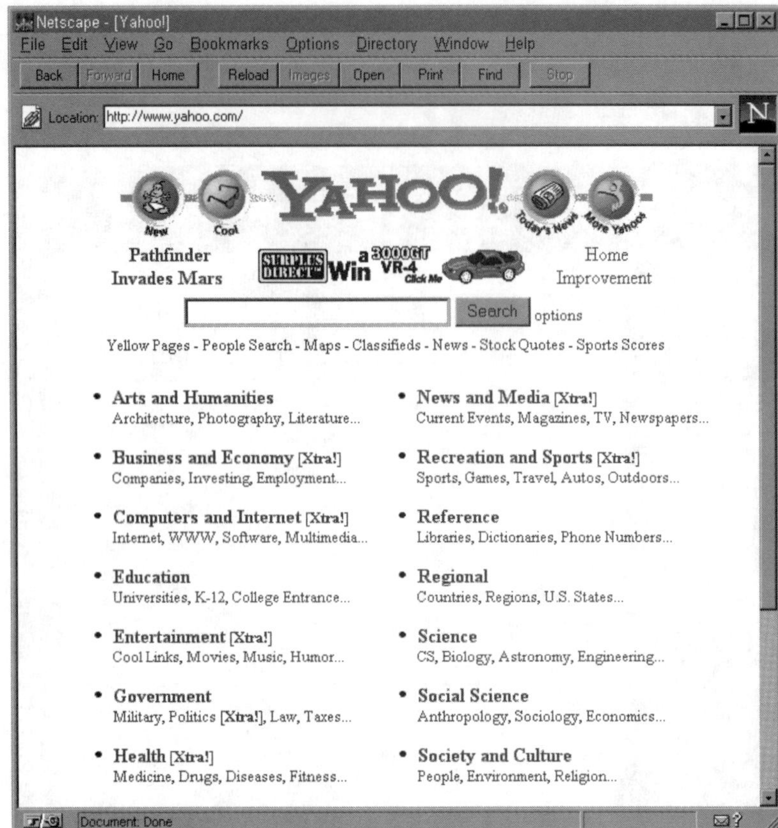

Figure 3.13
Yahoo! is the web's leading directory, relying on the human touch for its summaries and catetgorizations.

Adding Meta Tags

Adding meta tags for search spiders to find and use is quite simple. You'll place them in the HTML file's header area, one tag after the next.

The basic meta tag looks like this:

```
<META NAME="xxx" CONTENT="xxx">
```

- The tag's name is META.
- The first switch is Name. You use this switch because you are using the meta tag to store a set of information, not to pass a request or data along to a server.

The two most common values for the Name switch are "description" and "keywords."

- The second switch is Content. It tells the browser what data is stored in the meta tag.

  The content is the actual data that is being stored in the meta tag. For example, the content value for a description meta tag would be a brief description of the page. The content value for a keywords meta tag would be a list of possible search words or phrases, each separated by a comma.

The result of adding these tags is, ideally, that search spiders will describe your page the way you want it described, and display it as a search result high on its hit list.

None of these tags are "standards." They are simply names that many of the search spiders use. If the spider doesn't understand the name of a tag, it will simply ignore it, no harm done.

TIP: *The description and keywords meta tags are the most often recognized and most useful tags to use for enhancing the indexing of your pages.*

Using the Description Meta Tag

This is the basic structure of a description meta tag:

```
<META NAME="description" CONTENT="a short, but ap-
pealing, description of the page, usually less than
200-250 characters long.">
```

Normally, a search spider will use the first few words or first several hundred characters in the body of your HTML page as a sample of what a reader will find at the site. However, if you insert a description meta tag the spider will use the value in the Content switch as the page's description instead.

For example, a description meta tag for a South Florida Realtor might look like this:

```
<META NAME="description" CONTENT="Harry's Homes
brings you the finest waterfront properties in South
Florida." >
```

By using the meta tag, the description that appears after your site's name in a search result will be much more meaningful to potential readers.

Using the Keywords Meta Tag

This is the basic structure of a keywords meta tag:

```
<META NAME="keywords" CONTENT="words, simple phras-
es, items of interest, possible search terms">
```

The keywords meta tag lists words or phrases that a searcher might use in looking for your topic. The more words match, the better the odds are that your site will be in the top 10 matches. For example, a keywords meta tag for a South Florida Realtor might look like this:

```
<META NAME="keywords" CONTENT="South Florida, homes,
houses, waterfront, properties, realtors, condos,
dockage, waterside, canals, sunsets, water, ocean,
Atlantic, Biscane Bay" >
```

Now, the odds are improved that someone looking for "houses on the water" will find that site.

Using the Abstract Meta Tag

This is the basic structure of an abstract meta tag:

```
<META NAME="abstract" CONTENT="="A longer, more de-
```

```
tailed description of your site, an academic style
abstract.">
```

Sometimes a spider will also record an abstract, along with a description. The abstract is simply a longer description that summarizes the page. For example, an abstract meta tag for that same South Florida Realtor might look like this:

```
<META NAME="abstract" CONTENT="The most popular
place to retire and relax in the sun is South Flori-
da. Harry's Homes has the most complete listing of
waterfront property on ocean, bay, and canel. The
site includes links to MLS listings, information on
key communities, and a special search feature that
helps you work with Harry to find the home of your
dreams.">
```

Now readers using a service that supports the abstract meta tag will see a full and complete summary of your page.

Using the Author Meta Tag

This is the basic structure of an author meta tag:

```
<META NAME="author" CONTENT="Author/creator name">
```

The author meta tag lets you identify the author of the page. Sometimes this gets used; most often you'll be including it for your own benefit or for the benefit of anyone looking at your code. An author meta tag might look like this:

```
<META NAME="author" CONTENT="Jane A. Doe">
```

Using the Generator Meta Tag

This is the basic structure of a generator meta tag:

```
<META NAME="generator" CONTENT="program name">
```

You probably won't be inserting this tag yourself, but if you are using an HTML editor, you may see it when you view the document source code. Like a little advertisement, some HTML page editors automatically include a generator meta tag in every page they create. A typical generator meta tag looks like this:

```
<META NAME="generator" CONTENT="PageMill 2.0">
```

Using the Expiration Meta Tag

This is the basic structure of an expiration meta tag:

```
<META NAME="expiration" CONTENT="a date in time">
```

The expiration meta tag lets you identify the expiration date of the page. Sometimes this gets used; most often you'll be including it for your own benefit or for the benefit of anyone looking at your code. An expiration meta tag might look like this:

```
<META NAME="expiration" CONTENT="01 Jan 2000">
```

Meta tags that identify author or expiration date are most frequently used in conjunction with an HTTP server that expects to receive this data and produces automatic headers or reports based on the information. In these cases, you wouldn't use the Name switch; instead, you'd identify the type of meta tag with the Http-Equiv switch and you'd have a process set up with your web server to make use of the tags.

Avoiding Indexing

You can also use meta tags to avoid having your page indexed. Not all spiders honor the meta tag that does this, but several do today and more are rumored to be adding support for it in the future.

You avoid indexing by using a meta tag named *robots*. A robots meta tag looks like this:

```
<META NAME="robots" CONTENT="noindex">
```

Using a robots meta tag and setting its content value to "noindex" tells the search spider to skip this page when it builds its index.

USING META TAGS TO WORK WITH RATING SYSTEMS

This section shows you how to use meta tags to comply with emerging content-rating services.

A developing use for the meta tag involves content rating. Like movies and television, there is a growing accord that the best method of balancing freedom of expression with community concerns is a voluntary ratings system. The World Wide Web Consortium (W3C), the web's standards organization, responded to this by developing a system called *Platform for Internet Content Selection*, or PICS.

The PICS project was begun in mid-1995 and adopted as a standard in May 1996. It was designed to support more than filtering of "offensive" content. The PICS project intentionally did not define rating criteria, voting instead to create a judgment-free technology for supporting whatever ratings criteria individuals or groups want to use. This approach gives the PICS meta tags a hook for ranking site content in a variety of ways, and there is talk that the PICS meta tags could become an additional tool for building search indices and directories.

PICS ratings are currently offered by the nonprofit

Recreational Software Advisory Council (RSAC) and by the for-profit company SafeSurf. It is likely that others will also offering ratings codes in the near future. The W3C is keeping a list of groups offering self-rating services; if you're interested, drop by the W3C site for the most up-to-date information.

Each group devises its own rating scale and generates a meta tag for your site that ranks your content based on its criteria.

TIP: *To learn more about PICS and its ongoing development, you might want to visit the W3C PICS area at http://www.w3.org/pub/WWW/PICS/.*

The nonprofit Recreational Software Advisory Council supplies one set of self-rating criteria. It is located at http://www.rsac.org.

The for-profit company SafeSurf supplies a different set of self-rating criteria. It is located at http://www.safesurf.com.

Adding PICS Ratings to Your Site

Three things need to happen for the PICS security/ratings feature to work.

1. First, the reader needs to turn on Security in his or her browser. If readers don't have Security turned on in the browser, all the meta tags in the world won't make a bit of difference.

   Security is an option in Internet Explorer's View menu/Option selection. As of this writing, Netscape Navigator does not support the PICS meta tag.

2. Second, you need to register your site with the RSAC, SafeSurf, or any other group that creates rating values.

As part of registration with RSAC, you'll answer detailed questions about the scope of sex, nudity, language, and violence in your site. At the end of the questionnaire, the ratings system will assign you scores in each of the four categories.

SafeSurf uses 10 categories, including profanity, heterosexual themes, homosexual themes, nudity, violence, sex/violence/profanity, intolerance, glorification of drug use, other adult themes, and gambling. Like RSAC, SafeSurf will also provide you with numerical ratings based on your responses.

3. Third, you need to include the PICS meta tags in the header section of your HTML files.

   You'll receive your site's custom PICS meta tag directly from RSAC and/or SafeSurf via e-mail. You simply paste the code fragment into the header sections of your HTML files and your site is PICS compliant.

The tag you'll receive resembles this one:

```
<META http-equiv="PICS-Label" content='(PICS-1.0
"http://www.rsac.org/ratingsv01.html" l gen true by
"Microsoft Corporation" r (n 0 s 0 v 0 l 0))'>
```

Like other meta tag uses, PICS and site ratings are hardly a magic cure. PICS meta tags have an effect only in certain situations, with certain browsers and certain users. Look to your audience for guidance on using a rating system and the PICS meta tag. If you want to reach families and children, using PICS meta tags might be an ideal match. Or, if your site contains potentially controversial material, incorporating a ratings screening might offer you some degree of protection against critics.

The PICS project is interesting for more than what it does today. It opens up an interesting avenue to the use of meta tags and to a way of sorting out the massive volume of the web.

As you can see from this chapter, meta tags offer great potential in many areas, but can also be a bit frustrating because they are such a "nonstandard" standard. If your needs match one of the functions that meta tags can provide, give them a try. They are unlikely to do any harm, are easy to learn, and can be a valuable tool for enhancing your site.

4
ADDING SEARCH TO YOUR SITE

When most people think of *search,* they think of the tools that let them sort through all the information on the web and return a list of items that match their request. There are a number of major search services designed to let you do just that.

In the last chapter, you saw how to use meta tags to make your site be more accurately indexed by the web's search spider and how to enhance your chances of showing high up in a person's search results from one of the directory/search services. In this chapter, you'll see how to enhance your site by letting readers quickly and easily search for content within your site.

Not every site is a good candidate for adding search capabilities, but if you have a lot of content, a large site, or your readers are visiting you to find specific information, you might want to enhance your site by adding your own site search tools.

For example, suppose you are running an intranet for the company sales force. Salespeople don't use the intranet for casual browsing; they are typically seeking a specific piece of information to use in a sales presentation or to prepare for a customer meeting. They want the direct hit. They are less interested in attractive browsing paths than they are in having the ability to find and retrieve a specific item with a minimum of fuss. Enter *search*. By having a well-defined search interface, a well-indexed site, and understandable search results, you can meet your sales force's needs. They can always be a few clicks away from the specific document they want. They aren't searching the entire web; they are focusing on finding data from within your site.

Or suppose you are running a shareware site. Some of your readers might enjoy poking through the "shelves" and seeing what's available, but most people want to find and download something that meets their immediate needs. Again, a search feature is a way of delivering results, quickly.

Is your site a good candidate for a search enhancement? Ask yourself these questions:

- Do I have documents that others use as reference?
- Is it difficult to keep track of the information in the site or find a particular item there?
- Do I have more than one author? Is there an easy way for people to find things by author? How about by subject?
- Are people coming to my site to get something specific or are they there to spend entertainment time?
- Does my site have archived material that people want to sift through?

If you answered yes to any of those questions then you are a strong candidate for search enhancement.

Adding search to your site isn't difficult, but it does require that you select a specific search technology to incorporate and that you have some understanding about the makeup of your site and the needs of your audience. This chapter will show you how to get started, help you think about your search interfaces, and get you started down the search path.

One caveat: We can't possibly show you all of the different combinations of search software and web servers. You'll get specific software configuration information from the vendor of the search technology you select; at the end of this chapter, we'll highlight some of the most popular choices.

UNDERSTANDING YOUR SITE

Before you add search to your site, it is important to understand how the site is structured, and how people will expect to search for information within it. Search technologies offer many different features, some of which are best matches for certain environments, some of which are best matches for other environments. The way you implement search on your site is likely to vary, depending on your—and your audience's—needs.

Before you settle on a specific search technology, look at your site and consider the following:

- Where do your documents reside?
- In what format are these documents stored? HTML? ASCII text? PDF? Word processing files? Images with header data? Some combination thereof?
- Will readers be searching the document set or will the queries be passed onto a database?

- If a back-end database is involved, who understands its structure and will work with you on implementing search on your website?
- For what types of things are readers most likely to search? Will they be looking for downloadable files? For textual stories? For images?
- What type of results do you want to supply to your readers? How many matches do you want to offer?
- What added value will search bring to your readers?
- What is the background of your searching readers? Are they trained librarians? Are they impatient salespeople? Are they new computer users?

These are all things you'll need to understand as you select a search technology, index your site, and create a search interface that works for your audience and your content.

UNDERSTANDING SEARCH COMPONENTS

When you add search features, you'll really be adding four elements to your site.

1. A search engine
2. A search indexer
3. A search interface
4. A search results interface

These elements interact with each other and make the search powerful and useful to your audience.

The underlying search technology defines how your site is indexed and what approaches people can use when searching for information there. The search and search result interfaces are the ways your readers talk to the search tools; typically, you can adapt the off-the-shelf interface in a number of ways and it is a good idea to do so. The more understandable and specific the user interfaces are, the more likely your readers are to find what they are looking for and feel positive about the process.

Selecting a Search Engine

Search technology and search tools have grown and changed dramatically over the past decade. The need to manage huge databases coupled with research in language structure and meaning have resulted in better tools for both cataloging and retrieving information.

Historically, the most common style of search structure was a query method called *Boolean* search. Boolean search is derived from a symbolic logic system developed by mathematician George Boole. Boole, who lived from 1815 to 1864 is regarded as one of the greatest mathematical minds of the nineteenth century. This largely self-taught man was appointed professor of Mathematics at Queens College in Cork, Ireland. While there, his work on mathematical logic set the foundation for algebraic thought, and his books, *The Mathematical Analysis of Logic* (1847) and *An Investigation of the Laws of Thought* (1854) form the basis of present-day computer science and cybernetics.

George Boole: A nineteenth-century mathematician whose works form the basis of present-day computer science and whose name is attached to Boolean algebra and Boolean searching.

Boolean search uses a basic syntax of operators and search terms to define a set of data. The three basic operators are *and*, *or*, and *not*.

If you've ever used a search tool, you've probably encountered these three functions. By combining these ba-

Boolean Search: A method of searching data using a combination of three basic operators: and, or, not.

sic operators with groups, you end up with a very powerful way of defining sets. Of course, to use Boolean search methods effectively, you need to understand the dynamics of the operators and of grouping. The result is queries that look like this:

```
(cougar AND mustang) NOT (ford OR mercury)
```

For the average user who just wants to find mentions of interactions between wild cats and wild horses without reading about the automotive industry, this way of searching can sometimes feel a little obtuse . . . and not particularly user friendly.

Until recently, most data searching was done by librarians, archivists, or other trained individuals who spent time learning the intricacies of wording search queries. Finding specific data pieces from a massive databank was part of their job. But as data became more accessible to individuals, there was a growing demand for easier, "friendly" ways of searching.

The resulting research into information structure has led to a number of new concepts, which are incorporated into most of today's search tools. These include proximity, thesaurus, expansions, stemming, natural language query, relevancy ranking, and clustering, to name a few of the more common.

Proximity

The idea of *proximity* is that words near each other are more "valuable" than the same words simply existing in the same document.

For example, if you're searching for information about "growing orange trees," you're more likely to be looking for a document that uses the word "growing" and "orange" and "trees" within the same sentence, rather than one that talks about "growing up" in the first paragraph, drinking "orange juice" in the fifteenth paragraph, and "sitting under shade trees" in the forty-fifth paragraph. Proximity suggests that there is a relationship between the words, and that the relationship describes the idea for which you are searching.

Proximity: Words are more meaningful when used within the same sentence or paragraph.

Proximity is sometimes expressed by the operator "near." For example, this search query finds documents in which the words "orange" and "juice" appear within a predefined distance from each other.

```
orange NEAR juice
```

Thesaurus

Some search technologies use a *thesaurus* that compares similar words. A thesaurus feature lets your search respond with useful results in the case of a misspelling, typo, or use of a similar concept. Sometimes you build the thesaurus yourself; other times the software uses a standard thesaurus plus input from you.

Thesaurus: A dictionary of varitions on a search word or phrase.

Expansion and Stemming

The techniques of *expansion* and *stemming* let the search engine find a specific word and all its variations. For example, if your search tool incorporates expansion and stemming and you search for the word "dance," your search would also look for uses of "danced," "dancing," "dancer," and "dances."

Expansion: Looking for extended versions of a word.

Stemming: Looking for the root, or stem, version of a word.

Natural Language Query

In a technology that uses *natural language query*, the reader can type in a "normal" sounding question and the

Natural Language Query: Letting the search program interpret a human question into a search query.

search engine will parse and interpret it into a specific query, based on the words used and the way the words are assembled.

For example, the reader could type "tell me about vacations in places with beaches and sailing." The search engine would interpret this and bring back results from documents that seemed to show an intersection of "vacation," "beach," and "sailing." The idea behind natural query is to let the human ask questions like a human and give the computer the job of interpreting the text.

Relevance Ranking: Analyzing search results and suggesting possible best matches.

Relevance Ranking

In *relevance ranking*, or *weighting*, a combination of frequency and proximity of certain words is used to give each result a "score." The score, typically presented on a scale of 0 to 100 percent, indicates the likelihood that the result matches what the reader is seeking.

For example, if you were again searching for information about growing orange trees in a desert climate and you were using a search engine that employed relevance ranking, you might see a search result that resembles this:

```
98% Growing Oranges in the Desert
82% Cultivation of Orange Trees: A Study
63% More Trees Mean More Juice
51% Orange Juice Surplus Ahead?
34% Orange Juice is Good for Kids
```

The search engine counted the number of times the words "orange" and "tree" and "grow" and other search phrases were used, noted the proximity of the words to each other, and tried to apply some intelligence to tell you how likely it was that the different articles matched the idea of your search. The lower-ranked articles technically met the criteria of using the specified words and phrases, but the pattern of the word and phrase use suggested a different meaning to the search program.

Typically, you can set a minimum certainty or relevancy level so that you only see search results that receive a score of, say, 80 percent or more. The idea is that you see fewer but more meaningful results.

Clustering

Clustering: Analyzing documents and grouping them by similarity.

Clustering is a technique of analyzing documents to group like results together. It relies on notions such as frequency and proximity, as well as other techniques, and it is often presented to users as an option to "find more like these."

For example, in the search for information about growing orange trees, you could identify documents that most closely match what you are looking for and ask the search engine to "find more like these." It analyzes the patterns in the documents and returns results that seem to follow similar patterns.

These are just a few of the tools search engines use to analyze documents and return search results. It is helpful to have a little basic understanding of them because they impact how well search works within your site. Depending on the content of your site and the way people are searching it, you may want to be sure one feature or another is especially strong in the technology you select.

- For example, if you have a newspaper archive, you might want to be sure your technology of choice offers a customizable thesaurus. That way, you could ensure that readers searching for popular hometown ballplayer Jim "Spitball" Evans would get results whether they looked for "Spitball," "Spitbal," "The Spit," "Jim Evans," "Jimmy Evans," or "Big JE."

- If you know readers will be searching, then searching again for information, you might want to be sure the technology allows for clustering, so you can offer the "find more like this" option.
- If searches of your site are likely to yield large sets of results, then relevance ranking would be a good feature to include, to help readers sort through the results in a more meaningful way.

Thinking about Indexing

Searches can happen on several levels. At the most basic level, a search tool would go out and look at every document one by one. However, this quickly becomes a very tedious process.

Enter *indexing*. Instead of searching each and every document over and over, the indexing program compiles and routinely updates an index of all the information and searches this index instead of individual documents. The search index is a bit like a printed index in a book. Both contain a header, or a description of the information, and a locator, or a pointer to where that information is found. When the search engine finds a likely match from the index, it just zips on over to the document by following the locator information.

Indexer: The part of a search program that builds and maintains the search index.

Why should you care about indexing? For the same reasons you care about the underlying search tools of your selected search technology. Search engines will create somewhat different indices from the same set of data because each engine's indexer works a little differently. The indexer is the part of the program that builds the search index You want the best match between your data and the strengths of your search program's indexer.

Search Interface: The way you let your readers communicate with your search program.

Some indices are created around keywords. These usually require that a librarian or archivist create and assign sets of keywords to documents. A keyword-based system can be very fast, but it is also subject to the interpretation of the keyword assignor. Traditional text archive programs tended to rely on keyword indices.

More and more programs today rely on full-text indexing, in which the content of each document is evaluated automatically as it is indexed; common phrases such as "the" and "a" and "and" are ignored, and the document is distilled down to word or phrase components.

In addition, some search programs index only certain types of documents. Know what types of documents are part of your site and be sure that your selected search technology can handle them. For example, if your site includes PDF-formatted files, be sure you select an indexer that can process them.

If many of your documents are HTML files you may want to be sure that the indexer supports meta tags, so you can improve the accuracy of the index and search results by consistent coding on each page you create.

Thinking about Your User Interface

Your *user interface* is possibly the most important part of your search feature. It is entirely possible to have a very bad search experience with a very good search engine. It's easy to blame the search technology ("it's not fast enough," "it's not powerful enough," "it's not thorough enough") when all that may be at fault is the way you've asked for your readers to enter the search.

Think about the way you use information for a second—isn't it a little disconcerting to see an empty blank box staring at you, asking you to "type what you want" in it? What are the odds of spelling or typing each word exactly correct? How do you word the question? Can you use Boolean operators? How do you ask for orange trees without getting recipes for orange juice drinks? What if your mind just draws a blank?

The search results can't be any better than the search information you enter. Computers aren't psychic (yet!), and can only do what you tell them to do. The user interface is a way to make it easy for your reader to talk to the search engine and get results that feel satisfying and meaningful.

There are actually two parts to your user interface. The first is the way your readers ask search questions of your site. The second is the way the site returns the search results.

Designing a Search Interface

Most search tools for websites come with a "standard" search interface. This standard interface is typically a small box—a form that sends some typed text to the search engine for processing. If you have clear-thinking, rational readers who know exactly what they want and can articulate it clearly *and* you have a fairly small site, this might be enough. But more readers want—and most sites need—more.

The easier you make it for your readers to search, the more you anticipate their actions, and the fewest possibilities for mistakes you give them, then the more satisfied everyone will feel with your site's search features. Here's a few ideas to think about as you plan a search interface.

Searchers aren't browsers. They are searching because they want a specific bit of information. Now. Right now.

This is the most important thing to remember in designing a search interface. The interface you offer needs to be short, sweet, clear, and easy. If readers need to look at documentation or an FAQ in order to understand your search interface, something is wrong.

Searchers need help defining their searches. Often, searchers know what they want but aren't quite sure how to phrase it.

Clear options, like checkboxes or radio buttons, are fast, easy to use, and return consistent results. Just don't overwhelm with a vast number of disorganized choices!

Searchers need to know the rules. If there are guidelines to how a search should be worded, make the guidelines clear, brief, and obvious. For example, if you employ Boolean search, say so. State which operators you support. Don't hide information in some generic FAQ where no one will be looking.

Searchers aren't interested in scrolling through pages of input forms. Keep the search interface to one screen page or less. Short and sweet, but useful. That's the description of a good search interface. Don't make searchers feel as if they are completing a complex survey just to find an item on your site.

Searchers don't want to bond with the interface.

They want to get the search's result. Give them minimum interaction and maximum versatility.

Searchers want to know what they are searching through. If your site has multiple sections, consider offering an option that lets people search through a specific area or areas. For example, you might want to let your sales force search through product literature separately from engineering specs.

Searchers want search satisfaction. Don't make them wait.

Don't leave your readers puzzling over how they should phrase something or what to do with the search interface. Make the interface so obvious and intuitive that your audience barely feels it as they head on toward finding what they want.

The following sections show some examples that help to demonstrate how content, audience, and search interface can interact to make the search experience a fruitful one.

Example One: The Automobile Database

The problem: People want to search Joe's Auto Central for information about new cars. Most of the visitors to Joe's site are typical consumers who, when given a choice, can probably say they want A over B but they don't yet know they want a Volkswagen Cabriolet.

The audience: People who want to find cars that meet their general criteria.

The content: Information about different vehicle makes and models. There are standard categories of information that each piece of content shares.

The interface solution: A one-page checklist/radio box combo that complies a search query based on the selected options.

The resulting user interface, as shown in Figure 4.1, is presented in a way that nontechnical people can see and understand. It looks like a series of simple checkboxes—click on the features that are important to you. Readers can pick a single price range and several possible model options for each search.

The reader doesn't waste any time puzzling out how to say they are interested in convertibles that cost less than $20,000. It's obvious that they click on under $20,000 and convertible, and then start the search. Satisfaction is quick. Opportunity for reader error is low.

You can also see this interface as a working HTML page (using no graphics—all the typography is created through HTML tags, making the page perform quickly at modem speeds) on this book's companion website at http://www.projectcool.com/guide/enhancing.

Example Two: Sales Literature

The problem: A sales force wants to access the company's product spec sheets, brochures, and troubleshooting guides for its aquarium supplies and aquatic support equipment. The sales force is scattered across North America and receives the latest information through a password-protected site.

The audience: Highly motivated users who want to find a specific piece of information quickly; they are accessing the site from many remote locations.

The content: Product spec sheets, brochures, press releases, troubleshooting guides, and competitive bulletins.

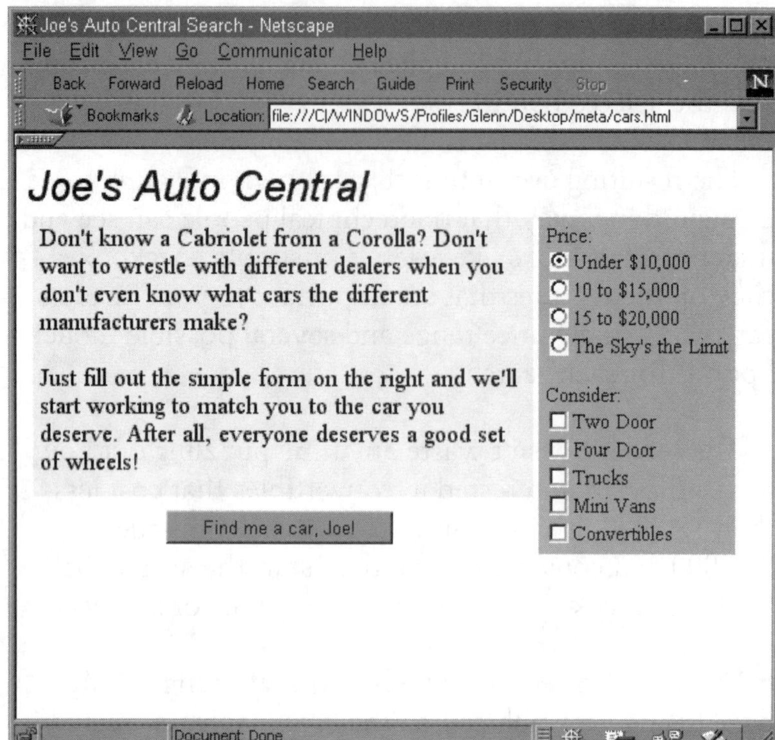

Figure 4.1
This checkbox interface works well for the casual user who wants to find information matching general criteria.

The interface solution: A type-in box for search terms coupled with a pulldown menu for selecting document type.

The resulting user interface, as shown in Figure 4.2, is small in size. It can be easily viewed on a laptop computer in the field. It also requires little download time. It combines a text box for specifying aquarium product name or other search terms. The pulldown menu lets the searcher specify one or more categories of document. In this case, Joe's aquarium sales force knows what it is looking for. Unlike the general audience, it knows the terms that are important and wants to target directly to a particular item. The sales force audience is also likely to want a specific type of document; for example, a cus-

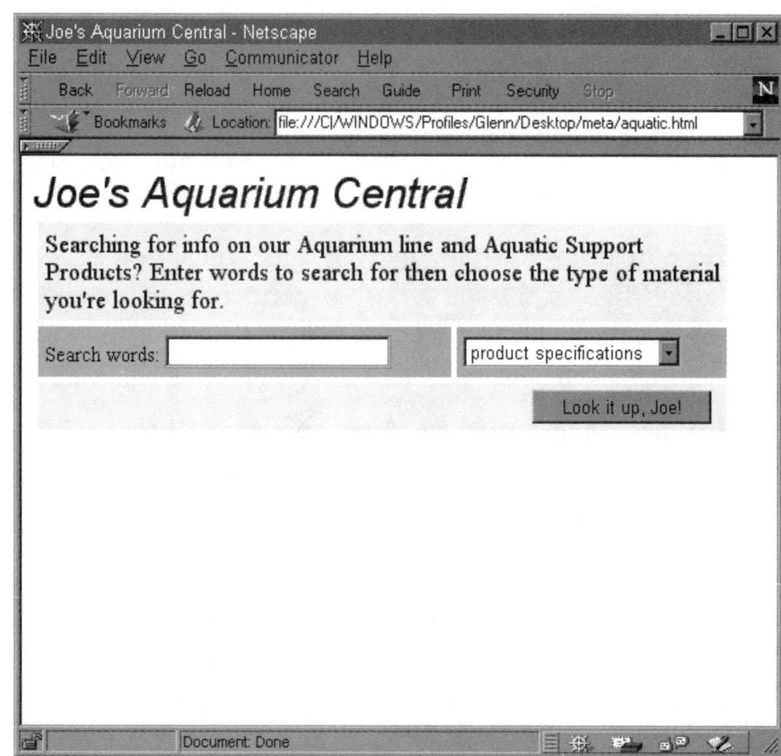

Figure 4.2
This interface works well for the motivated user who needs to find mission-critical information fast.

tomer is complaining about a newly purchased piece of equipment, so the salesperson might want troubleshooting or bug reports; or a competitor is pitching for the job and the salesperson wants competitive reports and product spec sheets.

You can also see this interface as a working HTML page on the companion website at http://www.projectcool.com/guide/enhancing.

Example Three: Complex Data

The problem: A financial data company sells people access to its archives of legal and technical documents. Readers can search for different document types by different criteria. The criteria vary depending on the type of document.

The audience: Paying customers who want accurate results sent to their e-mail accounts.

The content: Complex legal and technical documents about financial issues. The contents of the documents make any single one difficult to describe in short search phrases.

The interface solution: A combination of text entry boxes and checkboxes, which produce different search options through JavaScript variables.

The resulting user interface, as shown in Figures 4.3 and 4.4, is clean and straightforward, yet it handles a great deal of complex data. It responds to the user and lets him or her select information with a high level of specificity.

It lists the actions in step-by-step order, so that there is no confusion about what needs to be done. Each category of "alert" has several possible subcategories. If all the information for each alert and its subcategories were presented at one time on one page, it would be somewhat overwhelming. This approach lets the reader see only the options that are relevant to the immediate search.

This interface is controlled partly through a JavaScript script. JavaScript, which is covered in more detail in Chapter 5, is a scripting language that lets you create interaction between reader and browser. For example, if a reader clicks in a box about "general befuddlement," the browser automatically provides a subset of choices that are specific to the topic, as shown in Figure 4.4. This approach allows the reader to make complex choices with-

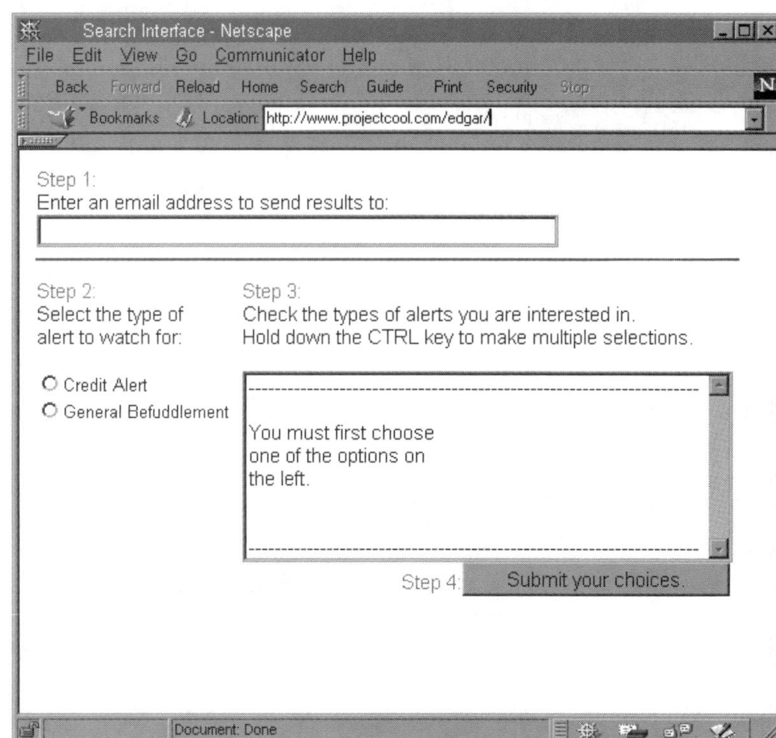

Figure 4.3
This interface works well for the paying customer who wants to define highly varying complex searches accurately.

out being overwhelmed by complex search phrases or an interface with far too many choices. Note how the subchoices change when the reader selects a differnt document type. This approach allows the search form to remain on one page, yet offers much flexibility and variation

For complex search patterns that will vary from reader to reader you may want to look at incorporating scripting to add a layer of interactivity (Figures 4.3 and 4.4).

You can also see this interface as a working HTML page on the companion website at http://www.projectcool.com/guide/enhancing.

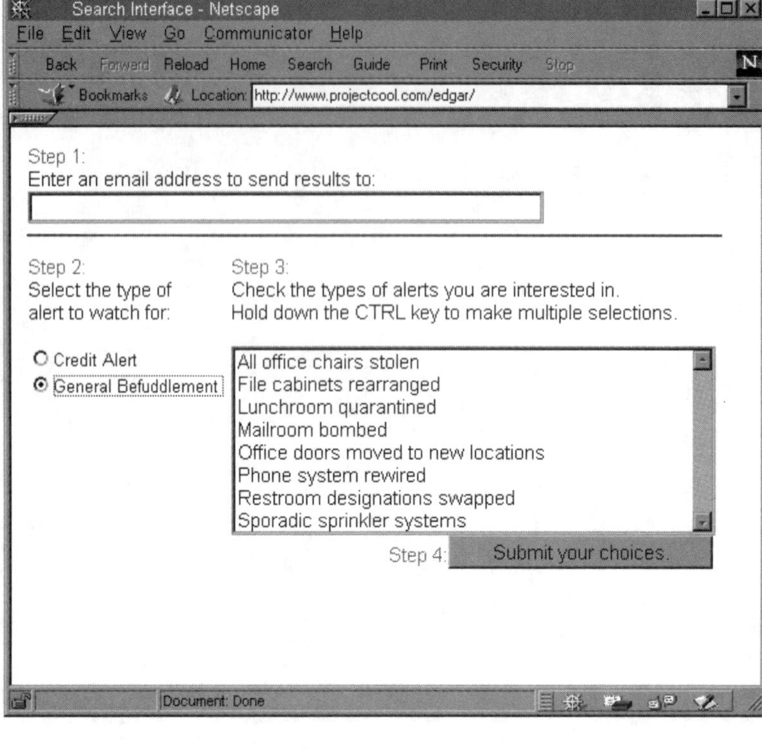

Figure 4.4
Note how the sub-choices change when the reader selects a different document type. This approach allows the search form to remain on one page, yet offers much flexibility and variation.

Designing a Search Results Interface

Once the reader has entered a search, he or she will be anxiously waiting for the search results. It is important that the presentation of the results be as clear and useful as the search query interface was. If the results page is muddy or confusing, the reader leaves frustrated and unsure if he or she has actually found anything of value. Here are some search results interface tips.

- No mud
- Clarity on next step
- Clutter-free

Here are a few ideas to think about as you plan a search results interface.

Don't hide the results. Make them plain and clear.

If possible, order the results in some meaningful way. A jumble of results can create a confused reader who thinks the search didn't work "right."

Make the next step obvious. Don't let the reader wonder what he or she can do next.

Does the reader click on a result to see the full document? Can he or she resubmit a different search? With one quick glance, the next step should be obvious.

Keep the results pages clean and simple. Don't clutter results down in graphics. Don't cram so many on a page that the forest overwhelms the individual trees.

For example, Figure 4.5 is the search results page from our DevSearch section. It uses color, relevancy, and a clean tabular structure to present the search results. The deeper the color of the relevancy cell on the left, the closer a match the item should be. This provides several types of visual feedback.

For items found in our Developer Zone, we display the page title to better describe the page content. When readers click on a choice, the item opens in a new window, leaving both the other search results and the search interface visible and immediately accessible.

Figure 4.5 shows this results page interface. Here, the reader searched for information about color and tables. The search found 38 possible matches and displayed the best-matching 20. This information appears at the very top of the results page.

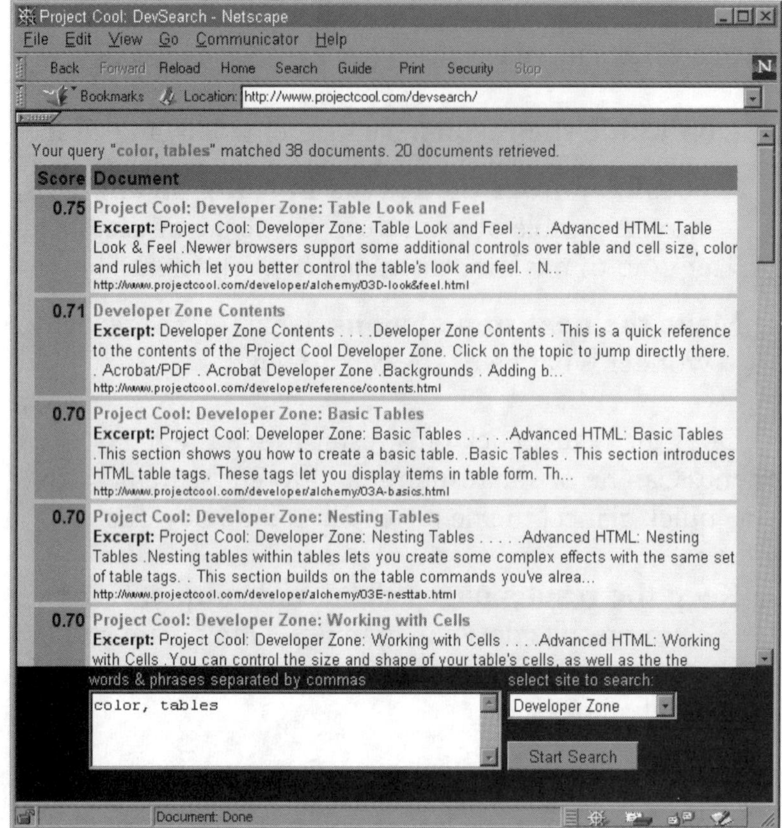

Figure 4.5
This search results page is clean, clear, simple, and obvious. It works.

You can test this search interface and results page by going to the Project Cool site at http://www.projectcool.com/devsearch and selecting the Search option.

Building the Interfaces

Although each search engine has slightly different requirements, the basic steps to creating custom interfaces are similar.

1. First, you'll design the interface and decide how it should look, what information it should collect or display, and how the reader will enter data. For the results page, you'll need to think about how the

data should be displayed and how the reader will get to the found items.

2. Next, you'll build an HTML form for collecting the data. The search programs will specify which variables they need and how the form must pass along the information. Some of the programs even supply you with templates that you can modify for your needs. For the results page, you'll need to build a similar HTML page, which will receive and display the information from the search engine.
3. Finally, if you are passing search information through to a database as well as to a search index, you'll need to work with your database programmer to create a CGI script that connects the search query to the database.

Interfacing with a Database

As is true with creating and implementing any form on your website, one important thing to remember about creating a search feature that interacts with a back-end database is this: You can't do it alone. You need to work with the people who run your database.

Databases are so varied that there is no way to describe this process properly within the confines of this book. If you are interfacing to a database, concentrate on creating your user interface from the website and trust your database programmers to help you create the connection between the website and the database.

INTRODUCING SEARCH VENDORS

Here, in alphabetical order, are some of the more popular search technology vendors. Their product offerings are subject to change, and no single technology is the best match for everyone. (We happen to use Verity because it works for us.)

The best way to select a technology is to first understand your needs and what will work for you and your site. Then, explore some of the vendors' websites to get a flavor for their areas of expertise and the markets they focus on. Ask people who are running sites with needs similar to yours what they do and don't like about their search engines. Finally, ask the vendors questions and request tests on datasets similar to yours. Find out—before you commit—what the nitty-gritty of setting up the engine and indexing your site entails, and what hardware platforms and server software will work with the search package. Up-front legwork is important because you don't want to be changing search technologies like yesterday's fashions. Find the best match, and grow with it.

Excite

Excite offers a package called EWS (Excite for Web Servers). As of this writing, a direct link to information about it is <http://www.excite.com/navigate>. EWS is described as an application that webmasters can download and install on their web servers to provide "intelligent, concept-based searching of the HTML and ASCII documents which are locally stored on their web server."

EWS is currently a free (and unsupported) product. The only price for use is that your site must link to Excite's site.

The product supports only HTML and ASCII documents; if you want to use this product and have other types of documents on your site (like word processing, spreadsheet, presentation, or PDF files), you'll need to convert them to HTML or ASCII in order for them to be indexed by EWS.

Fulcrum

As of this writing, Fulcrum is focusing on a product line called the Fulcrum Knowledge Network, with the idea that its technologies can tie multiple datatypes and locations together. It supports Lotus Notes documents, as well as the usual web documents. Its approach "maps" information to make it accessible and usable.

A current direct link to Fulcrum's product information is <http://www.fulcrum.com/english/products/prodhome.htm>.

Open Text Corp.

As of this writing, Open Text is focusing on intranet applications. Its online product listing is at <http://www.opentext.com/corp/otm_prod.html>.

Its primary product is called Livelink Intranet, which is a suite of applications for finding and managing information across intranets. The suite incorporates searching and indexing tools that handle more than 40 different file format types, including SGML, as well as workflow and document-tracking applications.

PLS

PLS is a vendor that came out of the text archive world (PLS once stood for Personal Library System). It offers tools for searching and indexing document collections.

As of this writing, its primary search product is called PLWeb Turbo. A direct link to its product page is <http://www.pls.com/products/>.

Verity

You're probably encountered Verity's search technology, but just haven't known it. The company's tools are embedded in many web and electronic publishing applications.

As of this writing, its search products are grouped under the name Search '97; a direct link is http://www.verity.com/products/family.html.

The Search '97 products are designed to be scaleable (in both price and function) and are adaptable to both intranet and Internet applications. Its agent technology lets you match incoming datastreams against a user's prerecorded preferences and immediately route matching data to an e-mail box or HTML page. Its Topics product lets you create complex searches that appear simple to the reader. It indexes most major file formats, including PDF.

Search can be a valuable enhancement to your website, especially if it is a large site, a site that serves as a reference or archive for readers, or a site from which readers are seeking specific information on demand. Doing search well requires that you spend time thinking, planning, and researching how you will implement it—but the time you spend is well worth your while given the value search can bring to your readers.

The search solution you find needs to fit both your content and your budget, as well as have the ability to grow with your site as you expand and add additional content. Once you select a search engine, you'll want to stick to it, so take the time upfront to explore different vendors and products and find the best match for your content, structure, and audience needs. With search, you are installing a framework that will be around for a long time.

And don't forget the elements of good user interface design when you implement your search feature. Your users' experience relies on it.

Above all, don't let the amount of work involved in setting up a solid search feature scare you off. If it is the right enhancement for your site, its value will pay off tenfold.

5

ADDING INTERACTIVITY WITH JAVASCRIPT

HTML lets you put different types of elements in a page and create hyperlinks, but it doesn't allow for much real interactivity based on the actions of the reader.

Yes, you can do some very basic cause-and-effect displaying of content with frames, you can accept input through forms, you can create links between pieces of data, and you can add visual elements, like GIF animations, that add motion but play alone. However, to add real interactivity, that is, actions that happen in response to something the reader does, you need to turn to some sort of scripting or programming language.

One of the most popular of these languages is *JavaScript*. JavaScript is an object-oriented scripting language that lets you build interactions between the contents and state of the browser and the actions of the reader. It was initially developed by Netscape but has become widely popular and seems to be on its way to becoming a *de facto* standard for scripting interactivity into web pages.

JScript is Microsoft's implementation of JavaScript.

JavaScript: A scripting language for the web, promoted by Netscape.

JScript: Microsoft's version of JavaScript.

You may see the two terms, JavaScript and JScript, used interchangeably on the web. In this chapter, we'll be using the term JavaScript, not because we prefer one version to another but because the term is in somewhat wider usage and more people are familiar with the word "JavaScript."

With just a few JavaScript snippets you can transform a static page into something extraordinary. JavaScript provides an accessible tool for enhancing your pages by adding real user interactivity. For example, you can use JavaScript to:

- Display different versions of a page, based on the browser the reader is using.
- Provide visual feedback to a reader when he or she puts the mouse over a menu option.
- Add a little explanatory text in the status bar when the reader moves his or her mouse over the button the text describes.
- Change the graphics on the screen as the reader moves his or her mouse around the browser.
- Do simple ad rotation.

Here's an example of JavaScript in action. This example shows a little of the potential of what JavaScripting can do.

TRY IT

To see a JavaScript in action:

1. Go to the companion website.
2. Move the cursor over the first menu option. Watch how the bar "lights up" and the graphic image changes.

3. Move the mouse to another option.
4. Move the mouse to a black area of the screen.

JavaScript made the appearance of the page change based on what you did with the position of your cursor.

In one version of the Project Cool homepage, readers first saw a page that looked like Figure 5.1. At first glance, this page looks like any other page with a list of choices.

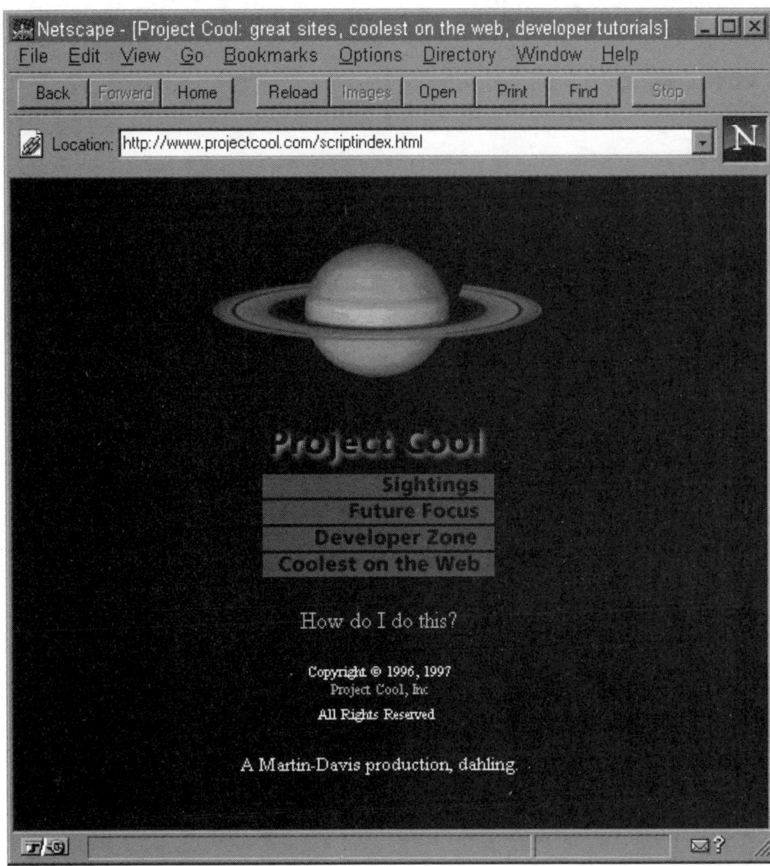

Figure 5.1
This page looks like a basic HTML page. It offers several options from which the reader can select.

But it is JavaScripted! As soon as the reader moves his or her cursor over one of the menu options, the page comes alive and reacts to what the reader is doing.

- The option "lights up" to show it can be selected.
- The image at the top of the page changes to reflect the section to which the option is linked.
- The status bar displays a brief textual description of the section.

Together, these responses provide the reader with valuable feedback about what he or she can do, and what each option offers.

For example, in Figure 5.2, the reader's cursor was on top of "Sightings," while in Figure 5.3 it was on top of "Future Focus." Notice how the page looks different, depending on where the reader has his or her cursor placed on the screen.

What to Expect from This Chapter

Whole books have been written on programming JavaScript. This chapter won't turn you into a JavaScript expert, but it will give you an understanding of what JavaScript is, what sorts of applications you can create , and how to use existing code and modify it for your own web pages.

This chapter also includes five scripts and directions for adapting them for your pages. You can use these scripts as a base and quickly and easily add additional functionality to your web pages. The five scripts in this chapter are:

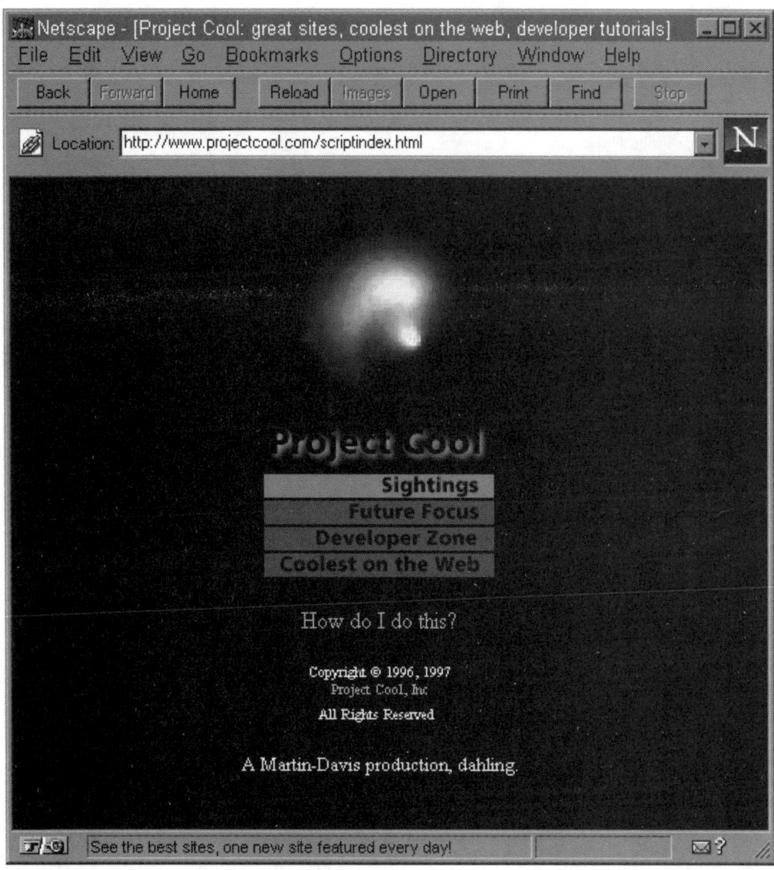

Figure 5.2
The Sightings option is highlighted, the image changes from Saturn to a comet, and the text description appears in the status bar at the bottom of the page.

- A script that lets you display different versions of the page based upon the browser the reader is using
- A script that lets you provide visual feedback to readers when they put the mouse over a menu option
- A script that lets you display text in the browser's status bar
- A script that lets you change graphics on a page, based on the location of the reader's cursor
- A script that lets you do simple ad rotation

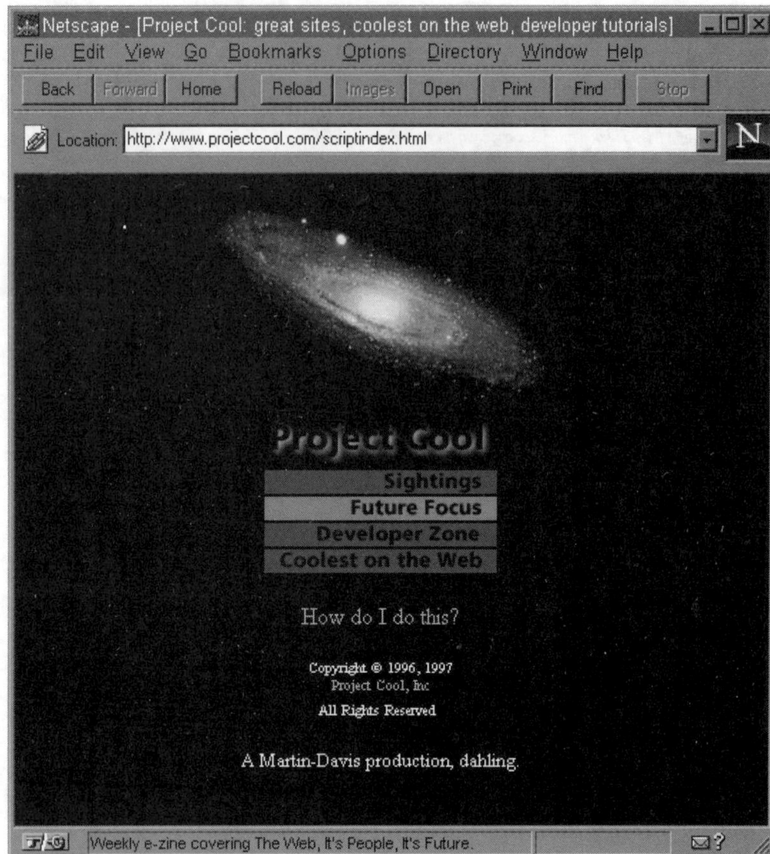

Figure 5.3
The Future Focus option is highlighted, the image changes to a galaxy, and the text description appears in the status bar at the bottom of the page.

These scripts are printed and documented in this chapter. They are also available in electronic form (which saves you some typing!) in the companion website (http://www.projectcool.com/guide/enhancing.) You can just download them, adapt them, and be up and running with them.

Ensuring Compatibility

Like a great deal of the web, it turns out that the JavaScript "standard" is a bit of a moving target. Netscape's version is called JavaScript. Microsoft's ver-

sion is called JScript. Each supports a slightly different set of commands from within their respective browsers.

Five major browsers currently support JavaScript in one form or another:

- Netscape Navigator 2.0
- Netscape Navigator 3.0
- Netscape Navigator 4.0
- Microsoft Internet Explorer 3.0
- Microsoft Internet Explorer 4.0

Naturally, the latest versions of each browser supports the most JavaScript commands. All of the JavaScript we cover will work on the latest versions of the browsers but we will lose some compatibility with older versions. We'll note what works with what as we cover it. When a browser doesn't understand a JavaScript command, it displays an error message and stops the script from running further. In general, it doesn't crash the browser or cause any other bad side effects.

TRYING A SIMPLE JAVASCRIPT COMMAND

This chapter focuses on writing and adapting full scripts. However, the latest versions of IE and Navigator offer some limited support for JavaScript commands within HTML tags. Here's one that you can try right now, to show how easy it can be to use JavaScript commands.

This command will let you create a clickable button that jumps your reader to a specific URL. The command is called an *event handler* (you'll learn more about these later) and it can be inserted in the HTML form tag.

TRY IT

1. Go to the Project Cool TRY IT page (http://www.projectcool.com/guide/enhancing).
2. In the text box, type the following text and code:

   ```
   <p>
   ```

   Click on this automatically generated button to jump to the Project Cool home page.

   ```
   <p>

   <form>

   <input type="button" value="Go to Project Cool"
   onClick="window.location='http://www.projectcool.com'">

   </form>
   ```

3. You'll notice that the form tags are just like the regular HTML form tags, except you have added a new switch. onClick is a JavaScript event handler that tells the browser to take this action when the reader clicks the mouse button. The action is to display the URL "http://www.projectcool.com>".

Click on the TRY IT button to see what this code looks like in a web page. It should resemble Figure 5.4.

You can insert this snippet of code inside your HTML text page to quickly create a linked button.

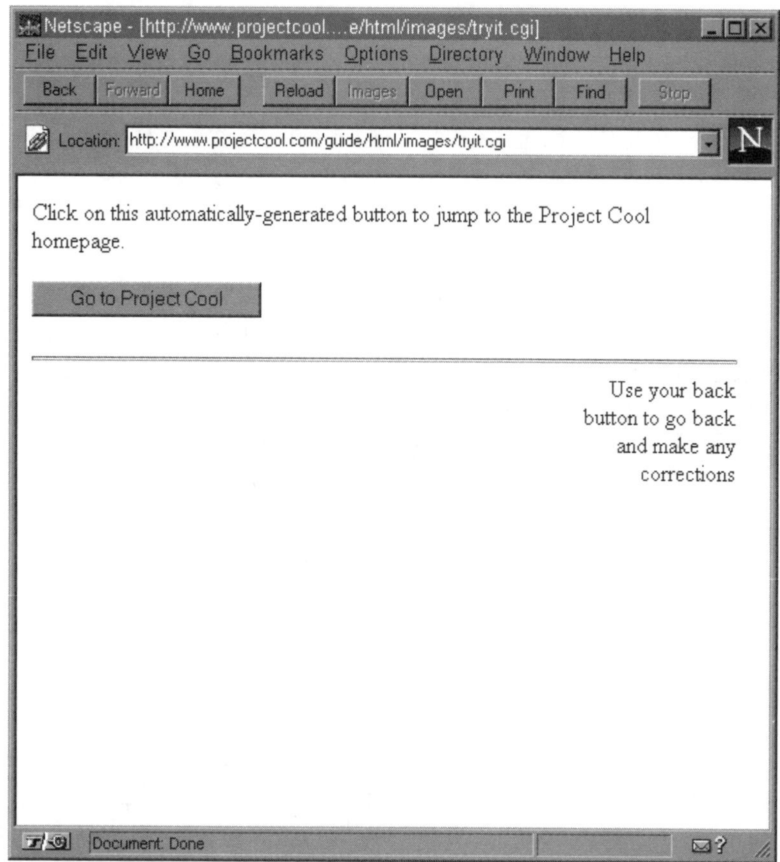

Figure 5.4
The code creates a button that your readers can click on to jump to a specified URL.

UNDERSTANDING JAVASCRIPT CONCEPTS

JavaScript is, as its name suggests, a scripting language. Scripts are simple sets of directions to a computer.

Scripting Language: Simple, noncompiled sets of directions to a computer.

Scripts have been used in different computer environments for a long time. They are often used to perform repetitive tasks. In the Unix world, many system administration tasks are handled through scripts. In the computer applications world, macros, like those found in Microsoft's Word or Claris' Filemaker Pro, perform script

Compiled: A type of computer program that can run as a standalone program on a computer. A compiled program is translated from text into machine language, which the computer can understand directly.

Interpreted: A set of computer instructions that run "as is" with the help of an interpretive program. An interpreted program has not been converted into machine language.

functions. In the web world, Perl is another common scripting language. It is often used to create CGI scripts that connect a web page to a server or database. Microsoft's VBScript is another web scripting language.

Scripts are *interpreted*, not *compiled*.

A compiled program is one that is written and then prepared to run on a certain type of computer. A compiled program is typically faster, larger, and more compact than an interpreted one. It can be easily moved from one computer to another. To edit a compiled program, you need special programming tools. Application programs, like word processors and spreadsheets, are compiled programs built with a language such as C or C++. The end user doesn't see any lines of code with a compiled language; the program just runs itself on the computer, using machine language.

An interpreted program is one that is just the raw lines of instructions to the computer. Interpreted programs tend to be small and can be quickly and easily created with just a text editor. They require an interpretive program, like a web browser in JavaScript's case, to translate the text directions into commands the computer can follow.

Understanding the Difference between Java and JavaScript

Many people confuse JavaScript/JScript with Java. It's an easy thing to do because the names are so similar, but the technologies are quite different.

Java is a compiled programming language, comparable to full-fledged programming languages such C,

C++, or Pascal. Everything from small "applets" (tiny programs) to entire shrink-wrapped applications are being created in Java. Many in the programming world predict that Java will eventually replace languages such as C and C++ as the language of choice for application development.

JavaScript is an interpreted scripting language, ideal for small nonstandalone programs within web browsers.

JScript is Microsoft's implementation of JavaScript. It lets you create functions similar to what you can build with Microsoft's VBScript. In fact, Microsoft supports both scripting languages in its Internet Explorer web browser.

Applet: A small program, often embedded in a web page, that runs locally on your computer.

Java

Within the web environment, the most common use of Java is to build applets, small programs that are automatically launched from within a web page. When the web page loads, these applets begin to execute themselves on your local computer. While the applet runs, your browser sits quietly by.

Running a Java applet doesn't consume server time. It makes it possible for small, self-contained programs to be delivered via the web, but run locally on individual computers.

However, the Java approach worries some people because it raises potential security issues. In some corporate environments, the *Information Systems* (IS) department has decided on a policy to screen out Java applets and prevent them from being downloaded. They often do this through their *firewalls*, the technology that controls who and what can access a network. These IS man-

Firewall: A combination of technologies that control access to a network.

agers fear (rightly or wrongly) that the applet could infect the system or be, in some way, a security threat to the network.

When you encounter a Java applet on the web, your computer's status bar may tell you that "applet XXXX" is running. If you are using a browser that doesn't support Java, that has Java turned off, or if you are working in an environment that screens out Java, you may see an error message telling you that you are not Java compatible—or you may simply see nothing at all.

Java is an exciting innovation for both application programming and the web. It offers the possibility of a true component environment and we're sure to be hearing more and more about Java as time goes on. But it offers something different from JavaScript.

JavaScript/JScript

JavaScript is an interpreted scripting language. When your browser encounters a JavaScript in the page, it performs the action the script specifies.

The code is typically placed directly in the web page. It requires a web browser in order to run and it is designed to be fully integrated with the browser.

JavaScript is fairly easy to learn (at least as compared with Java or another compiled programming language) and it is ideal for creating interactivity with a web page reader's actions.

Because JavaScript is physically located within the web page, firewalls can't screen it out. Individual browsers can, however, be configured to turn off JavaScript. Most browsers allow the individual user to turn Java and JavaScript/JScript on and off.

In Netscape Navigator, the JavaScript option is located in the Options menu, under Network Preference/Languages, as shown in Figure 5.5.

In Microsoft Internet Explorer, the JScript option is located in the Internet Properties menu, under Advanced, as shown in Figure 5.6.

JavaScript started out life as Livescript, a scripting language developed by Netscape to allow dynamic changes of web pages and communication between the web browser and plug-in applications. As originally conceived, one of JavaScript's main applications was to provide the "glue" that placed Java applets in a web page. In late 1995, Netscape got permission from Sun, the creators of Java, to use the word "Java," and Livescript became JavaScript.

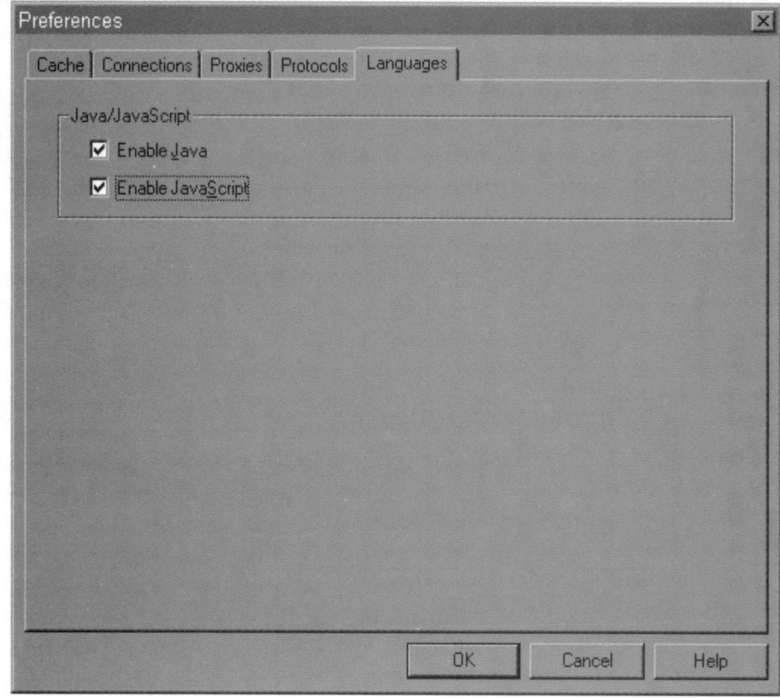

Figure 5.5
The Netscape Options menu.

Along the way, JavaScript took on a life of its own.

- It was easier for nonprogrammers to learn than Java.
- It could add a lot of interactivity with little overhead.
- Like HTML code, JavaScript is contained within the HTML text file, so it can be easily added and modified.
- It was an *open* language. Open means that the lan-

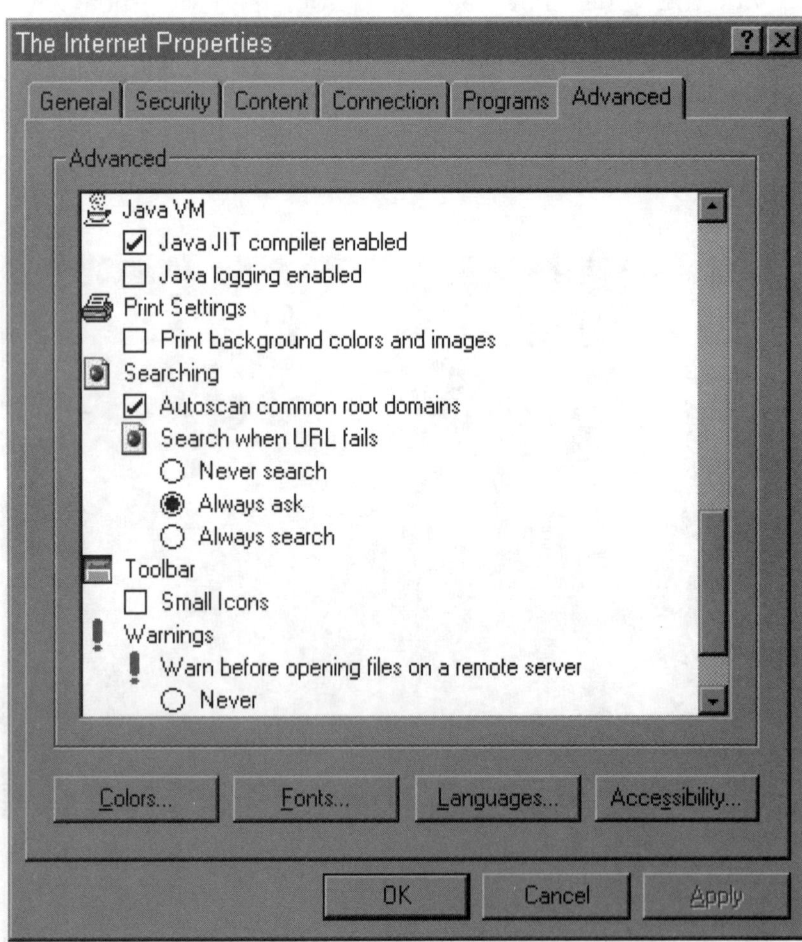

Figure 5.6
Internet Explorer's Internet Properties menu.

guage's creator has made the language's definitions and rules public, so that anyone can program with it.

Open Language: A programming language whose definitions and rules are publicly available.

As both Netscape Navigator and Microsoft IE grow more robust, their support for JavaScript/JScript increases, and JavaScript functions are becoming more and more common in web pages. Meanwhile, dozens of companies, including Apple, Oracle, and Silicon Graphics, have endorsed JavaScript as their choice for an open scripting language for the web. There is also a push underway for a standards body to "bless" a version of JavaScript and name it an official standard.

Understanding the Object Approach

Like Java, JavaScript is based on an *object-oriented* philosophy. In traditional programming, you tell the computer how to act and what to do sequentially. In an object-oriented approach, you create components, give the components characteristics and behaviors, and tell the computer how to act by describing the interaction of these reusable components. An object approach is potentially more flexible, more powerful, faster to develop, and easier to debug than a nonobject approach.

Object Oriented: A philosopy of programming that creates components and defines the interaction between them.

Java is a true *object-oriented programming language* (OOP). JavaScript is based on the OOP philosophy, but lacks some of the full OOP features. The underlying concept, however, is the same.

Objects

Objects are the central components of JavaScript. JavaScript has some standard, predefined objects. You

Objects: The basic building blocks of JavaScript

can also create custom objects for your own applications.

To think about the idea of objects, let's leave web pages and JavaScript behind for a moment and travel to a simplified videogame. To make this game work, you need to create a program that controls different spaceships. The ships will be chasing each other around the screen. You would have one model ship from which all other ships can be built. This ship is one of your objects, as shown in Figure 5.7.

Instances: A variation of the basic object.

Instances

You want to have several different types of ships in your game. You create each one by building an *instance* of the original ship.

Let's pretend we're working on that videogame. You want to create three different varieties of ship, each with its own name, color, and shape. Each of these ships is an instance of the original ship object, as shown in Figure 5.8.

Properties: Characteristics of an object.

Properties

Each instance of the object has one or more *properties*. Properties are characteristics of the object; they are a little like adjectives, describing the object.

Figure 5.7
One object is called "ship," and it is the master model from which all other ships can be built.

Ship

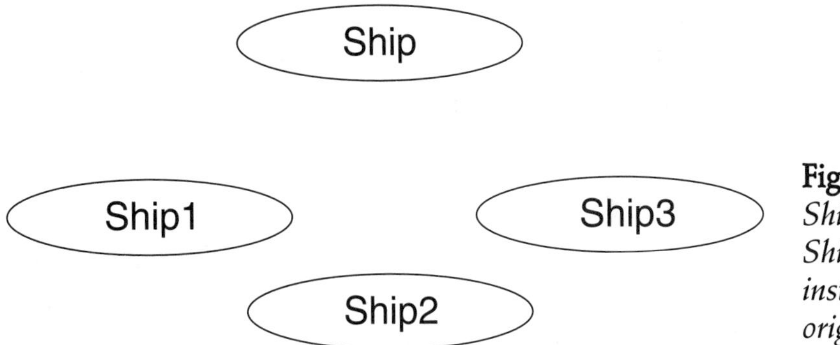

Figure 5.8
Ship1, Ship2, and Ship3 are each an instance of the original ship object.

Let's think again about those spaceships. Name, color, and shape are properties of the ship, as shown in Figure 5.9.

- Ship1 might have the name Eagle, the color blue, and the shape sphere.
- Ship2 might have the name Hawk, the color green, and the shape box.

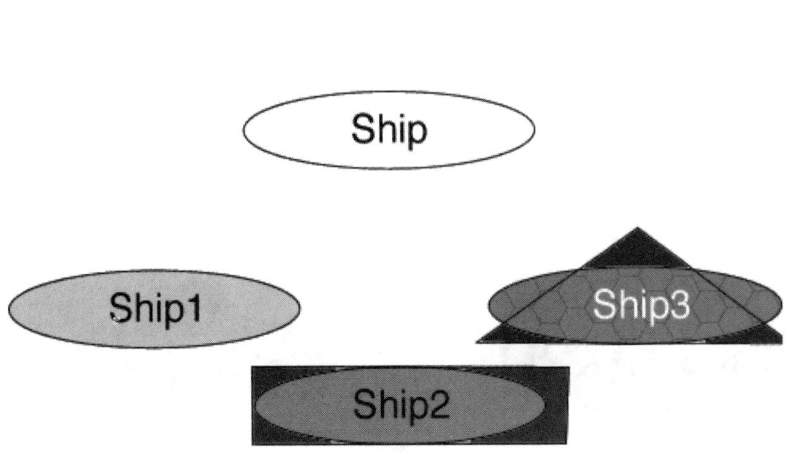

Figure 5.9
Objects have properties, which define their characteristics. The properties of name, color, and shape have a different value for each instance of the object ship. One instance, Ship 3, also has the property of texture.

- Ship3 might have the name Seagull, the color red, and the shape conical. Each instance of Ship3 might also have the additional property of texture.

Methods: Tasks which the object can perform.

Methods

In addition to having characteristics, each object can also do things or perform certain tasks. These tasks are called *methods*. Methods are a little like verbs.

Let's return to the ships again. Each ship object might have four methods: GoUp, GoDown, GoRight, and GoLeft, as shown in Figure 5.10. These methods describe what the object can do.

Functions: *Actions that perform a specific task.*

Functions

There's one more basic element in the JavaScript mix: the *function*. Functions are sets of code that perform specific tasks, but are not directly attached to objects the way that methods are. JavaScript includes several built-in functions and you can also create your own functions.

Let's return to the ships one final time. One function in this spaceship scenario might be "SpinAround," as

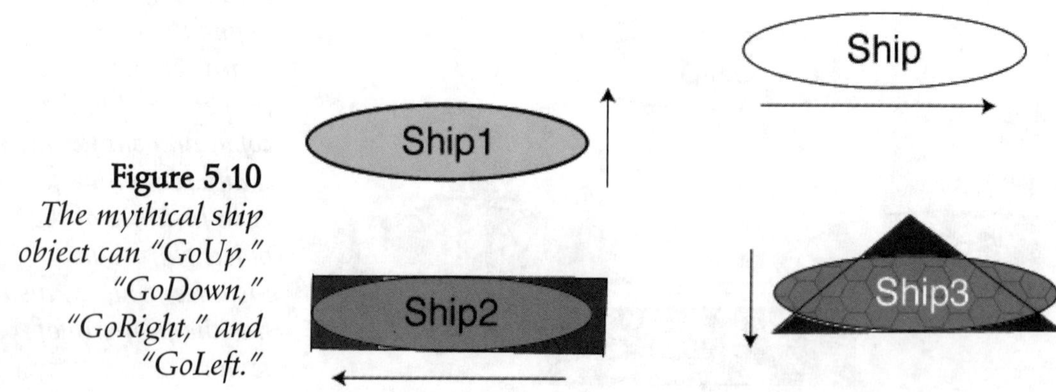

Figure 5.10 *The mythical ship object can "GoUp," "GoDown," "GoRight," and "GoLeft."*

shown in Figure 5.11. You'd create this function by writing four lines of code, calling the GoRight, GoDown, GoLeft, and GoUp methods, and then giving this set of code the name "SpinAround."

Understanding Other JavaScript Terms

In addition to the terms that describe the basic object world, there are some other programming/math concepts that are helpful to understand as you begin to tackle JavaScript. These terms will take you back to ninth-grade algebra—and you'll probably find them lurking somewhere in the dark recesses of your brain. They aren't complicated, but understanding them helps you make more sense of the way JavaScript "thinks."

Arguments

Arguments are a type of variable that you assign to objects, methods, and functions. The object, method, or function uses these values as they are processed. For example:

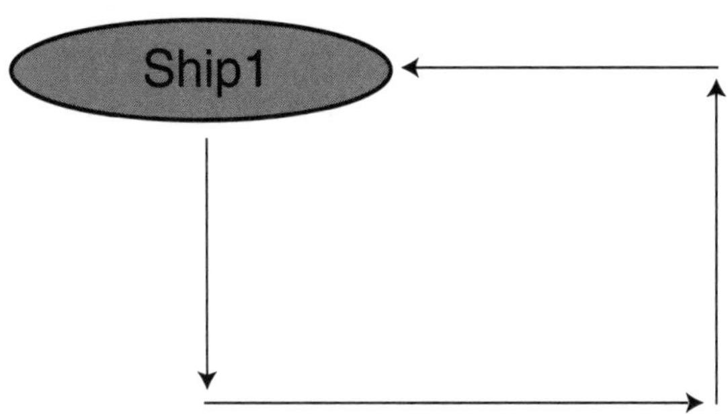

Figure 5.11
Functions can be groups of methods, combined under one handy, reusable name. The "SpinAround" function spins the spaceship in a circle.

Arguments: Values that get used by JavaScript methods, functions, and objects during processing.

- If you're telling the web page to display a line of text, you also need to tell it what that text should be. The "what" is an argument that gets passed along and processed when the script runs.
- If you're creating an instance of an object called "button," you might need to specify a color and width. The values "green" and "100" are two arguments that get passed along and processed when the script runs.
- If you're telling the browser to wait a certain amount of time and then open another, new, window, you need to define the amount of time to wait. The amount of time, 15 seconds, is an argument that is passed along and used when the script runs.

Operators: Mathematical verbs that describe relationships between different pieces of an expression.

Operators

Operators are mathematical verbs that describe the relationship between pieces of data and other components of a JavaScript. Operators are symbols like =, which sets one item to be the equivalent of another, and +, which says to calculate the sum of two items.

Sometimes operators go between two values, like this:

```
x=100
```

This sets the value of x to be 100. The equal sign is called a *binary* operator, because it can only be used between two values.

Other times, operators are used with a single value, like this:

```
x++
```

This means to increment the value x. The ++ is called a *unary* operator, because it works with one value at a time.

There are many operators in JavaScript. We'll talk about some of them in more detail later in this chapter.

Expressions

Expressions are somewhat like sentences, in that they combine variables, operators, and other expressions to evaluate something. For example:

- If you're telling an ad to rotate every 30 seconds, you'd use an expression to evaluate whether or not 30 seconds has elapsed.
- If you're displaying a greeting on the screen, and want to use a variable named "greeting" to hold the greeting message, you'd use an expression to set the name "greeting" to contain the value "Hello World! How are you?"

> **Expressions:** Mathematical sentences that evaluate a state or value.

Variables

Variables are containers that hold specific pieces of data. You give each variable a name and can then use the data by simply calling for the variable by that name. Sometimes the variable holds data that you have specified. For example:

- If you're displaying the name of your page throughout the script, you might assign the name to a variable. If you want to change the name, you have to change it only one time: in the variable.

At other times, the variable holds data that has been calculated by the script. For example:

> **Variables:** Containers that hold a piece of data. Each variable has a name and can be called repeatedly.

- If you're updating a frame every minute, you might use a variable named "time" to keep track of the clock.

Variable names are case sensitive. They must always begin with either a letter or the underscore (_) character. They cannot begin with a number or any other characters.

Local Variable: Variable for use only within a specific function.

You can use a variable at one of two levels: *local* or *global*.

A local variable is one that you use within a function. You create it specifically for the function, place it within the function, and call it from the function.

- For example, you might want to call a variable named "graphic" inside of a function that swaps graphic images. The variable doesn't have any use outside of that function.

Global Variable: Variable that can be used any place in the script.

A global variable is one that you can use anyplace in your scripts. You set it once and it is on call for you anywhere in the page.

- For example, you might want to call a variable named "readername" many different places within the script: in a greeting, "Hello Max!"; in a request, "How many copies do you want, Max¿"; in a response, "Thanks, Max! Your 27 sets of salt and pepper shakers will be arriving shortly"; and in a goodbye, "Good-bye Max. Come again soon!"

Arrays

Arrays are ordered sets of variables, saved under the same name. An array lets you cycle through a set of variables. One place you'll see an example of an array is in the script that lets you display a different graphic based on the location of the reader's cursor.

Arrays: Ordered sets of variables.

Loops

Loops are the "repeat key" of JavaScript. They are a way to keep reprocessing certain sections of the script until either specific conditions are met or an amount of loops have been made.

Loops: A way to repeat a section of a script.

Events

JavaScript is "aware" of certain interactions between the reader and the browser. These interactions are called *events*. Events include actions such as the reader putting his or her mouse over a link or changing the value in a form. You can use JavaScript to make different things happen when a specified event occurs.

Events: Interactions between reader and browser that are recorded by JavaScript.

Event Handlers

While it's nice that JavaScript knows about certain reader/browser interactions, unless you can make use of this knowledge you can't add interactivity to your web page. *Event handlers* are the scripts that let you create a response to an event and make your site responsive to reader actions. Some event handlers are built into JavaScript. In addition, you can create your own event handlers for your specific applications.

Event Handlers: Scripts that create a response to an event.

Inserting a JavaScript into an HTML Page

As you saw earlier, there is some limited support for JavaScript commands within HTML tags, but by far the more common use for JavaScript is as a language for writing full scripts that work within the HTML browser. That is the focus of the rest of this chapter.

Before you learn more details about the ins and outs of any specific JavaScript functions, let's take a moment and look at how to identify a script within an HTML page. Figure 5.12 shows what a very simple JavaScript looks like.

The script in Figure 5.12 is only a few lines long. It is easy to see where it is embedded; like other items in an HTML file, it is marked with beginning and ending HTML tags. The script itself is easy to find and can be seen by viewing the document's source file with your browser.

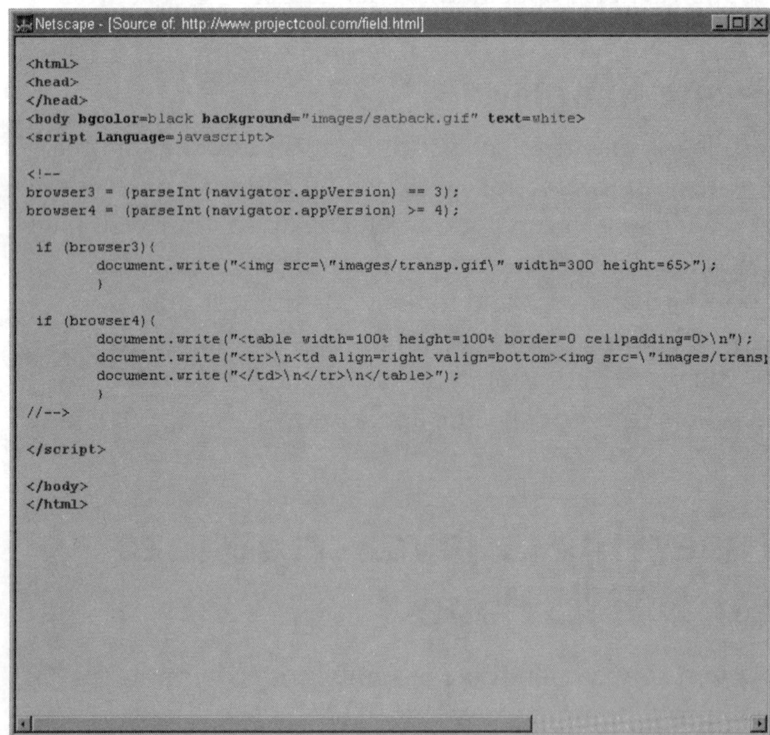
Netscape - [Source of: http://www.projectcool.com/field.html]

```
<html>
<head>
</head>
<body bgcolor=black background="images/satback.gif" text=white>
<script language=javascript>

<!--
browser3 = (parseInt(navigator.appVersion) == 3);
browser4 = (parseInt(navigator.appVersion) >= 4);

 if (browser3){
        document.write("<img src=\"images/transp.gif\" width=300 height=65>");
        }

 if (browser4){
        document.write("<table width=100% height=100% border=0 cellpadding=0>\n");
        document.write("<tr>\n<td align=right valign=bottom><img src=\"images/trans
        document.write("</td>\n</tr>\n</table>");
        }
//-->

</script>

</body>
</html>
```

Figure 5.12
JavaScript is typically embedded directly into an HTML page. You can see it when you "view source" from your browser.

TIP: *JavaScript is almost always embedded in the HTML text file. You can usually see a JavaScript script by viewing the document's source.*

The <script> Tag

It's easy to spot a JavaScript script. Just look for the <script language="JavaScript"> and </script> tags.

As you can see in Figure 5.12, the script is embedded in the HTML text. Whenever possible, you should place the script within the HTML page's header section. Some browsers on some platforms become confused when they encounter a script within the body of the HTML page. Additionally, many common uses of JavaScript require that the browser read the script before it displays the page.

TIP: *When possible, place JavaScript in the HTML header. Like the page's title, JavaScript is best located with the HTML header.*

This is the basic format for an HTML file that contains a JavaScript. The <script> tags are highlighted in bold to make them stand out.

```
<html>

<head>

<title>Frogs of the World</title>

<script language="JavaScript">

YOUR SCRIPT GOES HERE

</script>

</head>

<body>
CONTENTS OF HTML PAGE GO HERE
```

<script language="JavaScript">: The HTML tag that tells the browser a JavaScript is beginning.

</script>: The HTML tag that tells the broswer a script section has ended.

```
</body>

</html>
```

The <script> tag has two switches:

- **src="sourceURL"** lets you place the JavaScript code in a separate HTML file. This switch may not be supported by all browsers. At this time, it is a good idea to avoid this switch, although in the future it may become more common, enabling you to hide your JavaScript in a separate file and easily reuse the same JavaScript in multiple pages.
- **language="JavaScript"** tells the browser the script it is about to encounter is a JavaScript script, so it knows how to interpret it.

The Comment Line

You could just plunk the script down between the <script> and </script> tags, but what if a reader is using a non-JavaScript browser? That browser won't understand the tags and will ignore them as a working script. However, it *will* see the script as lines of HTML text and try to display them on the screen or process them in some way. To prevent non-JavaScript browsers from becoming confused by the script and trying to read it as text, it is good practice to put the script within an HTML comment area.

In addition, you will probably want to precede the script with copyright information or information about the script itself as well.

TIP: *By placing the body of a JavaScript script within a comment area, you'll avoid confusing non-JavaScript browers.*

To place the script within an HTML comment area:

1. Start the HTML comment area with the less than (<) symbol, an exclamation point (!), and two dashes (--).

```
<!--
```

2. Add JavaScript comments and the script itself. Precede each JavaScript comment with two slashes (//).

```
<!--
    //This page contains JavaScript.
    sample line of script
    sample line of script
```

3. End the HTML comment with two dashes (--) and a greater than (>) symbol.

```
<!--
    //This page contains JavaScript.
    //start the script

    sample line of script
    sample line of script

    //End of script-->
```

For example, this is the way we insert a JavaScript. The script area is in bold to make it stand out.

TIP: *Everyone who can view the source can also view—and borrow—your script. It's a good idea to include copyright or author information for your own protection.*

```
<html>

<head>

<title>Frogs of the World</title>
```

<!-- The code that starts an HTML comment area.

--> The code that ends an HTML comment area.

```
<script language="JavaScript">

<!--
//Copyright 1997, Project Cool Inc.
//This script makes the frog buttons light up
//start script

   THE SCRIPT GOES HERE

// end of script -->


</script>

</head>
```

The <noscript> Tag

IE 3.0 and Navigator 3.0 or later support the <noscript> tag. The <noscript> tag is a little like the <noframe> tag. It lets you display a text message for people with older browsers, and the newer browsers ignore it.

The message begins with the <noscript> tag and ends with </noscript> tag. For example, this HTML code lets people know they are missing a cool web effect. The noscript section is highlighted in bold to make it stand out.

```
<html>

<head>

<title>Frogs of the World</title>

<script language="JavaScript">

<!--
//Copyright 1997, Project Cool Inc.
//This script makes the frog buttons change based on
mouse location.
//start script

   THE SCRIPT GOES HERE
```

```
// end of script -->

</script>

<noscript>

If you were using a newer, JavaScript-enabled
browser (IE 3.0 or later, or Navigator 3.0 or
later), you'd be seeing a really cool web
effect. <br>
sigh!<br>
You might want to download the latest IE or
Navigator.<br>

</noscript>

</head>
```

WRITING JAVASCRIPT CODE

Once you understand the basic JavaScript structure, JavaScript will begin to seem a little clearer. This section outlines the basic rules for writing script code.

You write JavaScript as you do most programming language—in text format. You can use the same text editor that you use for writing your HTML pages.

The text is organized into single lines, called *statements* or *command lines*. Groups of commands can be organized together into blocks. Within each statement you use the elements described earlier: variables, operators, objects, methods, arguments, and expressions.

Statements

A *statement* is a single line of instruction to the computer. Each statement in JavaScript is structured in a similar manner.

- First, the command. Each command starts on its own line.
- Second, the concluding semicolon.

For example, a line of JavaScript that sets a variable resembles this:

```
var name="Young Explorer";
```

It creates a variable called "name" and sets the value of the variable to be the words "Young Explorer."

When a statement includes an object, method, and argument, the structure looks like this:

- First, the object's name, followed by a period and the method name, with no spaces between.
- Second, the argument that is passed on (in parentheses).
- Third, a concluding semicolon.

For example, a line of JavaScript that calls an object and method resembles this:

```
document.write("Hello World");
```

This line of JavaScript calls a standard JavaScript object (document) and a standard document method (write). It includes the argument "Hello World" to tell the script what to write. It ends with a semicolon.

Remember that in JavaScript, unlike HTML, everything is case sensitive. For example, each of these is perceived as a different item (and only the first is correct).

```
document.write
```

```
Document.write

Dcoument.Write
```

TIP: *Unlike HTML, JavaScript is case sensitive and will respond to uppercase and lowercase characters.*

Command Blocks

Command Block: A set of JavaScript command lines, grouped into one entity.

Sometimes individual lines are grouped into *command blocks*. The command block can then be treated as a separate entity.

When you are looking at a script, you can quickly identify command blocks; they are the section surrounded by braces.

A typical command block has three parts.

- It begins with a open brace, on its own line.
- The next lines contain one or more individual command lines.
- It ends with a closed brace, on its own line.

For example, a typical command block of JavaScript resembles this:

```
{
     document.writeln("Hello World");
     document.writeln("My name is Fred");
}
```

This simple command block has two lines of code. The first calls a standard JavaScript object (document) and a standard document method (writeln—write line). It includes the argument "Hello World" to tell the script what to write. It ends with a semicolon. The second also calls document.writeln, but it has the argument "My name is Fred." It also ends with a semicolon.

It is good style to indent the command lines within the command block. Doing so makes it easier to view the code and edit it if necessary. It is also good style to put the braces on their own lines. This makes it easier to see where each command block begins and ends. Technically, the code will work just fine without the indents and without the braces being on their own lines, but it will be much more difficult to read and edit your code.

It is important to remember that each command block must begin and end with matching braces. When you are nesting command blocks, this becomes especially important (and an easy mistake to make!). If you omit a closed brace, your script may not work.

TIP: *Be sure to include matching sets of braces.*

Make sure every open curly brace that begins a command block has a matching closed curly brace to end the command block.

Comments

You can include *comments* within the script. The comments can be either single lines or a comment block. Comments are a way for you to make notes about what the script is doing or when the script was created and by whom. It is good practice to include comments in your script, and reading the comments in other people's scripts can help you understand what the script is doing.

The comment line begins with a double slash (//). The script won't process anything between the double slashes (//) and the end-of-line character.

```
//This single comment line tells you something about
the script.
```

You can place many single lines together as in the following example. The two lines are comment lines, which JavaScript ignores when processing. The third is a line of code which JavaScript processes.

```
//The following line initializes a counter and sets
its value to 0.

//This counter tracks the number of times the form
was submitted.

var counter==0
```

Comment: A line or block of text that is not part of the script and is used as a place for you to make notes or comments about the script or its components.

Sometimes people put a command on the same line as a comment. For example, they type the command, and then type double slashes (//) to indicate that from this point to the end of the line is a comment. For example:

```
var counter==0  //initializes the counter
```

You can also create a comment block. The block starts with a slash (/) and an asterisk (*) and ends with an asterisk (*) and a slash (/), like this:

```
/*

This comment block. You can put many lines of text
together within a block to explain what the script
is doing. It is a good idea to make comments about
your script so that you can later make edits or
changes as necessary.

*/
```

Quotation Marks

You can use both single (' ') and double (" ") quotation marks when writing a JavaScript script. However, one of the most common mistakes people make when editing a script is inadvertently creating mismatched pairs of quotes.

Remember, in ASCII text, there is no difference between an open quote and a close quote the way there is in typography.

When the script sees a double quote, it notes the double quote as the start of something. That something ends when the script encounters the next double quote. But what if you're nesting a value inside a value? There's potential for confusion, even in a simple example like this:

```
document.write ("The Man in the Moon says "Good-
night" and winks!")
```

The script sees the first double quote and starts displaying characters. It sees the next double quote. "Oh, this is end of the quotation area," it says, and stops displaying characters. It then looks at Goodnight and tries to interpret it as an object or a variable and, when it can't interpret it, displays an error, as shown in Figure 5.13.

The solution is to surround one value with a set of

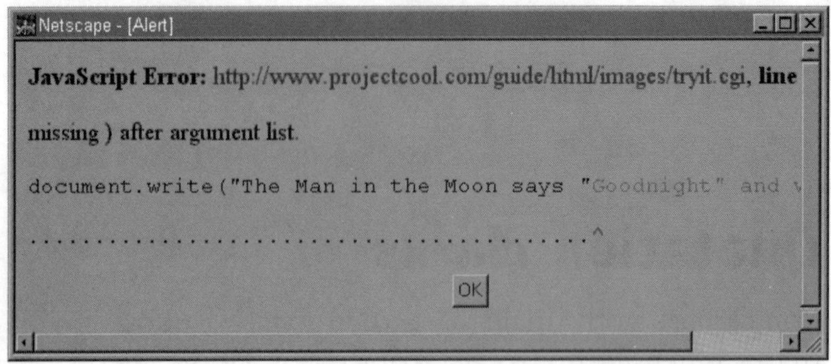

Figure 5.13
A small error in quotation marks creates a confused script.

double quotes and the other with a set of single quotes, and be careful to keep track of which is which. It doesn't matter if you put the double or the single quotes first. Either of these lines will produce the expected result:

```
document.write ("The Man in the Moon says 'Good-
night' and winks!")

document.write ('The Man in the Moon says "Good-
night" and winks!')
```

TIP: *Watch for the common error of accidently mismatching quotes.*

Another place to be aware of quotation marks is when you want to specify a variable, not a string. When you're referring to a variable name, use single quotes. Otherwise, JavaScript will assume you want to use the literal characters D-A-Y instead of the variable named "day."

TIP: *When passing a variable name, use single rather than double quotes.*

LEARNING STANDARD JAVASCRIPT COMPONENTS

As we noted earlier, JavaScript has some standard objects and functions. This section briefly overviews these. Please note that this is not intended to be a complete reference to JavaScript, but to simply give you a flavor of JavaScript's possibilities. For complete and most current information about built-in JavaScript and JScript objects and functions, visit the Netscape or Microsoft websites.

TIP: *In ASCII text, there is no difference between an open quote and a close quote, the way there is in typography.*

Objects

JavaScript has a handful of built-in *objects*. It also offers you the ability to create your own objects. Each standard object's name is written in all lowercase letters. For example, JavaScript will recognize "document," but it won't recognize "Document."

Each object also comes with its own standard set of properties and methods. We'll note some that might be especially useful here. In addition, you can create your own objects as needed.

Navigator

The *navigator* object records information about the browser in use.

Window

The *window* object is the top-most object in a hierarchy of objects that includes document, location, and history.

Some useful properties are:

- **window.frames**: Lets you control information in frames with a JavaScript.
- **window.name**: Assigns a name to a window or frame.
- **window.status**: Lets you display a message in the status bar.

Some useful methods are:

- **window.alert**: Lets you display a text message in an alert box.
- **window.confirm**: Lets you display a text message along with OK and CANCEL buttons.
- **window.open**: Lets you open a new window that displays a specific URL.

TIP: *You don't have to explictly specify the window object.*

When using a method of the window object, you can type just the method, not the full object.method, because window is the top-most object in the JavaScript hierarchy.

Because the window object is the top-most object, you can use its methods in a script by typing just the method name. For example, if you wanted to create an alert box that displayed the message "This page is JavaScript enabled," you could create a line of code that looks like this:

```
alert("This page is JavaScript enabled");
```

You don't need to include the full object.method (window.alert) because JavaScript assumes the object is window unless you specify otherwise.

By the way, that alert box would resemble the box you see in Figure 5.14.

Document

The *document* object lets you record HTML document attributes via JavaScript and control output to the document window.

Some useful properties are:

Figure 5.14
The alert method lets you create a separate alert dialog box.

- **document.cookie**: The cookie values for the current document. (This is a property you'll use only if you are doing fairly sophisticated user tracking; the "cookie" is the way Navigator accesses certain types of user data and actions that are recorded on the user's computer.)
- **document.images**: The set of images in the document.
- **document.links**: The set of links in the document.

Some useful methods are:

- **document.write**: Lets you display text and HTML tags in the document window.
- **document.writeln**: Lets you display text and HTML tags in a document window ("writeln" stands for "write line").

The document object also has a number of subobjects, including forms, links, anchors, and other HTML document components.

Location

The *location* object lets you record information about the current URL.

History

The location object lets you use JavaScript to work with the browser's *history* list of where the reader has been browsing. You can go back, forward, or to a specific numbered stop.

Date

The *date* object lets you use record, set, and date and time information.

Datatypes

JavaScript can handle four different types of data. All the values that you use in a JavaScript script must fall into one of these four categories: Strings, Numbers, True/False Boolean, or Null.

Strings

A *string* is a set of characters beginning and ending in quotation marks. We've been using string data for examples throughout this chapter. For example, the argument for this document.write command is a string value.

> **Strings:** A set of characters surrounded by quotation marks.

```
document.write("Hello World");
```

Numbers

Numbers are, obviously, numbers. Numbers can be positive or negative. This code creates a variable named "size" whose value is the number 155.

```
var size=155
```

Notice that there are no quotation marks around number values. If you put quotes around them, the numbers become a string, instead of a calculable number.

Boolean True/False

Another type of data you can use is a *Boolean true or false statement*. Although this category of data has only two possible values in JavaScript (true or false), it can be quite powerful. For example, it is used in the sample script that evaluates the reader's browser and displays the appropriate page based on the browser type. If certain statements are true, a certain page gets displayed.

You don't actually enter the values of "true" or "false" in a script. You create equations and tell the script to do certain things if the result is true or false. True and false states are passed along when the script is processed.

Null

Null: A variable that contains no value—an empty slot.

Null is the way you tell JavaScript that the variable is empty—there is no value for the variable.

The null value is not the same as 0. Zero is a number and can be used in calculation. Null is an empty slot.

Operators

JavaScript supports a range of *operators*. Remember, operators are mathematical verbs that assign values or perform mathematical functions. This section highlights some of the most common operators you might see as you look at JavaScript scripts.

Assignment

The most common *assignment* operator is the equal sign. It sets one item equal to another.

Operator	What It Does	Example
=	Sets one value equal to another.	Counter=0 Sets the counter to equal the number 0.

Comparison

The *comparison* operators compare two items and return a value of "true" if the conditions are true. Some of the most common are:

Operator	What It Does	Example
==	Generates a true value if the items are the same.	counter==10 Generates the value "true" if the counter's value is currently equal to the number 10.
!=	Generates a true value if the items are NOT the same.	counter!=10 Generates the value "true" if the counter's value is currently equal to anything except the number 10.
>	Generates a true value if the item on the left is greater than the item on the right.	counter>10 Generates the value "true" if the counter's value is greater than 10.
>=	Generates a true value if the item on the left is greater than or equal to the item on the right.	counter>=10 Generates the value "true" if the counter's value is greater than or equal to 10.
<	Generates a true value if the item on the left is less than the item on the right.	counter<10 Generates the value "true" if thecounter's value is less than 10.
<=	Generates a true value if the item on the left	counter>10 Generates the value "true" if

	is less than or equal to the item on the right.	the counter's value is less than or equal to 10.

Arithmatic (Computational)

The *computational* operators perform a mathematical function on a value or values, and return a single value. Some of the most common are:

Operator	What It Does	Example
+	Adds two values together.	var+2 Generates the sum of the variable plus 2.
-	Subtracts one value from another.	var-1 Generates the result of the variable minus 2.
*	Multiplies two values.	var*2 Generates the result of the variable times 2.
/	Divides one value by another.	var/2 Generates the result of the variable divided by 2.
++X	Increments the value, then returns the result.	++var Adds 1 to the variable value, then returns the result.
X++	Returns the current value, then increments the value.	var++ Returns the current value of the variable, then adds 1 to the variable.
--X	Decreases the value, then returns the result.	--var Subtracts 1 from the variable value, then returns the result.
X--	Returns the current value, then decreases the value.	var-- Returns the current value of the variable, then subtracts 1 from the variable.

The last four operators, the ones that increment or decrease a value, are often the cause of problems in a script. The script will run, but it won't work quite the way you expected.

Notice that the relative locations of the operator (the ++ or the - -) and the variable create a slightly different effect. When the operator comes first, the script will add or subtract from the current value, and then pass along the resulting new value to the rest of the script. But when the operator comes second, the script first grabs the current value and passes it along, and then adds or subtracts from it and uses that result as the new value for the variable, after the script is processed.

This is an important distinction. For example, suppose you are displaying a message each time the reader submits an answer to an online quiz you created. You have a variable that is tracking the number of submissions, so that the appropriate message will display each time. The value in the "submission" variable triggers the code that the displays the correct message. The first time you want to say "good first try!"

The variable starts out with the value of 0, because the reader hasn't submitted anything. When the reader submits an answer, the script checks the value in the variable.

- If you've used ++submission, the script first resets the variable value to 1, then passes along that value of 1. "Ah," says the script, "I've received a 1. That means I should display the message 'good first try!'" Your reader sees the message as you planned.
- However, if you've used submission++, the script first passes along the value. The current value is 0, so no message gets displayed. After it passes the

value, it then increments the variable from 0 to 1. Your reader sees nothing.

- After the second submission, the script again passes along the variable. This time the current value is 1. "Ah," says the script, "I've received a 1. That means I should display the message 'good first try!'" Your reader looks confused when this message pops onto the screen because he's just made a second try.

Subtle differences in the code, but a big difference in the end result.

Logical

The *logical* operators evaluate expressions and then return a true or false value. The two most common are:

Operator	What It Does	Example
&&	Returns a true value if both expression are true.	if day='friday'**&&**date=13 then alert("Are You Superstitious¿") This compares the value of the day and the value of the date. If it is true that today is a Friday and it is also true that the date is the 13th, then an alert box pops up with the message "Are You Superstitious¿").
||	Returns a true value if either expression is true.	if day='friday'**&&**date =13 then alert("Are You Superstitious¿") else if day='friday'**||**date=13

then alert("Aren't you glad it isn't Friday the 13th¿") This compares the value of the day and the value of the date. First it determines that both are not true, and passes along a false value. Then it does the second test and if it is true that today is a Fri day OR it is true that the date is the 13th, then an alert box pops up with the message "Aren't you glad it isn't Friday the 13th¿"

Functions

JavaScript includes a number of built-in *functions*. Some of these include:

- *Constructor* functions, such as "new." These functions let you create new objects, properties, methods, variables, and other items.
- *Evaluator* functions, such as "eval." These functions let you calculate and evaluate the results of expressions.

In addition, you can create your own functions. All function names are case sensitive and must begin with either a letter or an underscore (_). Later on, we'll show you how a custom function appears in a script so you can identify them when you are looking at a script.

Events

JavaScript includes a number of built-in *events*. Events are an awareness of a certain user action. Event names are in all lowercase characters. Some of these events include:

- **mouseover**.—JavaScript recognizes when the reader puts his or her cursor over a link in an HTML page.
- **mouseout**.—JavaScript recognizes when the reader moves his or her cursor off a link.
- **click**.—JavaScript recognizes when the reader clicks on a link.
- **load**.—JavaScript recognizes when an HTML page loads into the browser window.
- **submit**.—JavaScript recognizes when the reader submits an HTML form for processing.
- **unload**.—JavaScript recognizes when the reader exits a page.

Event Handlers

The JavaScript *event handlers* let you perform actions that respond to the reader's actions. Event handler names are a mix of uppercase and lowercase, as shown in the following list. Some of the event handlers are:

- **onMouseOver**.—Tells JavaScript to execute the command when the reader puts his or her cursor over the specified link.
- **onMouseOut**. —Tells JavaScript to execute the command when the reader moves his or her cursor off the specified link.

- **onClick**.—Tells JavaScript to execute the command when the reader clicks on the specified link, button, or option.
- **onLoad**.—Tells JavaScript to execute the command when the specified page loads.
- **onUnload**.—Tells JavaScript to execute the command when the reader exits the specified page.

CREATING YOUR OWN JAVASCRIPT

You can use any of the standard JavaScript components, but you really add value to your site when you can customize and create scripts specifically for your applications.

When you are first learning JavaScript, the best approach is to study existing scripts, understand what they are doing, and make small changes to adapt them to your content. A good place to start is with the five sample scripts at the end of this chapter. We've documented how they work and what you might want to do to customize them for yourself.

This section walks you through some of the common things you might need to do when creating or adapting a script. These include:

- Building a function
- Creating an object and its properties and methods
- Creating a new variable
- Creating an array

There are many other things you can do with a script. This section isn't designed to teach you how to create complex scripts; rather, it gives you a flavor of how to edit and work with some basic JavaScript commands.

Building New Functions

You can quickly and easily create new functions for your script. Building a function is quite straightforward. You call the function command, name the function, and create a command block that lists the different command lines that comprise the function.

This example creates a function that lets you click on a different line of text to turn the background black or to turn it white.

TRY IT

To see the result of this function, go to the companion website for this book and click on Chapter 5 examples.

This is what the code for that function looks like.

```
<html>
<head>
<title>Function Demo</title>
<script language=javascript>
<!--
function changecolor(newcolor){
  window.document.bgColor = newcolor;
  }
//-->
</script>
</head>
<body bgcolor=white link=888888
vlink=888888>
<h2><a
```

```
href="javascript:changecolor('black');
  ">Change Background to
Black</a></h2>
<h2><a
href="javascript:changecolor('white');
  ">Change Background to
White</a></h2>
</body>
</html>
```

To create a function:

1. Type *function* to call the function command.

```
function
```

2. Type the name you want to give to your new function. For example, you might want to create a function that displays a welcome box and call this function "changecolor."

```
function changecolor
```

3. Add open and close parentheses for holding arguments, and the argument, if any. In this example, the argument is a variable called "newcolor."

NOTE: *You always have to have these parentheses, even if your function doesn't use an argument. JavaScript expects to see them as part of the function definition.*

```
function changecolor(newcolor)
```

4. Start the command block with a curly brace.

```
function changecolor(newcolor){
```

5. Add each command line that makes up the function. Make sure to end each with a semicolon.

   And remember, it is good style to indent each

line. As your functions grow more complex and you are nesting items within each other, adding loops, and performing other tasks, a cleanly indented, neatly arranged structure will make it far easier to debug, test, and edit your work. It sounds a little dogmatic, but creating good habits from the beginning makes your job a lot easier down the road.

TIP: *Remember to indent each command line in a function. Indents prevent a tangle of unreadable "code spaghetti."*

6. End the command block—and the function—with a matching closed brace on its own line.

   Remember, every open brace must have a matching closed brace or the function won't work.

```
function changecolor(newcolor){
  window.document.bgColor = newcolor;
  }
```

   You now have a function named "changecolor" that you can use to change the background color of the window.document objects. This little function creates an effect as shown in Figures 5.15 and 5.16.

Building New Objects

There are several steps to building new objects.

1. First, you use a constructor function to create the object type and set its properties. Remember, the object type is sort of the template, the master model from which you create usable instances.
2. Next, you add methods to the object type, by again using the constructor function to define a

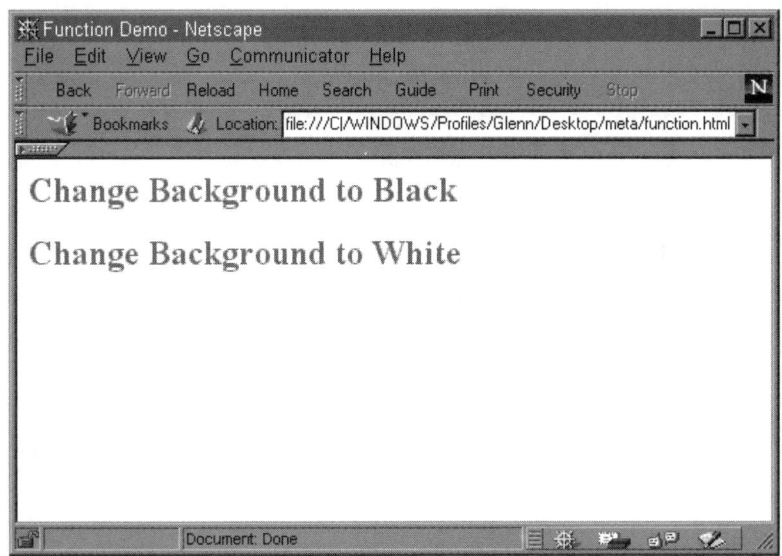

Figure 5.15
The function lets you create an option in your HTML page to turn the background black or white. Here is it white.

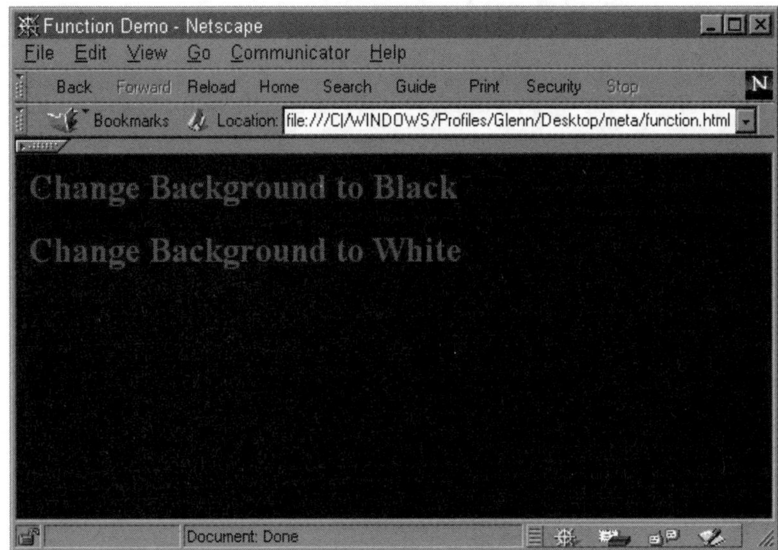

Figure 5.16
And here it is black.

method and then assigning the method to the object type.

3. Finally, you create instances of the object and use the instances within your script.

Creating the Object Type

To create an object type:

1. Type the word *function*.

```
function
```

2. Type a space.
3. Type the name you want to give to this new object type. In this example, the object type is called "Frog."

```
function Frog
```

4. Type an open parenthesis.

```
function Frog(
```

5. Type a placeholder word for each of the object type's properties. Separate each placeholder with a comma.

   Remember, the values for these properties can be a string, number, Boolean true/false, or null value. In this example, there are two string values: the Frog name and the URL at which its image is located; and one number value: its width.

```
function Frog(name,URL,width
```

6. When you've listed a placeholder for each property, close the list with a close parenthesis.

```
function Frog(name,URL,width)
```

7. Type a space and an open curly brace.

```
function Frog(name,URL,width) {
```

8. On the next line, type the word *this*, followed by a period, followed by the name you want to give the first property.

```
function Frog(name,URL,width) {
this.frogname
```

9. Then, type an equal sign and the name of the property's placeholder, followed by a semi-colon.

```
function Frog(name,URL,width) {
   this.frogname=name;
```

   This line of code has created a property called "frogname" for the object type "Frog" to match the placeholder of "name" in the argument area.

   Some people always give the placeholder for the argument and the property the same name. Others prefer to give them two different names. It is entirely up to you.

10. Repeat the process for each property of the object. When you've created each property, end the command block by typing a closed curly brace on its own line. The function that creates the Frog object type and its properties looks like this:

```
function Frog(name,URL,width) {
   this.frogname=name;
   this.frogpic=URL;
   this.frogsize=width;
}
```

Creating Methods

Once you have created an object type and its properties, the next step is to create methods for it.

1. Type the word *function*.

   ```
   function
   ```

2. Type the name you want to give to the method you are creating. For example, if you want to create a method that displays the frog's name in the browser window status bar, you might create a method named "FrogStats."

   ```
   function FrogStats
   ```

3. Add the open and close parentheses.

   ```
   function FrogStats()
   ```

   Remember, the function command expects to see the parentheses, even if you aren't putting any arguments in them.

4. Type an open brace to start defining the function.

   ```
   function FrogStats() {
   ```

5. Add each line of code that is part of the method. For example, this line of code tells the browser to display, in the status bar, the words "This frog's name is" and value of the property, "Frog.frogname".

   ```
   function FrogStats() {
      window.status="This frog's name is"+
      this.frogname;
   ```

6. End with the closed curly brace, on its own line as usual.

```
function FrogStats() {
   window.status="This frog's name is"+
   this.frogname;
}
```

7. Now go back and edit the object type definition to add the new method.

   ```
   function Frog(name,URL,width) {
      this.name=name;
      this.color=URL;
      this.shape=width;
      this.FrogStats=FrogStats;
   }
   ```

   Notice that you add the method at the end of the command block. You don't add a placeholder in the argument parentheses for it. When you want to use the method, you will call it by name: "Frog.FrogStats".

You can also assign the method to a particular instance of the object type. For example, if you wanted to create the FrogStats method of the object instance Frog1, you'd enter this code:

```
Frog1.FrogStats=new
```

and the method would be added to that instance.

Creating Instances

You can create as many instances of an object as you need. To create an instance:

1. Type the name you want to give to the instance. For example, we'll create a Frog called "Frog1".

   ```
   Frog1
   ```

2. Type the equal sign.

```
Frog1=
```

3. Type the word *new*.

```
Frog1=new
```

4. Type a space followed by the name of the object from which you are creating the instance.

```
Frog1=new Frog
```

5. Type an open parenthesis, followed by the value you are giving each property for this instance. Separate each value with a comma. Make sure the values are in the same order as the property names of the object.

```
Frog1=new Frog("common green","images/
   green.gif",100
```

6. End the list values with a close parenthesis and a semicolon.

```
Frog1=new Frog("common green","images/
   green.gif",100);
```

7. Repeat a similar command line for each instance. For example, this code creates three instances of the Frog object:

```
Frog1=new Frog("common green","images/
   green.gif",100);

Frog2=new Frog("american toad","images/
   atoad.gif",170);

Frog2=new Frog("bullfrog","images/
   bull.gif",200);
```

Using Variables

Variables are a handy way of storing values and working with these values.

Variable names are case sensitive. They must always begin with either a letter or the underscore (_) character. They cannot begin with a number or any other characters.

There are two parts to creating a variable. First, you *declare* it. That is, you state that there is a variable and assign a name to the variable. Second, you *define* it. That is, you give the named variable a value.

Declaring a Variable: Stating that the variable exists, `var varname`.

Defining a Variable: Giving the named variable a value, `varname="Happy Days Are Here Again!"`

To create a variable:

1. Type the command var.

   ```
   var
   ```

2. Type a space and then the name you are giving the variable. For example, to create a variable named "froggy" you'd type this:

   ```
   var froggy
   ```

   This part of the code is called *declaring* a variable. You are telling the script that the variable exits. Sometimes people declare a number of different variables that they plan to use at the beginning of the script. Then, later on, they define the variable as needed.

3. Type the equal sign.

   ```
   var froggy=
   ```

4. Type an open parenthesis, and the value you are

assigning to the variable. For example, to give froggy the string "Frogs are your little green friends," you'd type:

```
var froggy=("Frogs are your little green friends"
```

5. Finally, close the parenthesis and end the line with a semicolon.

```
var froggy=("Frogs are your little green
   friends");
```

You can now use that line of text in your script by calling for the variable named "froggy". For example, to write the message stored in the variable into the document, you could use a command like this:

```
docuument.write(froggy);
```

Remember, variables can be either *local* or *global.*

If you declare and define a variable within a function, you can use that variable only within the function.

If you just declare a variable at the beginning of your script, you can use the same variable name anywhere in the script, but you must remember to define it locally.

If you declare and define the variable at the beginning of your script, outside of any function, you can use the variable anywhere in your script and it will always have the same defined value.

Working with Arrays

Here are a few things to remember when you are working with arrays.

- An array is an ordered set of values.
- The set is referred to by a single variable name.
- Each entry in the set is assigned an *index number* and can be called specifically by that number.

Index Number: A number matched with an item in an array. Items are numbered sequentially, beginning with 0.

One place you'll see arrays is in the scripts that let you change graphics when the reader's cursor is on a different link. In these scripts, the arrays are used to store the URLs of the different graphics.

Creating Arrays

You'll create an array with the variable command: var.

To create an array:

1. Type the command var.

```
var
```

2. Type a space and then the name you are giving the array. For example, to create an array named "FrogPics," you'd type this:

```
var FrogPics
```

3. Type the equal sign and the word *new*. This tells JavaScript you're creating a new object (in this case, the object is an array.)

```
var FrogPics=new
```

4. Type the word *Array*.

```
var FrogPics=new Array
```

5. Now type an open parenthesis, and the value you are assigning to each item in the array. Separate each item with a comma. For example, to create an

array of four graphical frog buttons, your code would resemble this:

```
var FrogPics=new Array("images/button1.gif",
"images/button2.gif", "images/button3.gif",
"images/button4.gif"
```

6. Finally, close the parentheses and end the line with a semicolon.

```
var FrogPics=new Array("images/button1.gif",
"images/button2.gif", "images/button3.gif",
"images/button4.gif");
```

The first value in this array is called "button1.gif". Because it is the first value, its index number is 0. (Remember, computers start counting with the number 0 instead of the number 1.)

There's another way you could have created the array. You could have created the array name and then listed each value of the array as an equation. The double equal signs tell the script to assign the value on the right to the variable on the left.

```
var FrogPics=new Array();
FrogPics[0] == "images/button1.gif"
FrogPics[1] == "images/button2.gif"
FrogPics[2] == "images/button3.gif"
FrogPics[4] == "images/button4.gif"
```

PUTTING JAVASCRIPT TO WORK

When you think about adding JavaScript functionality to your web pages, use the same set of judgments you'd use when adding any other elements.

What value does this add for my readers?—Examine what the JavaScript script really does that makes your pages better to use. Don't include JavaScript just to show off.

Is this the best way to add the functionality?—Some functions can be added using different technologies. For example, if you are working with forms you can add interactivity with JavaScript, but you can often reach the same results through passing HTML form data to CGI scripts. Use JavaScript when it is the best tool for the problem.

Will my readers see this effect?—Remember, JavaScript acts a little differently on different platforms and different browsers. Be sure to test your JavaScript effects under the conditions in which your readers are likely to encounter them.

This section includes five scripts that you can easily adapt for your pages.

- A script that lets you display different versions of the page based upon the browser the reader is using.
- A script that lets you "highlight" a menu option.
- A script that lets you display text in the browser's status bar.
- A script that lets you change graphics on a page, based on the location of the reader's cursor.
- A script that lets you do simple ad rotation or other object rotation.

Feel free to use these scripts and adapt them for your pages. Each script includes a tutorial that points out what you need to change to make it work for you. Go ahead and give these a try, even if you aren't ready to write your own scripts from scratch. They provide a way to learn JavaScript by implementing it—and an easy way to enhance a site.

In addition to being printed on these pages, each of these scripts is also available in electronic form on the companion website.

Script #1: Browser Detection Script

As we know all too well, different versions of different browsers support different features. The name of the game is "browser wars," and it is driving everyone who builds web pages crazy.

If you have made a decision to support several different browsers and browser versions, this simple browser detection script will let you serve the correct page to each browser.

We use this code on our main navigational page. On that page, we use a JavaScript script to display information about the different sections. However, the different browsers handle JavaScript frame placement data differently, and so we need to serve a different version of the page for the different browsers.

Online Location

You can find this code on this book's companion website. It is in the JavaScript Templates area.

The Code

This is what the code looks like. The script is highlighted in bold. Each line of the code, both HTML and

JavaScript script, is numbered for reference. You won't have these reference line numbers in your real working script.

```
01    <html>
02    <head>
03    </head>
04    <body bgcolor=black background="images/sat-
back.gif" text=white>
05  <script language=javascript>
06  <!--
07  browser3 = (parseInt(navigator.appVersion) ==
3);
08  browser4 = (parseInt(navigator.appVersion) >=
4);

09  if (browser3){
10   document.write("<img src=\"images/transp.gif\"
width=300  height=65>");
11   }

12  if (browser4){
13   document.write("<table width=100% height=100%
border=0 cellpadding=0>\n");
14   document.write("<tr>\n<td align=right
valign=bottom><img src=\"images/transp.gif\"
width=300 height=65></td>");
15   document.write("</td>\n</tr>\n</table>");
16   }
17  //-->
18  </script>

19  </body>
20  </html>
```

Customizing the Code

Line by line, this is what the code does:

Line 1:—Starts an HTML page as normal.

Line 2:—Starts and ends the header section. In this case, the page does nothing but load an image and perform a browser detect routine, so we don't need any header information.

Line 3:—Ends the header section.

Line 4:—Starts the body, sets a black background and white text, and calls a background image.Customization options: You'll put in your own page's body infomation here.

Line 5:—Announces that a JavaScript script is beginning.

Line 6:—Starts an HTML comment area, so that the script won't confuse older browsers that don't understand the script tag.

Lines 7 and 8:—Check to see which version of browser the reader is using. The object.method navigator.appVersion is the built-in JavaScript object.method that does the checking.

- The object.method to test for browser name is navigator.appName.
- The object.method to test for browser version is navigator.appVersion.

NOTE: *The word "navigator" in "navigator.appVersion" and "navigator.appName" does not refer to the specific browser Netscape Navigator. It is the name for the general browser object. Netscape wrote JavaScript, so it got to name the object and (can you blame it?) it used the name "navigator."*

In this case, we are checking to see if the browser is a 3.0 version of any browser, or version 4.0 or higher of any browser. For this page, the differences in JavaScript support happen to fall across the 3.0/4.0 line of both Navigator and IE.

- If the browser is a 3.0 version, variable "browser3" will be used. We used the variable name "browser3" because it helps us remember what the variable contains.

▶ If the browser is a 4.0 version, variable "browser4" will be used. We used the variable name "browser4" because it helps us remember what the variable contains.

Customization options: If you want to check for other browsers, you can add browser variable lines. The items you need to change are the variable name and the value for which it is testing.

For example, this code segment checks for Navigator 3.0 or greater, or IE 4.0 or greater, and delivers the same pages for these newer browsers. Older versions would receive a different page. If the response is true to either of these, the variable "newer_browser" will be activated.

```
newer_browser = (((navigator.appName == "Netscape")
&& (parseInt(navigator.appVersion) >= 3 )) || ((nav-
igator.appName == "Microsoft Internet Explorer") &&
(parseInt(navigator.appVersion) >= 4 )))
```

The following code segment checks to differentiate between Netscape Navigator 3.0 /IE 3.0 browsers. If the response is true to both Netscape and 3, the variable "NN3browser" will be activated. But if the response is true to both Microsoft Internet Explorer and 3, the variable "IE3browser" will be activated.

```
NN3browser = ((navigator.appName == "Netscape") &&
(parseInt(navigator.appVersion) = 3 ))

IE3browser = ((navigator.appName == "Microsoft In-
ternet Explorer") && (parseInt(navigator.appVersion)
= 3 ))
```

Lines 9, 10, and 11:—Specify the image and HTML tags to use if browser3 is the selected variable.

Customization options: You'll change the information in the document.write argument to reflect the image or page that you want to display in the browser window when the specified browser is being used.

Lines 12, 13, 14, and 15:—Specify the image and HTML tags to use if browser3 is the selected variable.

Customization options: You'll change the information in the document.write arguments to reflect the information that you want to display in the browser window when the specified browser is being used.

Line 16:—Ends the function.

Line 17:—Ends the HTML comment.

Line 18:—This line is the normal HTML tag that ends a script.

Lines 19 and 20:—These are the normal HTML tags that end an HTML file.

Script #2: User Feedback to Mouse Over a Menu Option

This script goes into the head area of the HTML page that uses it. It puts a little marker in front of a selected menu choice when the reader puts his or her cursor over the choice.

Figure 5.17 shows what the "static" page looks like. Figure 5.18 shows how the marker appears when the reader moves over the menu choice. (To see this effect in *glorious, full, glowing interactive color*, visit the Project Cool Daily Sightings page at http://www.projectcool.com/sightings.)

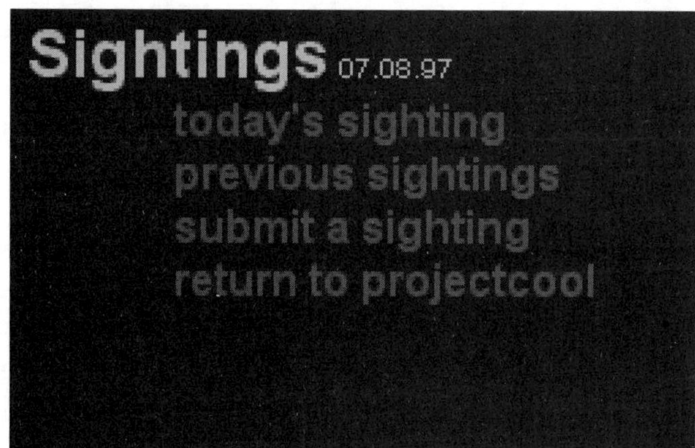

Figure 5.17
This is the basic HTML page.

Online Location

You can find this code on this book's companion website and download it from there. It is in the JavaScript Templates area.

The Code

Using this script is a two-step process.

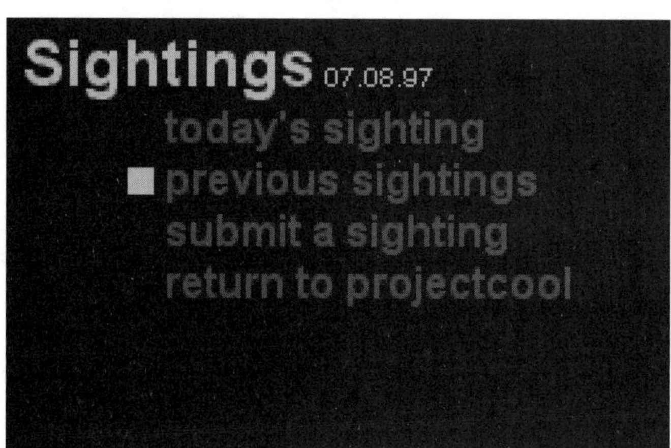

Figure 5.18
Now readers get feedback when they move their cursor over the menu option.

1. First, you place the script in the HTML page head area.
2. Second, you add event handlers to the menu option anchor tags in the body of the HTML page.

The mouseover script shown here is a very basic script, easily adaptable for your own use. Insert it into your page's head area, just after the title, as shown here. The script itself is highlighted in bold to make it stand out. All lines are numbered as reference; don't put these reference line numbers in your actual code.

We are actually using two scripts here. The first is a browser detection script. It checks to be sure the reader is using Navigator 3.0 or higher, or IE 4.0 or higher. We do this check because this particular mouseover effect requires Navigator 3.0 or IE 4.0 to support the JavaScript commands.

```
<html>
<head>
<title>contents</title>
<script language=javascript>
<!--
browser = (((navigator.appName == "Netscape") &&
(parseInt(navigator.appVersion) >= 3 )) || ((naviga-
tor.appName == "Microsoft Internet Explorer") &&
(parseInt(navigator.appVersion) >= 4 )))

if (browser){
 markeron = new Image();
 markeron.src = "images/gold.gif";
 markeroff = new Image();
  markeroff.src = "images/black.gif";
}

function msover(num) {
 if (browser){
       document.images[num].src = markeron.src;
     }
}
```

```
18  function msout(num) {
19  if (browser){
20          document.images[num].src = markeroff.src;
21          }
22  }
23  //-->
24  </script>
25   </head>
```

Customizing the Code

Line by line, this is what the code does:

Line 1:—Starts an HTML page as normal.

Line 2:—Starts the header section.

Line 3:—The normal HTML title tag. In this case the page's title is "contents."

Line 4:—Announces that a JavaScript script is beginning.

Line 5:—Starts an HTML comment area, so that the script won't confuse older browsers that don't understand the script tag.

Lines 6:—Checks to see which version of browser the reader is using. It activates the browser variable if the result is Netscape 3 or higher, or IE 4.

Lines 7–11:—If the correct browser is being used, this segment sets two states:

- One is called "markeron" and it uses the source image called "images/gold.gif". This is the gold marker that appears when the reader's mouse is atop the menu option.
- One is called "markeroff" and it uses the source image called "images/black.gif". This is a black box that blends in with the background and hides the

gold marker when the reader's mouse is not over the menu option.

Customization options: If you want to use your own graphics, just change the name of the source image.

For example, this code segment uses images named "arrow.gif" and "no_arrow.gif". The changes are in bold to highlight them.

```
if (browser){
   markeron = new Image();
   markeron.src = "arrow.gif";
   markeroff = new Image();
   markeroff.src = "no_arrow.gif";
}
```

Line 12:—Ends the function.

Lines 13–17:—This function identifies what happens during a mouseover event. If the correct browser is being used and the mouse is over the specified image, then the markeron graphic will be displayed.

Lines 18–22:—This function identifies what happens during a mouseout event. If the correct browser is being used and the mouse is off the specified image, then the markeroff graphic will be displayed.

Line 23:—Ends the HTML comment.

Line 24:—This line is the normal HTML tag that ends a script.

Line 25:—This line is the normal HTML tag that ends the head section.

That was the script. But the script alone won't create the mouseover effect; you must also tell the browser when to use the script. You do this by making the event handler part of the menu selection's anchor tag.

This is the code we use on our Daily Sightings page, slightly simplified for this example. It is in the body of the page, where we want the menu choices to appear. The event handlers are highlighted in bold. The menu choices are HTML text.

```
<img src=images/black.gif width=10 height=10 alt=""
> <a href="http://www.today.com/"
onmouseover="msover(0) ; return true"
onmouseout="msout(0)">today's sighting</a>

<img src=images/black.gif width=10 height=10
alt=""> <a href="months.html"
onmouseover="msover(1) ; return true"
onmouseout="msout(1)">previous sightings</a>

<img src=images/black.gif width=10 height=10
alt=""> <a href="submit.html"
onmouseover="msover(2) ; return true"
onmouseout="msout(2)">submit a sighting</a>

<img src=images/black.gif width=10 height=10
alt=""> <a href="/home.html"
onmouseover="msover(3) ; return true"
onmouseout="msout(3)">return to projectcool</a>
```

We use four menu options.

- Today's sighting
- Previous sighting
- Submit a sighting
- Return to projectcool

You can see that each menu option has an accompanying event handler in its anchor tag.

Let's walk through one of the menu options. For purposes of explanation, this code is broken into numbered segments. These reference numbers will not be in your real code.

```
01  <img src=images/black.gif width=10 height=10
alt="">

02   

03  <a href="http://www.today.com/"
onmouseover="msover(0) ; return true"
onmouseout="msout(0)">

04  today's sighting

05  </a>
```

Line 1:—The first component is the image that goes with the menu option. When the page first loads, the image will be the one named “black.gif”. When the reader mouses over the option, this graphic will be swapped as defined in the script.

Line 2:—The second component is a nonbreaking space. This puts a little distance between the image and the menu option.

Line 3:—The third component is the anchor tag for the menu option.

- It starts out giving the URL for the link, in normal href manner.
- Then it adds event handlers: onMouseOver and onMouseOut. When the mouse is over the first graphic on the page, the browser will look to the script to see what to do. It will see that when a mouseover event is recorded, it should display a different graphic. And, when a mouseout event is recorded, it should again display a different graphic.

Line 4:—The fourth component is the text that is serving as the menu option and is the item that appears as the link on the reader's page.

Line 5:—The final component is an end anchor tag, as normal.

There is one other very important thing to remember

when using a mouseover event: *The browser tracks each graphic on the page*. It numbers them sequentially, based on the order in which they appear in the HTML code. The first graphic is numbered 0. (Computers start counting at 0, not at 1.) The second is numbered 1. The third is numbered 2, and so on. In this example, the phrase "onmouseover="msover(0)" is saying that the graphic swapping will happen with image number 0.

A common mistake that people make is confusing the numbering of the graphics on their page. You'll note that in the example code, the image in front of each menu option is identified by number.

Our menu options are HTML text. But what if they were graphical buttons? We'd have to watch our counting even more carefully. The first marker image would still be image number 0. The next image would be the button for menu option 1. That would be image number 1. The second marker image would then be image number 2, and the msover reference would need to change to reflect that.

Script #3: Displaying Text in the Status Bar

This code displays text in the status bar at the bottom of the browser when the mouse is over the specified link.

You add this JavaScript notation directly into an HTML anchor tag. You do not need a separate script for it.

Online Location

You can find this code on this book's companion website and download it from there. It is in the JavaScript Templates area.

The Code

Here's the status bar script. It's all contained within an anchor tag. The JavaScript code is highlighted in bold to make it stand out. For purposes of explanation, this code is broken into numbered segments. These reference numbers will not be in your real code.

```
01 <a href="http://www.projectcool.com/"
02       onmouseover="window.status ='Go to Project
Cool';return true"
03      onmouseout="window.status = 'Nothing select-
ed'; return true">
04  Touch your mouse here</a>
```

Customizing the Code

Line by line, this is what the code does:

Line 1:—This starts an HTML anchor tag as usual. The link in the anchor is to the Project Cool homepage.

Line 2:—When the browser detects a mouse over this link, it tells the window status bar to display the text "Go to Project Cool." When the reader mouses over this link, this text appears in the status bar at the bottom of the browser window, as a subtle prompt.

Line 3:—When the browser detects that the mouse has left this link, it tells the window status bar to display the text "Nothing Selected." When the reader is not over this link, this text appears in the status bar at the bottom of the browser window, as a subtle prompt.

Line 4:—This is the linked text and the normal end anchor HTML tag.

Customization options: To use your own links and

messages, just substitute the linked text and the message text with your own content.

For example: This code segment displays the message "Eat at Joe's!" when the reader mouses over the graphic for Joe's Diner. No text appears when the reader's mouse is elsewhere. The changed elements are noted in bold to make them stand out.

```
<a href="http://www.projectcool.com/"
        onmouseover="window.status ='Eat at
Joe's!';return true"
        onmouseout="window.status = ''; return true">
<img src="joes.gif"></a>
```

Script#4: Changing Graphics Based on the User's Actions

This is the JavaScript that creates the mouseover effect you saw first thing in this chapter, back in Figures 5.1, 5.2, and 5.3. When the reader moves the mouse over a menu item, the menu button changes to one that is "lit up," and the graphic on top of the page changes to reflect the section the button selects.

Online Location

You can find this code on this book's companion website and download it from there. It is in the JavaScript Templates area.

The Code

As with the other mouseover script (Script #2), using this script is a two-step process.

1. First, you place the script in the HTML page head area.

2. Second, you add event handlers to the menu option anchor tags in the body of the HTML page. You do this in same way you did in Script #2, so we aren't repeating the HTML body content in this example.

We are actually using two scripts here. The first is a browser detection script. It checks to be sure the reader is using Navigator 3.0 or greater, or IE 4.0 or greater. We do this check because this particular mouseover effect requires Navigator 3.0 or IE 4.0 to support the JavaScript commands. For purposes of explanation, this code is broken into numbered segments. These reference numbers will not be in your real code.

```
01  <script language="Javascript">
02  <!--
03  /* NOTE:  New Browser detection code, more effe-
cient and allows Netscape 4.0 and the new IE 4.0
which now supports image arrays.
This code is now being used throughout the net, but
this is the source
you should refer to for updates.  We're modifying it
as the net changes.
Copyright 1996-97 Project Cool, Inc.  Used by the
net, with permission but we would appreciate it if
you would give us credit in the source or a link
from your site.*/

04  browser = (((navigator.appName == "Netscape")
&& (parseInt(navigator.appVersion) >= 3 )) || ((nav-
igator.appName == "Microsoft Internet Explorer") &&
(parseInt(navigator.appVersion) >= 4 )))

05  if ( browser) {
06  normal = new MakeArray(5)
07  over = new MakeArray(5)
08  picture = new MakeArray(6
09        blurb = new MakeArray(6)

10  normal[1].src = "images/menu1.gif"
11  normal[2].src = "images/menu2.gif"
12  normal[3].src = "images/menu3.gif"
13  normal[4].src = "images/menu4.gif"
```

```
over[1].src = "images/menu1a.gif"
over[2].src = "images/menu2a.gif"
over[3].src = "images/menu3a.gif"
over[4].src = "images/menu4a.gif"

picture[1].src = "images/1.jpg"
picture[2].src = "images/2.jpg"
picture[3].src = "images/3.jpg"
picture[4].src = "images/4.jpg"
picture[5].src = "images/0.jpg"

blurb[1] = "See the best sites, one new site
featured every day!"
blurb[2] = "Weekly e-zine covering The Web,
It's People, It's Future."
blurb[3] = "An easy to understand guide to
building great websites."
blurb[4] = "Our picks for the cream of the crop
of websites."
blurb[5] = ""
}

    function MakeArray(n) {
            this.length = n
            for (var i = 1; i<=n; i++) {
                    this[i] = new Image()
                    }
            return this
    }

function msover(num) {
        if ( browser) {
        document.images[num+1].src =
over[num].src
window.status = blurb[num]
document.images[0].src = picture[num].src
}
}

function msout(num) {
if ( browser) {
                    document.images[num+1].src =
normal[num].src
                      document.images[0].src =
picture[5].src
                      window.status = blurb[5]
        }
}
```

```
50  // -->
51  </script>
```

Customizing the Code

Line by line, this is what the code does:

Line 1:—Announces that a JavaScript script is beginning.

Line 2:—Starts an HTML comment area, so that the script won't confuse older browsers that don't understand the script tag.

Line 3:—This is a comment block. It is a good idea to add comment blocks and comment lines to your script.

Line 4:—Checks to see which version of browser the reader is using. It activates the browser variable if the result is Netscape 3 or greater, or IE 4 or greater.

Lines 5–9:—Assuming the browser is one of the valid browsers, this segment sets controls for four elements.

- The first two elements, normal and over (Lines 6 and 7), will swap a menubar graphic based on the reader mousing over and mousing off the menu option. There will be five possible image combinations: all unmoused, mouse over first menu button, mouse over second menu button, mouse over third menu button, or mouse over fourth menu button.
- The second two elements (Lines 8 and 9) rotate images and status bar text based on the mouse location. There will be six possible combinations for these: the default state when the page loads, all buttons unmoused, mouse over first menu button, mouse over second menu button, mouse over third menu button, or mouse over fourth menu button.

Customization options: You can change the variable names and the number of menu choices to match your page's need.

Lines 10–27:—This segment defines the source images and status bar text for each of the variable states.

- The first state, normal.src (Lines 10–13), is an array that contains the names of the four menu buttons.
- The second state, over.src (Lines 14–17), is an array that contains the names of the four menu buttons that appear when the mouse is over the button. These are the "lit up" buttons.
- The third state, picture.src (Lines 18–22), is an array that contains the names of the five images that appear at the top of page, one of each of the menu options and one when the mouse isn't over any menu option.
- The fourth state, blurb.src (Lines 23–27), is an array that contains the text that will appear in the status bar during the different mouseover states, one phrase each of the menu options and one when the mouse isn't over any menu option.

Customization options: You can change the image source files and the blurbs to reflect your own content. If you changed the variable names in the first part of the function, you must also change them here. If you have added or deleted images, make sure the numbers of images and blurbs continue to match (for example, if you are using only three menu options, you'll only need three menu button graphics).

Line 28:—Ends the function.

Lines 29–35:—This is the function that actually

makes the array. Don't change this portion of the code.

Lines 36–49:—This creates two functions: one that describes what happens when the mouseover event happens and one that describes what happens when the mouseout event happens.

Customization options: If you have added or deleted images, make sure the numbers of images and blurbs continue to match (for example, if you are using only three menu options, you'll only need three menu button graphics).

Line 50:—Ends the HTML comment.

Line 51:—This line is the normal HTML tag that ends a script.

Doing Simple Ad Rotation

You can use JavaScript to write a script that does basic ad rotation on your pages. It is not a full-featured ad tracking/ad management script by any means, but it provides some basic ad swapping capability.

TRY IT

To download and learn how to adapt the script that does simple ad rotation, go to this book's companion website and download it from there. It is in the JavaScript Templates area.

The ad rotation script is quite detailed and the interactive tutorial demonstrates how it works in real web time.

As you can see, with JavaScript you can create simple interactive functions, like alert boxes and status bar text. You don't need to be a programmer to incorporate basic

JavaScript functions. Just a little creativity and thought can start to bring your pages to life.

You can also use JavaScript to write complex programs, like ad rotation or other programmed interactivity. If you are hooked on the possibilities of JavaScript, go out and look at as many scripts as you can. Visit the Project Cool JavaScript Developer Zone, which is a constantly expanding resource for new scripts. Visit your bookstore and pick out other JavaScript-specific books to expand your knowledge.

Try deconstructing scripts that you like. Once you know the basic "grammar" of JavaScript, all you need is some time and patience to work your way through even the most complex script. Scripts that work follow the rules and you can decode them.

Tweak existing scripts, adapting them for your own content and pages. One of the best ways to get a feel for scripting is by editing existing scripts—you'll be more likely to see working results sooner than if you struggle to write your own complex script line by line.

Of course, once you feel comfortable with JavaScript, you probably will start creating your own code from scratch . . . and then you'll be the one sharing it with the web and serving as inspiration for other web builders.

That's the way to enhance both your site . . . and the web world.

6 USING CASCADING STYLE SHEETS

You've probably been here: You made a decision to use the color blue-green for all your level-three heads. It looked nice on your page. It fit your tone and mood. It didn't require any server overhead. It seemed like a wonderful decision. But somewhere around the 32nd time you created an H1 and a font color, a little voice inside began to scream—loudly and persistently—"There has to be an easier way!"

Or, you've just finished the last of 103 pages for a client. You carefully set a link color in each. It looked good. You were finished. And then your client told you "Gee, I'd really like to see how this looks with a link color of green . . . and then how it looks with a link color of light green . . . and what if . . . ." Part way through the conversation that loud little voice inside probably shrieked and said "Give me some global style control!!!!"

You're not alone. The push for more style control, both locally and globally, has been in the works for several years, and the advent of *Cascading Style Sheets* is a step toward a solution.

Cascading Style Sheets (CSS, for short) became a "W3C Recommendation" in December, 1996. Translated, that means the web's standards organization agreed the style sheets were a good thing, and released a specification outlining how it would like to see them implemented.

Of course, in today's web marketplace there are the standards . . . and there's the real-life support for them. The two are not always in synch and CSS is no exception. But with the release of the latest versions of IE and Navigator/Communicator, support is growing. This chapter tries to be browser agnostic and defers to the W3C specifications for using CSS, rather than tracking down the latest—and ever-changing—support decision from Microsoft or Netscape. As always, the best rule for ensuring compatibility is to test your pages with different browsers—with the browsers your readers will be using.

TIP: *When in doubt, test. With newer web page features, never assume that any given browser will support them exactly as you expect. The browser releases happen quickly and support can literally change from month to month. The best route is to test, test, test your page.*

UNDERSTANDING BASIC CSS

Cascading Style Sheets aren't nearly as complicated as their specs would have you believe. Most of the complexity comes from trying to figure out which browser supports which style attributes in exactly which manner. In addition, the specs present so many options for achieving the same result that the tree gets lost in the forest.

At its core, CSS is fairly straightforward, as long as you remember two basic rules:

- **First, and most important, CSS is very finicky about syntax.** One misspelling, one misplaced semicolon, and the whole style can go kaput and not reflect your chosen attributes. Unlike straight HTML, which will just skip what it doesn't understand, CSS won't work at all if it encounters something it doesn't understand.

- **Different browsers react just a bit differently with CSS styles.** We're going to show you the syntax that works best across different browsers, which will make cross-platform development easier. But even then, there are no guarantees. The software keeps changing and the best rule of thumb is to test, test, and test again.

So when something doesn't work as expected, don't panic. You probably have the basic idea down right and have just made some tiny stylistic error. You might spend some tedious time debugging your work, but using CSS can be worth the effort, especially as more browsers support it and as editing tools begin to emerge for it.

Defining Style

What exactly does the word "style" mean? Well, in the case of CSS, style means everything that defines how your web pages look. This includes fonts, spacing, color, indents, and line height, among other features. You can define the look of each type of tag you use in your web page.

For example, if you wanted all your paragraph tags to display on the screen at 12-point type size, in the Times New Roman font, and have a first line that indents 12 points, you could set up a style to do just that. In fact, here's what the code would look like:

```
P  {font-size: 12pt;
       font-family: "Times New Roman";
       text-indent: 12pt}
```

The result would resemble that in Figure 6.1.

It's pretty simple, isn't it? We specified the font size, the font family, and the text indent. The syntax may look a bit different from what you are accustomed to seeing, but then, it's not HTML—it's CSS.

In this example:

- The letter P tells the browser that this style is describing the paragraph (<p>) tag.
- The curly braces start and end the style rule.
- Semicolons separate each of the style properties. Take special note that the last item closes with a close brace, not a semicolon.

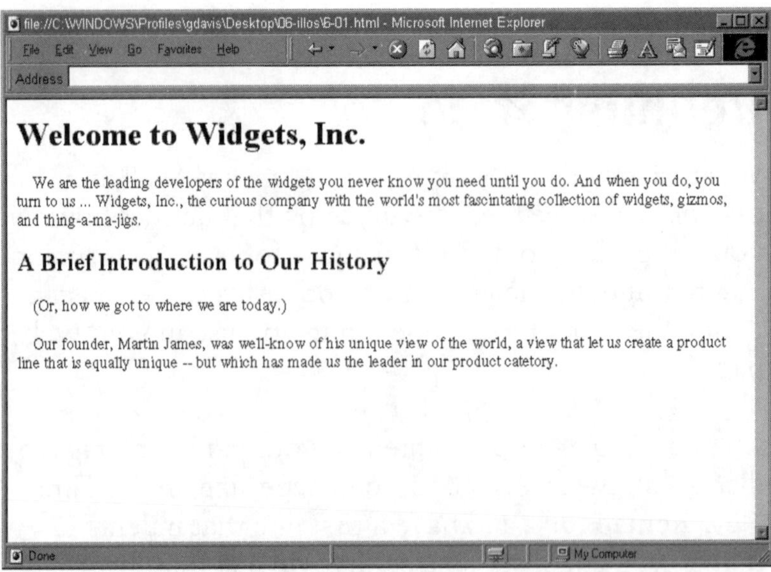

Figure 6.1
In this page, the paragraphs have been given a style of 12-point type, Times New Roman font, and a first line indent of 12 points.

- Each property has a name, followed by a colon, followed by a space, followed by the property's value.

  (In this example, 12pt stands for 12 point. One of the CSS measurement units and the standard unit of print typography, the point is about 1/72 of an inch.)

Inserting a Style in Your Web Page

There are several options for placing your styles in your web page.

- You can set up an external file to hold your style definitions.
- You can declare your styles in-line with the tags.
- You can set them up in a style definition in the head of your document.

The third method, setting styles in the document's head area, is the most common. To get the feel for using CSS, let's focus on this process; we'll return to the other options later in the chapter.

Style Declaration: The CSS code that describes the rules of a style.

Setting Up a Style Declaration

To use styles in an HTML file, you'll need to create a *style declaration*. A style declaration is just a listing of the different style rules you'll be using.

The style declaration typically goes in the HTML page header. It starts and ends with a <style> and </style> tag.

To create a style declaration:

<style>: Starts a style declaration.

</style>: Ends a style declaration.

1. Put the cursor in the head area of your HTML page. Type the start style tag, <style.

```
<head>
<title>Here comes the CSS</title>
<style
```

2. Finish the style tag by telling the browser that this style is a CSS style. Do this by using the Type= switch and the value "text/css" and then closing the tag.

```
<head>
<title>Here comes the CSS</title>
<style TYPE="text/css">
```

3. Next, type an HTML remark tag. This hides the CSS information from browsers that don't support it.

```
<head>
<title>Here comes the CSS</title>
<style type="text/css">
<--
```

4. Declare each of the styles you want to use within this HTML page. For example, this style sets a style for the body tag, a style for head level-one tags, and a style for paragraph tags. Each time the browser displays one of these tags, it will use the display information you note here, in the style declaration.

```
<head>
<title>Here comes the CSS</title>
<style type="text/css">
<--
BODY {font-size: 12pt;
     font-family: "Times New Roman";
     line-height: 15pt}

  H1 {font-size: 24pt;
     font-family: "Arial";
     font-weight: bold;
     color: ffffff;
     background-color: 9966cc}
```

```
  P  {font-size: 12pt;
      font-family: "Times New Roman";
      line-height: 15pt;
      text-indent: 12pt;
      margin-top: 2pt}
```

5. Close the HTML remark.

```
<head>
<title>Here comes the CSS</title>
<style type="text/css">
<--
BODY { font-size: 12pt;
      font-family: "Times New Roman";
      line-height: 15pt}

  H1 {font-size: 24pt;
      font-family: "Arial";
      font-weight: bold;
      color: ffffff;
      background-color: 9966cc}

  P  {font-size: 12pt;
      font-family: "Times New Roman";
      line-height: 15pt;
      text-indent: 12pt;
      margin-top: 2pt}
-->
```

6. Type the end style tag.

```
<head>
<title>Here comes the CSS</title>
<style type="text/css">
<--
BODY { font-size: 12pt;
      font-family: "Times New Roman";
      line-height: 15pt}

  H1 {font-size: 24pt;
      font-family: "Arial";
      font-weight: bold;
      color: ffffff;
      background-color: 9966cc}

  P  {font-size: 12pt;
      font-family: "Times New Roman";
      line-height: 15pt;
```

```
        text-indent: 12pt;
        margin-top: 2pt}
-->
</style>
```

7. End the head section as usual, with the end head tag.

```
<head>
<title>Here comes the CSS</title>
<style type="text/css">
<--
BODY { font-size: 12pt;
       font-family: "Times New Roman";
       line-height: 15pt}

  H1 {font-size: 24pt;
       font-family: "Arial";
       font-weight: bold;
       color: ffffff;
       background-color: 9966cc}

  P  {font-size: 12pt;
       font-family: "Times New Roman";
       line-height: 15pt;
       text-indent: 12pt;
       margin-top: 2pt}
-->
</style>
</head>
```

Let's take a look at what this example style defined.

- The default body text has a size of 12 points, a font of Times New Roman, and a line height of 15 points. Line height is the space from one baseline to the next. This is roughly the equivalent of leading or line spacing in print typography.

```
BODY { font-size: 12pt;
       font-family: "Times New Roman";
       line-height: 15pt}
```

- The default values for all <h1> text is 24 points in size, the font Arial, the font style bold, and the color white with a background color (which appears in the form of a bar the depth of the headline) of purple.

```
H1 {font-size: 24pt;
       font-family: "Arial";
       font-weight: bold;
       color: ffffff;
       background-color: 9966cc}
```

- The default values for all <p> tagged text is 12 points in size, a font of Times New Roman, and a line height of 15 points. The first line will be indented 12 points from the margin and there will be an extra two points of space before each paragraph.

```
P  {font-size: 12pt;
       font-family: "Times New Roman";
       line-height: 15pt;
       text-indent: 12pt;
       margin-top: 2pt}
```

Don't worry if you don't understand all of the attributes right now. Later in the chapter, each one is defined in more detail and the table in Appendix A summarizes them as well.

Using a Style

Once you've set up the style declaration in the file's header, you don't need to do anything special to use it. The browser will automatically display each tagged element as you've specified in the style.

TRY IT

Try creating a style to see how easy it is.

1. Go to the TRY IT section on the companion website.
2. Type this text. Make sure what you type is exactly as you see it here. Remember,

CSS is very particular about syntax. You must have an IE 4.0 or Netscape Communicator 4.0 or higher browser to see the results.

```
<head>
<title>A CSS Test</title>
<style type="text/css">
<--
  H1 {font-size: 36pt;
      font-family: "Arial";
      font-weight: bold;
      color: ffffff;
      background-color: 9966cc}

  H2 {font-size: 16pt;
      font-family: "Arial";
      font-weight: bold;
      color: 00ff00}

  P  {font-size: 12pt;
      font-family: "Times New Roman";
      line-height: 14pt;
      text-indent: 12pt;
      margin-top: 24pt}
-->
</style>
</head>
<body>
<h1>Head Level One, We've Just
Begun!</h1>
<p>
With CSS you can define the look of any
tag in your page. You can set a value
for all the paragraphs, for example.
<p>
That's what you'll be seeing here in a
moment. Each paragraph will conform to
the style you have just set.
<h2>True for H2, Too!</h2>
<p>
Not as hard as it seems. You can do the
basics quickly, easily, and painlessly.
</body>
```

3. Click on the TRY IT button and look at the results.

USING CSS AT DIFFERENT LEVELS

As we mentioned earlier, you can use style declarations at three levels.

The most common way to use them is to put them into the head area of your HTML page. When the browser reads the page, it also reads the style declaration and displays the tags as they are described in the style.

But what if you want to override your styles for a specific instance inside the body? Maybe you want one H1 to be green instead of the default purple. Or maybe you want one paragraph to be 14 point instead of 12 point in size. No problem! You can use a style declaration within the body of an HTML page.

In-line Styles

In-line styles, as you might guess from the name, are used within HTML tags, within the body of an HTML document. They override any document-level styles and apply just to the single use of the tag in which you include them.

The code of an in-line style looks like this:

```
<H2 style="font-family: helvetica, arial; color:
red;" >
```

This code produces the text you see in Figure 6.2.

With a CSS-compliant browser, you can add the Style switch to any HTML tag to which style elements apply.

To add an in-line style:

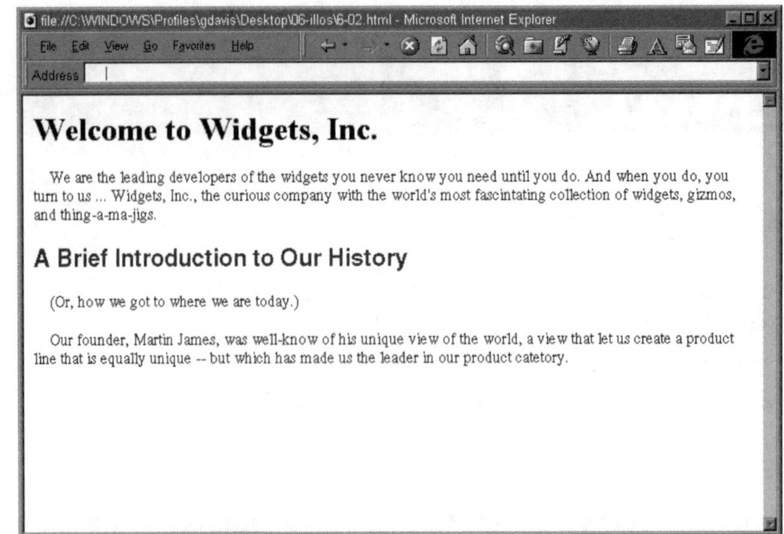

Figure 6.2
This level-2 HTML head is now in a Helvetica face and colored red.

1. Type the opening HTML delimiter, followed by the normal HTML tag. For example:

   ```
   <H1
   ```

2. Type a space and the Style= switch.

   ```
   <H1 style=
   ```

3. Type a double quotation mark.

   ```
   <H1 style="
   ```

4. Type the first style element, followed by a colon, a space, and the element's value.

   ```
   <H1 style="font-size: 36pt
   ```

5. Type a semicolon, and the second element, followed by a space and the element's value.

   ```
   <H1 style="font-size: 36pt; font-family: helveti-
   cal, arial
   ```

   Note: You can put a space after the semicolon or not. This is one of the few places where it doesn't matter. The semicolon is seen as the breaker between elements.

6. Add other values to the list if you want. When you have added all the style elements and their values, end with a double quotation mark, and then end your HTML tag as usual.

```
<H1 style="font-size: 36pt; font-family: helveti-
cal, arial; color: blue;">
```

Linked Style Sheets

So you now know how to control styles within an individual HTML file. But in the real world, we are often working with groups of documents, and want them all to be consistent. Again, no problem.

You could, of course, cut and paste the same style declaration into the header of each file. But there is an easier way. You can create a single style declaration, save it in a special kind of file, and call that one file from all your HTML pages. This is far easier than cutting and pasting the same declaration over and over, or maintaining a declaration in 43 different HTML files.

.css Files

The first thing to remember about linked style sheets is that they are saved in a file with a .css file extension.

- house_style.css
- new.css
- mystyle.css

> **.css Files:** ASCII text files that contain only style-sheet information.

Much as HTML files need the extension .html or .htm for the browser to recognize them, so too do style files need that .css extension. Without it, they'll just be ignored.

Each .css file is simply an ASCII text file with nothing

in it except for the style rules. There are no HTML tags, no scripts; nothing except the style rules, like this:

```
H1 {font-size: 36pt;
      font-family: "Arial";
      font-weight: bold;
      color: ffffff;
      background-color: 9966cc}

 H2 {font-size: 16pt;
      font-family: "Arial";
      font-weight: bold;
      color: 00ff00}

 P  {font-size: 12pt;
      font-family: "Times New Roman";
      line-height: 14pt;
      text-indent: 12pt;
      margin-top: 24pt}
```

Once the file is created, it can be called from multiple HTML documents. When you update the style file, all the HTML documents to which it is linked will also change. You can create a totally different look and feel to the exact same file just by linking to a different .css file.

The <link> Tag

<link>: Links to the specified .css file stylesheet.

You link to a .css file by adding a new HTML tag—the link tag—to the HTML file's head area.

To link to a style file from an HTML document:

1. In the head of your HTML file, type the link tag.

   ```
   <link
   ```

2. Type the Rel switch, an equal sign, and the word "stylesheet" to tell the browser it will be finding a style-sheet file.

   ```
   <link rel=stylesheet
   ```

3. Type the Type switch and the value "text/css" to

tell the browser the type of style sheet file it will be using:

```
<link rel=stylesheet type="text/css"
```

4. Type the Href switch followed by the URL where the .css file is stored. You can use either full or relative linking, as with any Href switch.

```
<link rel=stylesheet type="text/css"
href="/styles/alpha.css"
```

5. End the tag as usual.

```
<head>
<title>Alpha Version of Client Pages
</title>
<link rel=stylesheet type="text/css"
href="/styles/alpha.css">
</head>
```

Cascading

Now that you know the three different ways of specifying styles, you should also be familiar with the way styles "cascade" from one level to the next. In W3C-speak, the term "cascade" describes "the ordered sequence of style sheets where rules in later sheets have greater precedence than earlier ones."

In reality, this means that:

- The highest-level of style is the style within the first linked .css file. If the HTML document links to a .css file, this is the first place the browser will look for style information. It will use that information to display the HTML element unless . . .
- There is a second linked .css file. The browser (if it supports multiple linked .css files—at this writing it is not clear which do and don't) will cycle through any linked .css files in the order in which they are

linked in the HTML file, and aggregate the style rules in each. If there are duplicate rules, the rules in the last listed style sheet will be in effect for the entire HTML document unless . . .

- There is a style declaration in the document header. Any style elements in a style declaration will override the same style elements specified in the .css files. The elements will be in effect for the entire HTML document unless . . .
- There is an in-line style specified for an individual element on the page. This will override any style declarations for this specific use of this element.

For example, suppose your HTML document is linked to a .css file that describes level-one heads as being bold Helvetica, level-two heads as being bold Times, and body text as being 12-point Times with 14 points of line height with no paragraph indent.

The document displayed with this linked style sheet resembles the one in Figure 6.3.

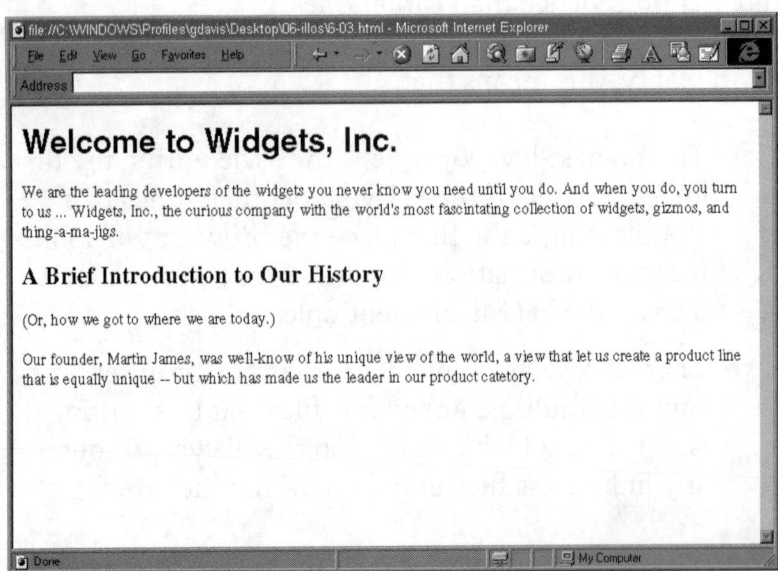

Figure 6.3
This HTML document uses all the attributes defined in the linked style sheet.

But what if you wanted one of your HTML documents to be just a little different? Say, you wanted its level-one heads to be green and its level-two heads to be in Helvetica instead of in Times? You'd simply create a style declaration in that document's head.

The declaration would look like this:

```
<head>
<style type="text/css">
<--
  H1 {color: green}

  H2 {font-family: "Helvetica, Arial"}

  P  {text-indent: 6em}
-->
</style>
</head>
```

You'll see that we didn't re-create every style property for the HTML elements; we just added new ones (green H1, 6 em paragraph indent) or changed the one we wanted changed (Helvetica). The styles inherit all the characteristics in the linked file and then update based on the style declaration in the HTML document head.

The same page displayed with the linked style sheet plus the style declaration resembles the one in Figure 6.4.

Ahh, but what if you want just one of those level-one heads to really stand out and be extra, extra large? You'd use an in-line style, as part of that one element's H1 tag, like this:

```
<H1 style="font-size=72pt;">
```

For that one instance of the level-one head, the headline would have the added style characteristic of being 72 points in size.

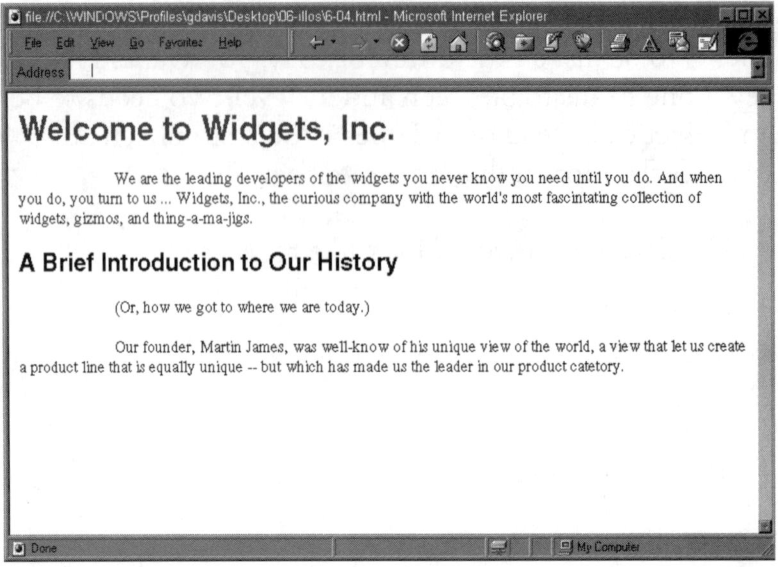

Figure 6.4 *This HTML document uses all the attributes defined in the linked style sheet, plus the addition of any elements or changes in the style declaration.*

The same file you saw in Figure 6.4 with this in-line style element addition would look like the one in Figure 6.5.

Inheritance

Another way that elements can acquire a style characteristic is through the notion of *inheritance*.

CSS is loosely based on an object hierarchy. That is, certain objects are "parents" and other objects are "children" of those parents. The children elements automatically inherit the style attributes of their parents, unless you override them with another set of style attributes.

For example:

- An HTML element is the parent to any subclasses of that element. The classes inherit all the character-

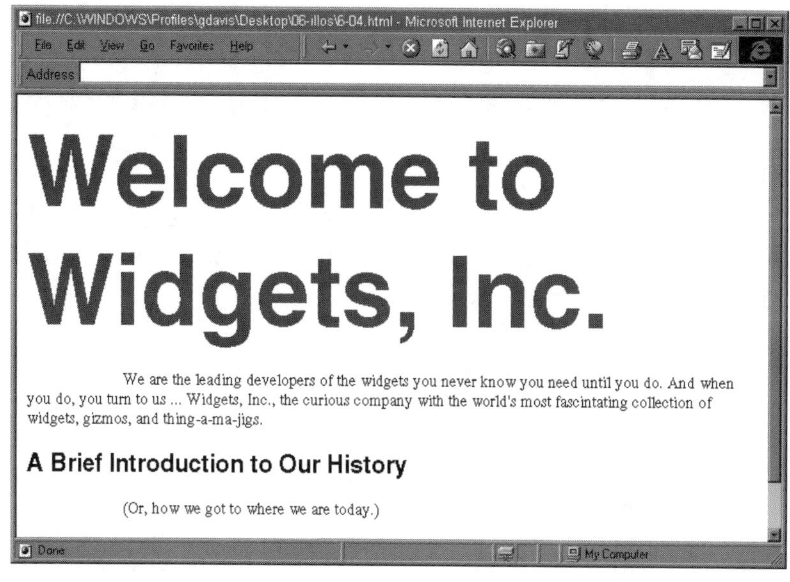

Figure 6.5
This HTML document uses all the attributes defined in the linked style sheet, plus inline style information.

istics that were set for the element. For example, if you specify a style for the paragraph tag and also create a class of paragraph called "first-graph," the "first-graph" class will inherit all of the paragraph style attributes automatically.

- If an HTML tag is contained within another HTML tag, the inner tag is considered a child and inherits the outer tag's characteristics. For example, if your paragraph is 14-point Helvetica and is blue, the contents of a bold tag inside that paragraph will also be 14-point Helvetica and blue, as well as bold. The contents of the bold tag inherit the style attributes of the parent paragraph tag.

WRITING CSS CODE

This section talks about creating styles and some of the factors you may want to take into consideration as you add them to your website.

Building Basic Styles

It is quite straightforward to create and use basic style commands.

First, look at your HTML page or pages and see which elements you are using, and think about how you want these elements to look.

- Do you want all your paragraphs to have an indented first line?
- Do you want block quotes in a larger, different color font?
- Do you like the default headlines, or do you want your H1s and H2s to use a different font?

If you are creating styles for a whole site, take note of what style decisions you are making. It is good policy to have an old-fashioned style guide—the kind that doesn't have anything to do with HTML but which is a central list of how your site, document, publication, or pages will look. Having this information—in writing and in a central spot—will make your life much easier when you update, add elements, or pass along site maintenance duties to someone else.

TIP: *An old-fashioned style guide—a simple reference list of what's what on your site—will help you maintain consistency.*

Style Declaration: A description of the style information for an HTML page.

Once you have decided what style changes you want to make to the different HTML elements, you are ready to create a *style declaration*. The style declaration contains a description of all the style information for the HTML page.

The declaration, you'll remember, goes in the header of the HTML file.

Declarations

Each *declaration* is made of one or more rules. Together, the rules define the "look" of the HTML page.

The declaration begins with the style tag and ends with the end style tag. Between the two tags are the rules.

The style tag has one switch, Type. Type should have the value "text/css" within double quote marks.

It is a good idea to put the style rules within comment markers. That way non-CSS browsers won't try to display the style rules as HTML text. This code shows a sample declaration with three rules.

```
<style type="text/css">
<--
  H1 {font-size: 36pt;
      font-family: "Arial";
      font-weight: bold;
      color: ffffff;
      background-color: 9966cc}

  H2 {font-size: 16pt;
      font-family: "Arial";
      font-weight: bold;
      color: 00ff00;

  P  {font-size: 12pt;
      font-family: "Times New Roman";
      line-height: 14pt;
      text-indent: 12pt;
      margin-top: 24pt}
-->
</style>
```

Rules

Each rule describes a set of style properties for one HTML element. A property is some feature about the element that you can control through a style.

This is the format for a rule:

1. Type the HTML element tag. For example, paragraph.

   ```
   P
   ```

   The tag can be in either uppercase or lowercase.

2. Type a space and then an open brace.

   ```
   P {
   ```

3. Type the first property, followed by a colon.

   ```
   P {font-size:
   ```

4. Type a space and then type the value you are assigning that property.

   ```
   P {font-size: 12pt
   ```

5. End with a semicolon.

   ```
   P {font-size: 12pt;
   ```

6. If you want to add another property to the rule, type a space, that property's name, a colon, and its value. Visually, you may want to place each property on a separate line in the rule.

   ```
   P       {font-size: 12pt;
     font-family: "helvetica, arial";
   ```

7. End the rule with a close bracket. Note that the last property in the rule does not end with a semicolon.

   ```
   P       {font-size: 12pt;
     font-family: "helvetica, arial"}
   ```

Style Property: An attribute or feature that you can control through a style command.

Properties

CSS gives you five general categories of features that you can control through a style sheet. Each of these features is called a *style property*.

These five basic categories are:

- **Text properties**, which control the way the browser displays text. These include wordspacing, letterspacing, text decoration (underline, overline, strike-through, or blink), text transformation (all caps, upper/lowercase, all lowercase), vertical alignment to the baseline, horizontal alignment, indent, leading.
- **Font properties**, which control how fonts are called and used. These include font size, font family, font style (normal or italic), font variant (normal or small caps), and font weight (normal or bold).
- **Color and background properties**, which control foreground and background colors and images. These include text color, background color, background image, repeat pattern for background image, and positioning of background image.
- **Placement properties**, which define the element's relative location on the web page. These include margins, borders, and padding.
- **Classification properties**, which define the category of an element. These include display classifications and display attributes of different classifications, such as lists or blocks.

The specific properties and their values are detailed later on in this chapter. In addition, Appendix A in this book has a reference chart of the properties and what each does.

Creating Classes

When you create a rule for an HTML element, that rule applies every time you use the element in your page. But

Class: A variation of a style.

sometimes you'll discover that you need variations of certain styles. For instance:

- You might need two different styles of anchors, one that is the default style, and another with a variation for a different section of the same page.
- You might need two different paragraph styles, one that you use as the first paragraph after a headline and one that you use the rest of the time.

Classes are a way of creating variations on the standard style. They are easy to set up and use.

- To create a class, you'll just add another rule to your style declaration.
- To use a class, you'll just add the Class switch to the HTML element tag when you call the element in your HTML file.

TIP: *If you are using classes, it is a good idea to keep a reference list for your own development efforts, noting the variations and when you want to use them.*

Creating a Class

To create a class:

1. In your style declaration, begin a style rule as usual. For example, to create a style for your anchor tags, you'd type A.

```
A
```

2. Type a period. This tells the browser that you are creating a class, a variation of style for this element.

```
A.
```

3. Type the name you want to give to this class. For

example, you might be creating a highlighted anchor link.

```
A.highlighted
```

4. Now, finish the rule, entering the property and its value. In this case, we're setting the background color of the "highlighted" anchor link.

```
A.highlighted {background-color: ffff00}
```

Using a Class

To use a class style:

1. In the body of your HTML document, start the HTML tag as you normally would. For example, if you want to use the "highlighted" anchor tag:

```
There is much more information about frogs. Click
<a
```

2. Type the Class= switch.

```
There is much more information about frogs. Click
<a class=
```

3. In double quotes, type the name of the class that you created in the style declaration and that you want to use at this point in your HTML page. In this example, we created—and will now use—a class of anchor tag called "highlighted."

```
There is much more information about frogs. Click
<a class="highlighted"
```

4. Finish the element tag as usual. In the case of the anchor tag, you'll add the Href switch.

```
There is much more information about frogs. Click
<a class="highlighted"
href="frogs2.html">HERE</a> to learn more.
```

The class you create inherits all the attributes of the

parent element, plus the attributes you specify in the class's style rule. This means that you don't have to recreate all the properties for each class of the element.

This code is an example of how you might use two different types of paragraphs. The regular paragraph is used most of the time. The "first" paragraph class is the first paragraph that follows a headline. It isn't indented and it has a larger line-height property.

Figure 6.6 shows the resulting HTML page.

```
<html>
<head>
<title>Course Listings</title>
<style type="text/css">
<--
  H1 {font-size: 24pt;
      font-family: "helvetica, arial";
      font-weight: bold;
      color: #ffffff;
      background-color: #9966cc}
```

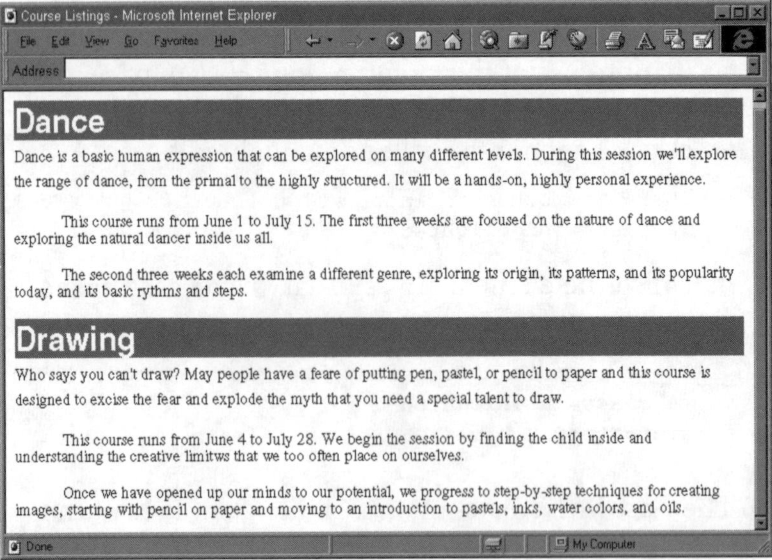

Figure 6.6 *This HTML document uses two variations of the paragraph: The "first" paragrah has a greater amount of spacing between lines and no indent. The normal paragraph has a first line indent and a lesser amount of spacing between the lines.*

```
P  {font-size: 12pt;
      font-family: "Times New Roman";
      line-height: 12pt;
      text-indent: 3em}

P.first  {font-size: 12pt;
      font-family: "Times New Roman";
      line-height: 18pt;
      text-indent: 3em;
      margin-top: -12pt}
-->
</style>
</head>
<body>
<h1>Dance</h1>

<p class="first">

Dance is a basic human expression that can be ex-
plored on many different levels. During this session
we'll explore the range of dance, from the primal to
the highly structured. It will be a hands-on, highly
personal experience.

<p>

This course runs from June 1 to July 15. The first
three weeks are focused on the nature of dance and
exploring the natural dancer inside us all.

<p>

The second three weeks each examine a different
genre, exploring its origin, its patterns, and its
popularity today.

<p>

<a href="registration.html">To register for the
classs, click on this link.</a>

<h1>Drawing</h1>

<p class="first">

Who says you can't draw? Many people have a fear of
putting pen, pastel, or pencil to paper and this
```

```
course is designed to excise the fear and explode
the myth that you need a special talent to draw.

<p>

This course runs from June 4 to July 28. We begin
the session by finding the child inside and under-
standing the creative limits that we too often place
on ourselves.

<p>

Once we have opened up our minds to our potential,
we progress to step-by-step techniques for creating
images, starting with pencil on paper and moving to
an introduction to pastels, inks, water colors, and
oils.

<p>

<a href="registration.html">To register for the
classs, click on this link.</a>
```

<div></div> : Creates a division on an HTML page.

Adding Divisions and IDs

The <div> tag is a standard HTML element. It lets you create a section within an HTML page and apply attributes to just that section.

For example, to create an area within a page in which everything is centered, you could add a Center switch to each element. Or, you could create a division and give it the Center switch once, like this:

```
<div align=center>
```

Everything between the <div> tag and the </div> tag is centered.

For example, this code creates the page you see in Figure 6.7.

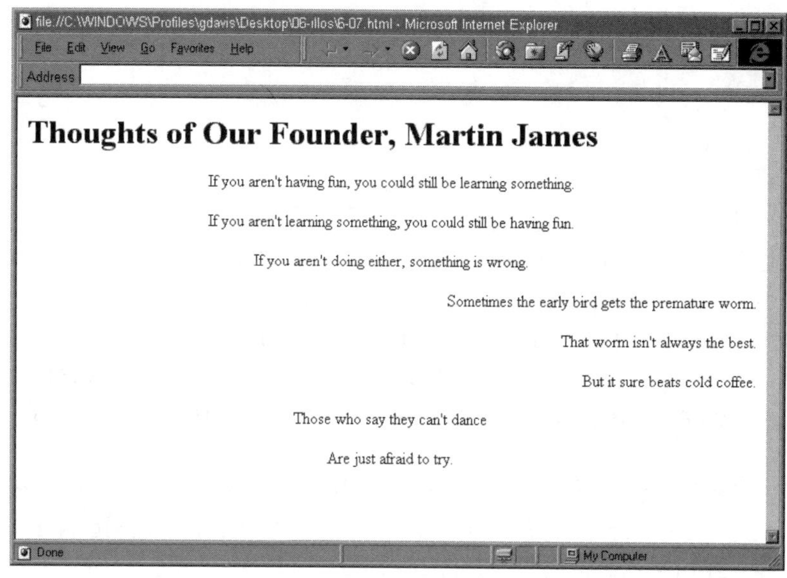

Figure 6.7
This page has three divisions. The first and third have an alignment of center. The second has an alignment of right.

```
<body>
<h1>Thoughts of Our Founders</h1>

<div align=center>
<p>
If you aren't having fun, you could still be learn-
ing something.
<p>
If you aren't learning something, you could still be
having fun.
<p>
If you aren't doing either, something is wrong.
</div>

<div align=right>
<p>
Sometimes the early bird gets the premature worm.
<p>
That worm isn't always the best.
<p>
But it sure beats cold coffee.
</div>

<div align=center>
<p>
```

```
Those who say they can't dance
<p>
Are just afraid to try.
</div>
</body>
```

The div tag is already a useful HTML tool, but with CSS—and later on, with Dynamic HTML—the division tag can become even more powerful. It essentially creates a mini-page nested within your main page. You can create and name different divisions, and assign different styles and JavaScript functions to the different divisions.

ID: *An attribute that assigns a name to an object on an HTML page.*

To harness the power of the div tag, you'll need to use a function called *ID*. An ID is an attribute that assigns a reference name to a division in an HTML page. Once you know a division's ID, you can set specific styles for the division or manipulate it with a bit of JavaScript code.

To see how this works, let's look at those Founder's Quotes again, and see how we can enhance the page using CSS, divisions, and IDs.

- First, we created a style declaration. In the declaration, we created two classes of style for the <div> element. The "quote1" class centers the text and makes it Palatino bold, 14 point. The "quote2" class aligns the text right and makes it Helvetica, red, and 18 point.

  The classes can be used over and over again and called, as switches, in many different divisions.

- After we created the classes, we told the style that there are some named divisions—IDs—and that each of those divisions has its own attribute of background color.

  Each ID can be used only once. It refers to a single specific use of the division element. It is the ID that lets us call the worm quote by name. We can change its appearance and, eventually, manipulate it in other ways.

This is the style declaration in the header:

```
<style type="text/css">
<!--
div.quote1 {font-family: times;
                font-size: 12pt;
                text-align: center}

div.quote2 {font-family: helvetica, arial;
                font-size: 18pt;
                text-align: right}

#fun {background-color: ffff00}
#worm {background-color: 00ff00}
#dance {background-color: 0000ff}
-->
</style>
```

Now, this is the body of that HTML file. You'll see that we made each quotation its own division. We used the Class switch to assign specific style information to the divisions. And we used the Id switch to assign the ID name to the division and to call in the ID-specific information from the style sheet.

Figure 6.8 shows the resulting HTML page. The page is also "live" on the companion website to this book.

```
<body>
<h1>Thoughts of Our Founders</h1>

<div id="fun" class="quote1">
<p>
If you aren't having fun, you could still be learn-
ing something.
<p>
If you aren't learning something, you could still be
having fun.
<p>
```

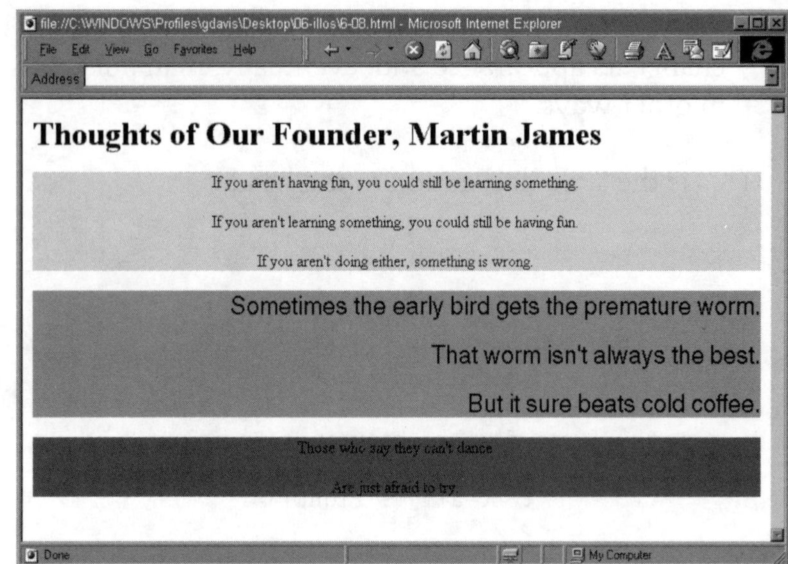

Figure 6.8
This page has three divisions. Each is assigned its own unique ID name, which allows it to be treated as a manipulatible object.

```
If you aren't doing either, something is wrong.
</div>

<div id="worm" class="quote2">
<p>
Sometimes the early bird gets the premature worm.
<p>
That worm isn't always the best.
<p>
But it sure beats cold coffee.
</div>

<div id="dance" class="quote1">
<p>
Those who say they can't dance
<p>
Are just afraid to try.
</div>
</body>
```

Using the Span Tag

CSS support also includes support for an HTML tag named <span>. The span tag essentially creates an in-line division.

Figure 6.9 shows the span tag in use. In this example, the span tag lets you make the first few words of the paragraph larger than the rest.

<span></span>: Creates an in-line division.

This is the code that created the effect. It used in-line style properties.

```
<h1>The Princess and the Rain Cloud</h1>
<p>
<span style="font-size: 14pt; font-family: helveti-
ca, arial; color: blue;">Once Upon A Time </span>
there lived a beautiful princess. Her skin was soft
as the morning dew and her hair was all the hues of
the rainbow. Her smile touched everyone she met, as
if the first rays of the morning sun were somehow
directed by her very glance.
```

You could have also used a style declaration to create the same effect. If you were using the effect several times in the same HTML file, a style declaration would be a better choice than an in-line style. The code, with a style declaration, would look like this:

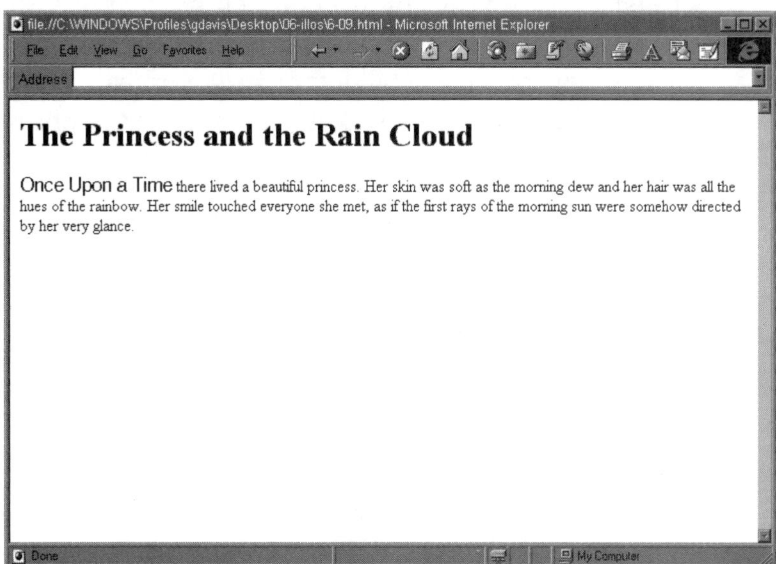

Figure 6.9
This page uses the span tag to create a different effect for the first few words in the paragraph.

```
<head>
<title>The Princess and the Rain Cloud</title>
<style type="text/css">
span {font-size: 14pt;
      font-family: helvetica, arial;
      color: blue"}
</style>
</head>

<body>

<h1>The Princess and the Rain Cloud</h1>
<p>
<span>Once Upon A Time </span> there lived a beauti-
ful princess. Her skin was soft as the morning dew
and her hair was all the hues of the rainbow.
```

USING STYLE PROPERTIES

The CSS specification divides style properties into five categories.

- **Text properties**, which control the way the browser displays text. These include wordspacing, letterspacing, text decoration (underline, overline, strike-through, or blink), text transformation (all caps, upper/lowercase, all lowercase), vertical alignment to the baseline, horizontal alignment, indent, leading.
- **Font properties**, which control how fonts are called and used. These include font size, font family, font style (normal or italic), font variant (normal or small caps), and font weight (normal or bold).
- **Color and background properties**, which control foreground and background colors and images. These include text color, background color, background image, repeat pattern for background image, and positioning of background image.

- **Placement properties**, which define the element's relative location on the web page. These include margins, borders, and padding.
- **Classification properties**, which define the category of an element. These include display classifications and display attributes of different classifications, such as lists or blocks.

This section of the book details the properties and how to use them. Appendix A of this book lists a summary of each property, its values, and what it does.

Individual versus Summary Commands

All of the property categories let you specify each property one by one. Several also allow you to specify several property values with one summary command.

This code shows how three font properties are defined one by one for the H1 HTML element.

```
H1 {font-family: helvetica, arial; font-size: 72pt;
font-weight: bolder}
```

This code shows how the same three font properties are defined by the summary command.

```
H1 {bolder 72pt "helvetica, arial"}
```

For several reasons, it is currently a good idea to specify each property separately, rather than using the summary command. First, browser support for the summary command is currently mixed and not predictable. In addition, a string of values after a summary command can be difficult for someone else to interpret later on down the road, unless you add comment lines to explain what you have done. Thus, we recommend that for the time, at least, you consider specifying property values using individual property commands.

TIP: *More specificity makes for easier editing. In general, try to list the individual properties rather than stringing them together in one command line.*

Units

You can specify the values of properties in two ways:

- As *absolute* values
- As *relative* values

Absolute values describe the property as having a fixed, specific value. The font size might be 12 point. The text indent might be 4 centimeters. The absolute value lets you—the page creator—be very specific about how the reader will see your content. For people who are accustomed to working in print, it also feels very comfortable, natural, and normal.

If you want that level of control and if you know a great deal about the environment in which your readers are working, absolute values are wonderful and give you a great deal of control over your pages' look and feel. However, when you are using absolute values always remember that the reader might be viewing your page in a different environment from what you expect. For example, if you specify 12-point type, the page might display wonderfully on a high-resolution computer monitor, which the reader is viewing at a distance of 18 or 24 inches. But what if that reader pulls up your page on his or her WebTV and is watching it from the sofa at a distance of six feet? Suddenly, your 12-point type doesn't seem like such a good choice.

Relative units describe the values in comparison to the current value. For example, the type size might be larger, smaller, bolder, or lighter. The indent might be specified in em spaces, which vary with the display size of the text. Because web pages are viewed in so many different ways, it is often a good idea to use relative values. It gives you less control but it could create a better experience for your readers.

The decision comes down to knowing your audience: Who are they? What do they expect? In what type of environment will they be working? It also involves a sense of balance: Is controlling the look more important than allowing web pages to flow within the user environment? Ultimately, the decisions you make will be based on your expectations for your pages.

Text Properties

CSS lets you assign a variety of other characteristics to an HTML text element. These include:

- Wordspacing
- Letterspacing
- Text decoration (underline, overline, strike-through, or blink)
- Text transformation (all caps, upper/lowercase, all lowercase)
- Vertical alignment to the baseline
- Horizontal alignment

- Indent
- Line spacing/leading

> **Point:** Traditional print unit of measurement. There are 72 points to an inch.

Measurement of Text

Most text properties can be measured by the absolute value of points, abbreviated as pt. There are 72 points to an inch. Points are the traditional U.S. method of measuring printed type height.

Other absolute units are:

> **Pica:** Traditional print unit of measurement. There are 12 points to a pica, 6 picas to an inch.

- **picas**, "pc" (There are 12 points to a pica, or 6 picas to an inch; picas and points together are the traditional print measurement of column width.)
- **inches**, "in"
- **centimeters**, "cm"
- **millimeters**, "mm"

When specifying an absolute unit, do not put any space between the value and the unit abbreviation. For example, to specify 14-point leading ("line height"), you'd type this code:

```
P {line-height: 14pt}
```

> **Em Space:** An amount of whitespace equal to the width of the capital letter M in the current font size and style.

Many text properties can also be measured as a relative percentage, such as 120% or –10 percent.

Width text properties, such as line indents, can be measured as *em units*. The em is the width of the capital letter M in the current type size and style. An em unit measurement scales with the size of the text.

You might also see the value "ex." This refers to the x-height of the current type size and style. It is not a good unit for measuring length.

The third width measurement you can use is *pixel*, abbreviated as px. The pixel unit scales with the type of monitor the reader is using. Some web builders suggest that if your readers will be using many different types of display devices, you might want to try using pixels as your measurement unit.

Pixel: One "picture element" on a monitor. The number of pixels per inch varies from monitor to monitor. A typical range is between 72 and 90 pixels per inch.

Wordspacing

```
{word-spacing: normal/XXunit/%}
```

You can set a style to control the amount of space between each word in a text block. For example:

```
P {word-spacing: -10%}
P {word-spacing: normal}
P {word-spacing: 150%}
```

Note: At the time of this writing this property is not supported by any commercial browser, although it is in the W3C spec and will likely be supported in future browser releases.

Letterspacing

```
{letter-spacing: normal/XXunit/%}
```

If you are a print person, don't let your print background confuse you—the CSS use of the term "letter spacing" is somewhat different from the print definition. With CSS you are setting the amount of space between each letter from scratch; you are not adding or deleting ("loosening or tightening") intraletter space from a pre-set typographically defined space. For example, if you set the CSS letter spacing value to 0, all of the letters will sit atop each other. If you set it to five pixels, there wil be five pixels between the left starting point of one letter and the left starting point of the next.

You can use literal units, relative units, or percentages as letter space values.

For example:

```
P {letter-spacing: -5px}
P {letter-spacing: 1 em}
```

At the time of this writing this property is not supported by any commercial browser, although it is in the W3C spec and will likely be supported in future browser releases.

Text Decoration

```
{text-decoration: underline/overline/line-
through/blink}
```

The *text-decoration* property lets you create underlined, overlined, strike-through, or blinking text. Vendors may be adding their own decoration support as well.

Figure 6.10 shows an example of some text decoration values. Remember, just because you can use them does not necessarily mean that you should. There was a recent news-wire story about a man who shot his computer four times at close range. We suspect he saw one too many blink tags on his web browser. . .

Text Transformation

```
{text-transformation:none/capitalize/uppercase/low-
ercase}
```

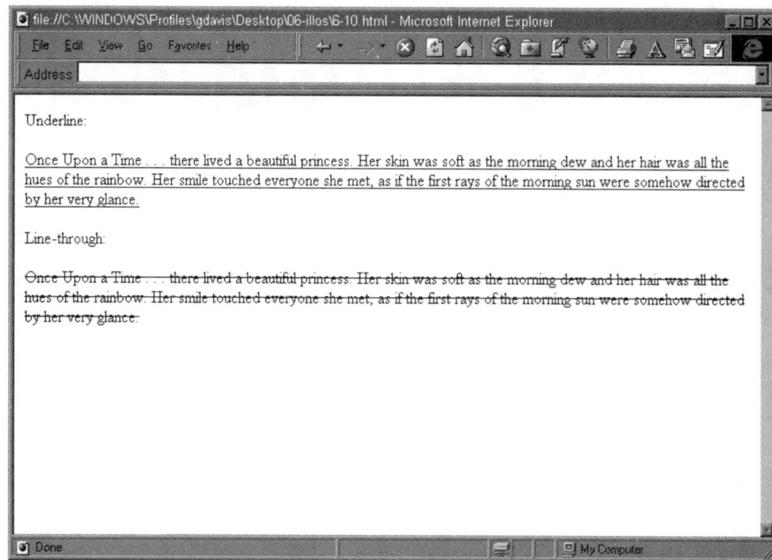

Figure 6.10
Underline and line variations of text decoration.

The *text-transformation* property lets you create text with the first letter of each word capitalized, all the letters in uppercase characters, or all the letters in lowercase characters.

Figure 6.11 shows an example of each of the text transformation values.

Vertical Alignment

```
{vertical-align: baseline/sub/super/top/text-
top/middle/bottom/text-bottom}
```

The *vertical-alignment* property defines the relationship of the element to the text baseline. You can use this property to define not only text elements, but also image elements. If you use it for images, it can be a useful way to gain more control over image alignment.

For example, an image style that text-top aligns image elements looks like this:

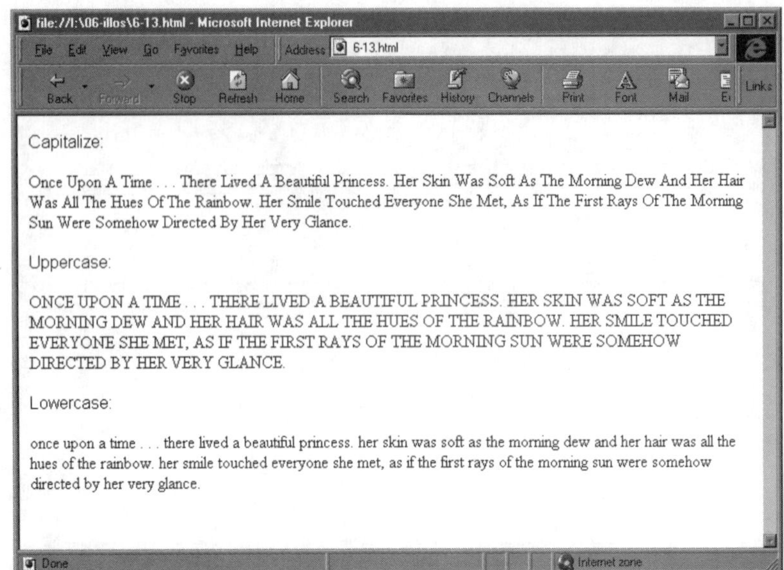

Figure 6.11
An HTML document with variations of text transformation.

```
img {vertical-align: text-top}
```

Note: At the time of this writing this property is not supported by any commercial browser, although it is in the W3C spec and will likely be supported in future browser releases.

Horizontal Alignment

```
{text-align: left/right/center/justify}
```

The *horizontal-alignment* property aligns the elements horizontally across the page or within the division.

For example, Figure 6.12 shows division aligned left, right, and center.

Text Indent

```
{text-indent: XXunits/%}
```

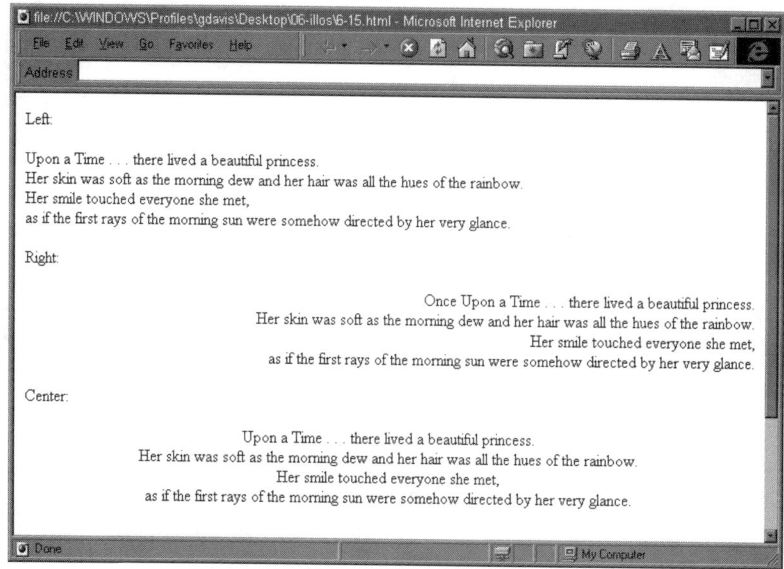

Figure 6.12
This HTML document shows different text alignment options.

The *text-indent* property lets you create an indent for the first line in a block of text. You can specify the indent in either absolute or relative units. Many people find that a 2- or 3-em space indent works well and scales with the text size.

For example, the first paragraph in Figure 6.13 has a style that sets a text indent of 2 em spaces; the second has a text indent of –10 percent (which creates a hanging indent), and the third has a text indent of 100 pixels.

The style definition for the first paragraph is:

```
P {text-indent: 2em}
```

The style definition for the second is:

```
P {text-indent: -10%}
```

The style definition for the third is:

```
P {text-indent: 100px}
```

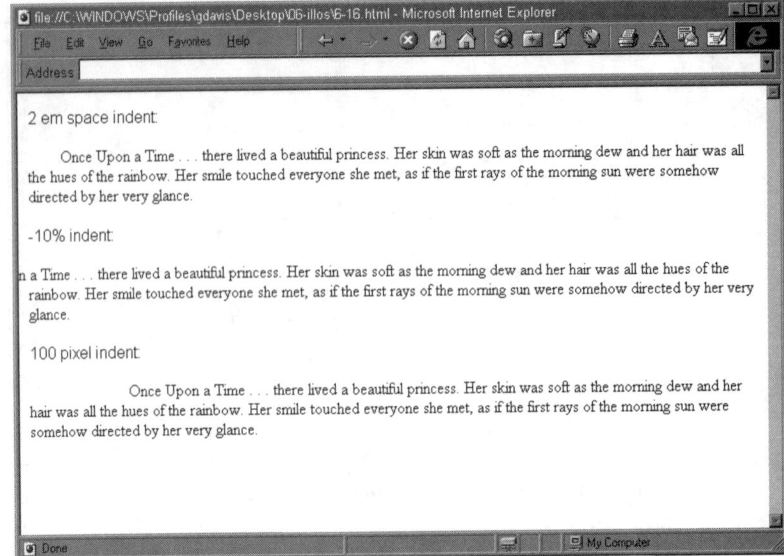

Figure 6.13 *This HTML document shows different text indent styles.*

Leading

```
{line-height: normal/XXunits/%}
```

The *line-height* property specifies the space from one baseline to the next. In print, this is traditionally called *leading*. In desktop publishing it is often called *linespacing*. Figure 6.14 shows how line height is measured.

You can specify this property as either an absolute or relative value. If you are specifying the type size as a relative value, you will probably also want to specify the line height property as a relative value.

The line-height value will depend, in some part, on the typeface you are using. Some typefaces look better with more space between lines while others are more readable when displayed more tightly. You'll want to look at some test styles under different conditions and see which works best for your application.

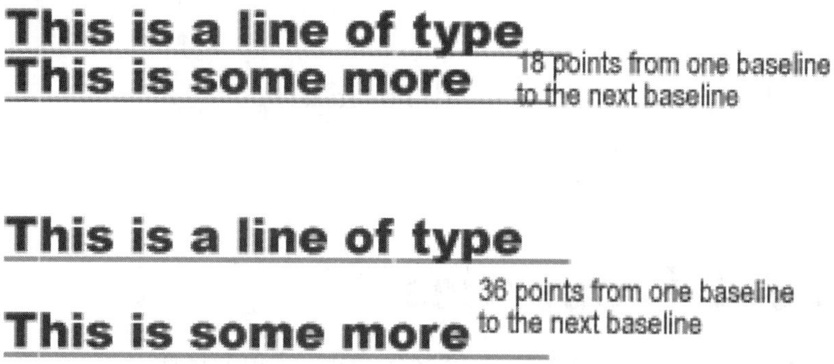

This is a line of type
This is some more
18 points from one baseline to the next baseline

This is a line of type
36 points from one baseline to the next baseline
This is some more

Figure 6.14
The line-height property describes the space from baseline to baseline.

Figure 6.15 shows three paragraphs, each with a different line-height value. In each case, the type size is 12 point.

The style definition for the first paragraph is:

```
P {line-height: 18pt}
```

The style definition for the second is:

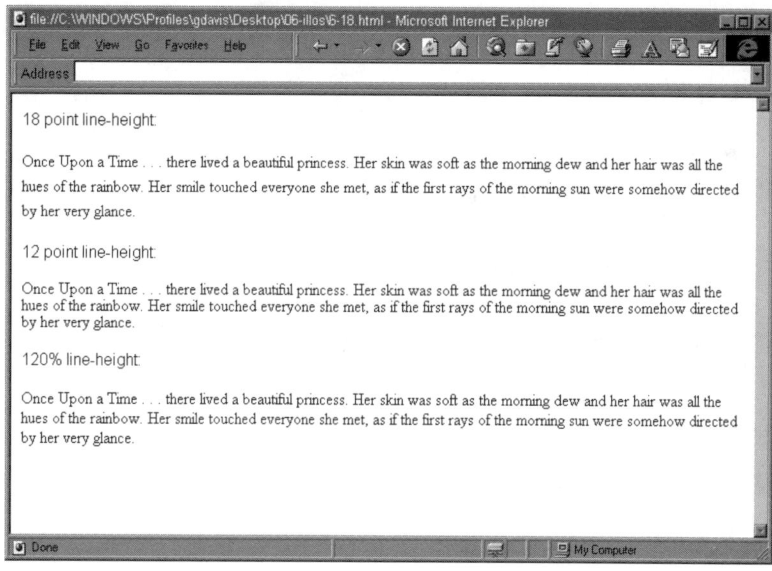

Figure 6.15
This HTML document shows the effect of different line-height styles.

```
P {line-height: 12pt}
```

The style definition for the third is:

```
P {line-height: 120%}
```

Font Properties

CSS lets you assign a variety of font characteristics to an HTML element. These include:

- Font size
- Font family
- Font style (normal or italic)
- Font variant (normal or small caps)
- Font weight (normal or bold)

Measurement of Fonts

Most font properties use the same measurement units as do text properties. The standard absolute values are:

- points, "pt"
- picas, "pc"
- inches, "in"
- centimeters, "cm"
- millimeters, "mm"

The standard relative values are:

- %
- em space, "em"
- pixels, "px"

Font Size

```
{font-size: XXunits/%/sizevalue}
```

The *font-size* property lets you specify the size of the text. There are a variety of values you can use to specify size.

First is as an absolute unit value, for example, 12-point type:

```
P {font-size: 12pt}
```

Second, as an absolute CSS value—CSS offers seven size options that you can specify by name.

```
P {font-size: xx-small}
P {font-size: x-small}
P {font-size: small}
P {font-size: medium}
P {font-size: large}
P {font-size: x-large}
P {font-size: xx-large}
```

Figure 6.16 shows the CSS code and the HTML results of different font sizes for a paragraph.

A third option is as a CSS relative size, that is, as a size larger or smaller than the default size.

For example, if the default size of the paragraph tag is medium, setting a style to make it "larger" will bump it up one size, effectively making it the equivalent of the absolute value "large." If you set a style that makes it "smaller," the size gets bumped down one size, making it the equivalent of the absolute value "small."

Figure 6.17 shows the CSS code and the HTML page that results from using relative sizes.

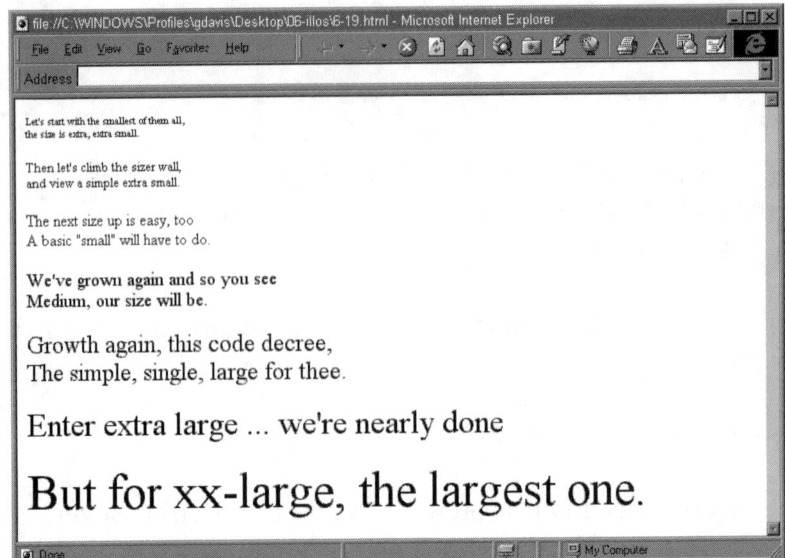

Figure 6.16
This HTML page shows the variation among the different absolute HTML font sizes in CSS. The first is xx-small; the last is xx-large.

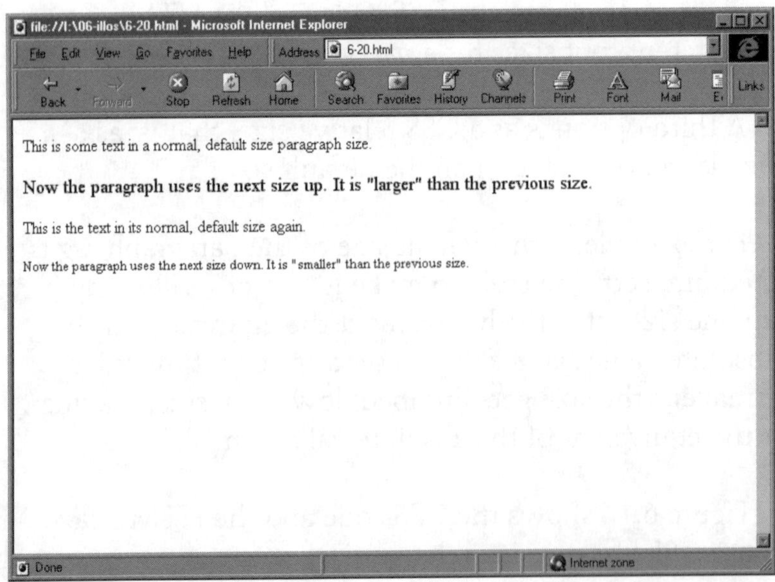

Figure 6.17
Relative font sizes in CSS are based on the element's parent size.

```
<p>
This is some text in a normal, default size para-
graph size.

<p style="font-size:larger;">

Now the paragraph uses the next size up. It is
"larger" than the previous size.

<p>
This is the text in its normal, default size again.

<p style="font-size:smaller;">
Now the paragraph uses the next size down. It is
"smaller" than the previous size.
```

A fourth option is to specify a percentage of the default size. For example, you could make the style size be 300 percent of the default size or 50 percent of the default size.

Figure 6.18 shows the CSS code and the HTML page that results from using percentage sizes.

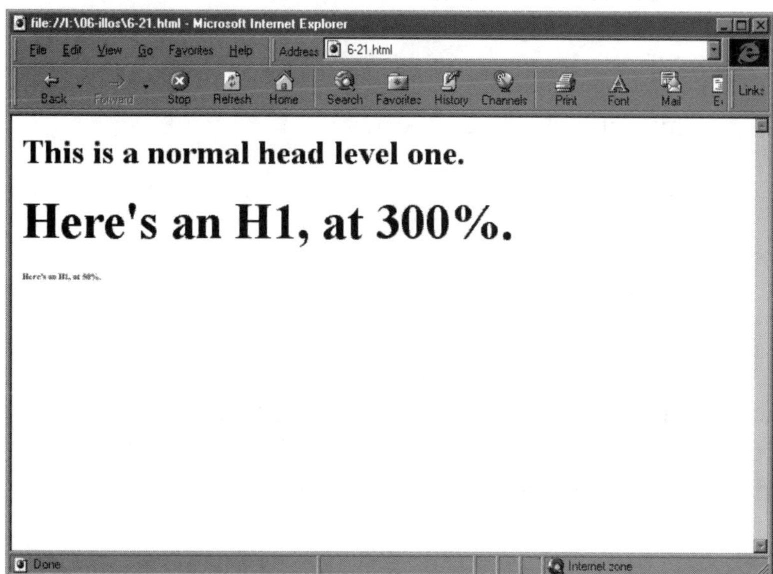

Figure 6.18
Percentage font sizes in CSS are based on the element's parent size.

```
<h1>This is a normal head level one.</h1>

<h1 style="font-size: 300%;">Here's an H1, at
300%.</h1>

<h1 style="font-size: 50%;">Here's an H1, at
50%.</h1>
```

Font Family: A specific typeface design.

Font Family

```
{font-family: "name,name"generic name}
```

The *font-family* property lets you specify a typeface by font name. The browser looks in your reader's system to find the specified font. You can list a number of different fonts in the style and the browser will look for each, in order, until it finds a match.

CSS gives you the option of using both a specific font name and a generic font name as a value. For example, you can specify Futura, Univers, or Palatino.

You can also specify a font family by generic family name. CSS defines five generic names.

- Serif
- Sans-serif
- Cursive
- Fantasy
- Monospace

It is a good idea to list one of these generic names as a last alternative in the style rule. You don't put the generic names inside of quotes as you do for the real font names. For example:

```
body {font-family: "univers, helvetica, arial" sans-
serif}
```

If the reader doesn't have any of the specified faces, the browser will look for something it thinks is a sans-serif face and use that as a last resort.

When you are using different typefaces, think about how they will look on a computer screen at different resolutions—they won't look quite the same as they look in a printed type sample book. Clean, open faces tend to work best. If you are familiar with type history, think about fonts that were designed for letterpress printing; they often translate well to the monitor. There are also designs, such as Stone, which were created specifically for lower-resolution display.

Remember, too, that your readers aren't likely to have the same selection of interesting fonts that you might own. Font embedding, a process in which font description data is embedded into a page, is coming, but isn't in common use yet. So, although it may seem boring, it's often a good idea to stick with the most common Macintosh and PC system fonts.

Font Style

```
{font-style: normal/italic/oblique}
```

The *font-style* property selects a font from the defined font family that is italic or oblique. For example, if you wanted to specify the font Palatino Italic for the block quote, you'd create two rules—one for font family and one for font style—like this:

```
blockquote {font-family: "palatino", serif; font-
style: italic}
```

Font Variant

```
{font-variant: normal/small-caps}
```

The *font-variant* property selects a font from the defined font family that is small caps in style. For example, if you wanted to specify the font Century Small Caps for the block quote, you'd create two rules: one for font family and one for font style. If the reader's computer has Century Small Caps installed, that's what will display. If not, the browser will scale an existing serif face into a small caps presentation.

```
blockquote {font-family: "century"; font-
variant:small-caps}
```

Font Weight

```
{font-weight: normal/bold/bolder/lighter/XXX}
```

The *font-weight* property selects the weight of the font. You can use either the words "normal," "bold," "bolder," or "lighter," or a numeric value from 100 to 900 to specify the font's boldness.

You can use the word "bold," in combination with a font-family rule to specify the bold version of a face. For example, to select Future bold as the font for your block quotes, you might set rules like this:

```
blockquote {font-family: "futura", san-serif; font-
weight: bold}
```

But, to make the block quote darker or lighter than the default block quote element, you'd use a rule like this:

```
blockquote {font-weight: bolder}
```

or

```
blockquote {font-weight: lighter}
```

The browser then darkens or lighten the boldness of the text based on the parent block quote element.

You can also specify weight numerically. A value of 400 is equivalent to a medium or book-weight font. A value of 700 is the equivalent of a bold font.

```
blockquote {font-weight: 400}
```

Colors and Backgrounds

CSS lets you assign a variety of color and background characteristics to HTML elements. These include:

- Text color
- Background color
- Background image
- Repeat pattern for background image
- Positioning of background image

Measurement of Color

You have four options for specifying color:

- As a standard color name
- As a hexadecimal value
- As an RGB percentage
- As RGB decimal numbers

The standard color names are a set of names that have been agreed upon and are in common use. For example, this rule makes the paragraph text red.

```
P {color: red}
```

Hexadecimal (Hex) Value: An alphanumeric code used to represent a specific color.

RGB Value: A description of a color based on the amount of red, green, and blue that it contains.

The hexadecimal value is a numerical representation of a color. In a style rule, you precede a hex value with the pound sign (#). For example, this rule specifies the color white for the paragraph text:

```
P {color: #000000}
```

The RGB percentage defines the color as a combination of red, green, and blue, the three colors that are used to display an image on a monitor. If all three are set at 100 percent, you'll get pure white. If all three are set at 0 percent, you'll get pure black. For example, this rule specifies the color green-with-a-little-blue for the paragraph text:

```
P {color: rgb(0%, 100%, 25%)}
```

You can also specify RGB values as decimal numbers instead of RGB percentages. If you are working with an image program such as Photoshop, you are probably used to seeing color specified this way.

For example, this rule creates red text, with a value of 100% (255) for red and 0 for blue and green:

```
P {color: rgb(255, 0, 0)}
```

In the companion website to this book (http://www.projectcool.com/guide/enhancing), you'll find an interactive color chart that lists the standard colors, as well as their hex values. You can click on any color and it will fill the background, and you can try out different color text with different backgrounds. (The effect, by the way, was created using standard JavaScript.)

Appendix B in this book also contains a listing of the standard color names and their hexadecimal values.

There are also a number of programs that let you calculate your color hex values. Some of these are shareware and others are sold commercially. If you are interested in a color-specific tool, use one of the web search tools to find options that are appropriate to your platform.

TRY IT

1. Go to Try It section of the companion website.
2. Type this style:

```
H1 {color: 100%, 0%, 00%}
```

3. Then type:

```
<h1>All the colors of the video rain-
bow...</h1>
```

4. Click on TRY IT to see the results. You should see a red headline.
5. Now, change the the percentage values. Play with different numbers to see the result. Try 50%, 50%, 50% and click on TRY IT. What about 0%, 100%, 25%? Or 80%, 0%, 80%?

   Working with RGB percentages is a little like playing with finger paints or water colors and building a whole palette by mixing together just three basic colors.

Text Color

```
{color: name/#hex/R%, G%, B%}
```

The *color* property specifies a foreground color. Typically, this will be the color of the text in the HTML element. For example, this creates purple text for the block quote element:

```
blockquote {color: #9966cc}
```

Background Color

```
{background-color: value}
```

The *background-color* property specifies a background color. The background of an element is the space around the element. For example, the background of a headline is a bar the depth and length of the headline text. The background of the body is the entire page.

For example, this code sets a style rule for the background color of the body of a page:

```
body {background-color: #9966cc}
```

And this sets a style rule for the background color of a level-one head:

```
h1 {background-color: maroon}
```

Background Image

```
{background-image: url(URL name)}
```

The *background-image* property specifies a background image to display in the element's background area.

For example, this code sets a style rule that calls an image named "ocean.gif" as the background for the table element:

```
table {background-images: url(../images/ocean.gif)}
```

Background Repeat

```
{background-repeat:repeat/repeat-x/repeat-y/no-re-
peat }
```

The *background-repeat* property specifies how and if a background image is repeated in the element's background area. The image can repeat in both X and Y direction, in just the X or just the Y direction, or you can prevent it from repeating at all.

For example, this code sets a style rule that calls an image named "ocean.gif" as the background for the body element and repeats it in both the X and Y directions:

```
body {background-image: url(../images/ocean.gif);
background-repeat:repeat}
```

Background Attachment

```
{background-attach: scroll/fixed}
```

The *background-attachment* property specifies whether a background scrolls with the element or remains fixed in the same location on the page.

For example, this code sets a style rule that calls an image named "ocean.gif" as the background for the body element and prevents the background image from scrolling with the page:

```
body {background-image: url(../images/ocean.gif);
background-attach: fixed)}
```

Background Position

```
{background-position: %/top/center/bottom/
%/left/center/right}
```

The *background-position* property lets you place a background image at a specific spot in the element's background.

You can specify its placement in two ways:

- As two percentages, one from the top of the element and one from the right of the element.

  For example, this code places an image named logo.gif 20 percent from the top of the page, 30 percent from the left of the page, and fixes it in place:

  ```
  body {background-image: url(../images/logo.gif);
  background-position 20% 30%;background-
  attach:fixed}
  ```

- As it is aligned to the element, vertically and horizontally.

  For example, this code places an image named logo.gif on the page, placing it at the top vertically and centering it horizontally:

  ```
  body {background-image: url(../images/logo.gif);
  background-position top center}
  ```

Note: At the time of this writing this property is not supported by any commercial browser, although it is in the W3C spec and will likely be supported in future browser releases.

Placement ("box") Properties

CSS lets you assign a variety of *placement* characteristics to an HTML element. These include:

- Margin
- Padding
- Border
- Height and width
- Float

Measurement of Placement

Most placement properties use the same measurement units as do text and font properties. The standard absolute values are:

- points, “pt”
- picas, “pc”
- inches, “in”
- centimeters, “cm”
- millimeters, “mm”

The standard relative values are:

- %
- em space, “em”
- pixels, “px”

Understanding Placement

The placement, or “box” as the W3C specification calls it, properties describe where the element is placed on the page, relative to other elements. If you think of different elements as being nested items in one big table, the idea of the W3C’s box makes a little more sense.

The body is the whole page. Within the body are divisions, and headlines, and other elements. Some of these elements sit inside the page. Others sit inside another element that sits in the page; for example, you might have a headline inside a table, inside a division, inside the body.

The placement properties let you specify how each element should be placed relative to the elements surrounding it.

The best way to understand these properties is to play with them and see which ones work on your browser and how changing them changes the appearance of your page.

Margins

```
- {margin-top: XXunit/XX%/auto}
- {margin-bottom: XXunit/XX%/auto}
- {margin-left: XXunit/XX%/auto}
- {margin-right: XXunit/XX%/auto}
```

The *margin* properties—margin-top, margin-bottom, margin-left, and margin-right—specify the margin space to leave around the element.

For example, this code creates a 2-em space margin at the top of the division and a 6-em space margin at the bottom of the division.

```
div {margin-top: 2em;
    margin-bottom: 6em}
```

Padding

```
- {padding-top: XXunit/XX%/auto}
- {padding-bottom: XXunit/XX%/auto}
- {padding-left: XXunit/XX%/auto}
- {padding-right: XXunit/XX%/auto}
```

The *padding* properties—padding-top, padding-bottom, padding-left, and padding-right—specify the padding to leave around the element. Padding is the space between the border and the content. You are probably most used to seeing padding used with tables—cellpadding is one of the standard table switches.

This code creates 12 points of padding at the top of a table and 2-em spaces of padding on the left of the table.

```
table {padding-top: 12pt;
    padding-left: 2em}
```

Border Width

```
{border-width: thin/medium/thick/none}
```

The *border-width* property specifies the thickness of the element's border. The border value can be:

- Thin
- Medium
- Thick
- None

For example, this code creates a table with a thick border.

```
table {border: thick}
```

Border Style

```
- {border-style:
none/dotted/dashed/solid/double/groove/ridge/inset/o
utset}
```

The *border-style* property specifies the style of the border. The border can be:

- A dotted line
- A dashed line
- A solid line
- A double line
- A grooved line

- A ridged line
- An inset line
- An outset line

Figure 6.19 shows some of the varieties of border styles. Remember, not all browsers may support all border styles. For example, as of this writing dotted and dashed lines do not appear to be supported.

Height and Width

```
{height: XX units}
{width: XX units}
```

The *height* and *width* properties set the default height and width of the element.

This can be useful if you are inserting multiple images—say, buttons—that are the same size into your

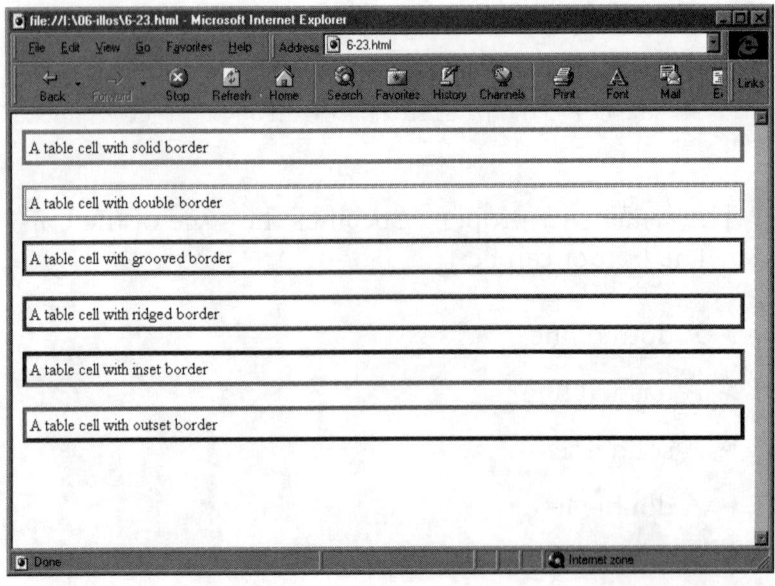

Figure 6.19
You can specify different border styles with the border-style property.

HTML page. You might even set a different class of <img> style rules for the different types of images. Doing this will save you from typing a Height and Width switch into each image tag.

This code creates a class of the <img> tag called "buttons," which has a default height of 75 pixels and a default width of 100 pixels.

```
img.buttons {height: 75px;
             width: 100px}
```

Float

```
{float: right/left/none}
```

The *float* property is also best used with images. It places the element to the left or right of its area and allows text to flow around it.

This code pushes the image left and lets text flow around it.

```
img.buttons {float: left}
```

Clear

```
{clear: right/left/none}
```

The *clear* property is much like the float property, except it prevents text from flowing around the element. It gives you the effect of using the HTML tag <br clear=all>.

This code pushes the image left and prevents text from flowing around it.

```
img.buttons {clear: left}
```

Classification Properties

The *classification* properties describe the category to which an element belongs or whether it should be displayed or hidden. These properties come into play when you are working with Dynamic HTML and want to display or hide an element based on the user's actions.

Display

```
{display: none/""/block/inline/list-item}
```

The *display* property serves two functions. First, it can be used to define the category to which an element belongs. There are three categories of elements:

- **Block.** A block is typically text, headline, or another element that is displayed as a unit.
- **In-line.** An in-line element lives inside of a block.
- **List-item.** A list item element is an item within a list tag.

Second, it can be used to hide or show an element:

- None will hide the contents of the element.
- "" is the null command. It will show a previously hidden element's contents.

When you work with Dynamic HTML, you will likely be using the display property to hide and display content based on the user's actions.

White space

```
{white-space: normal/pre/nowrap}
```

The *white space* property controls the placement of extra white space in a block element. Normally, the white-space is evenly distributed between words and at the end of lines.

- A value of "no-wrap" prevents the block element from automatically breaking into separate lines and keeps its content in one long string unless you manually insert a <br> tag.
- A value of "pre" is the equivalent of using the <pre> tag in HTML; it displays the element with the spaces that appear in your HTML text file.
- A value of "normal" returns the element to a normal whitespace distribution.

List Type

```
{list-style-type: disc/circle/square/decimal/lower-
roman/upper-roman/lower-alpha/upper-alpha}
```

The *list-style-type* property defines the type of bullet that is used in a list item element.

For example, this code tells the browser to display a circle for the bullets in front of each list item.

```
li {list-style-type: circle}
```

List Image

```
{list-style-image: url(URL name)}
```

The *list-style-image* property lets your list display a specific image in place of a standard bullet character.

For example, this code creates a class of list item that

uses the image "logo.gif" as a bullet in front of each list item.

```
lil.logo {list-style-image:url
(../images/logo.gif")}
```

List Position

```
{list-style-position: outside/inside}
```

The *list-style-position* property lets you control the way your list and bullets align. Figure 6.20 shows the difference between outside and inside values.

CSS is not difficult, but it is particular about syntax. And it isn't a fixed standard that you can memorize—as of this writing it is an evolving set of functions. All of which can feel frustrating at times.

But the benefits of CSS—making your site easier to manage, adding visual control without adding file size overhead, making your site's visual appearance more

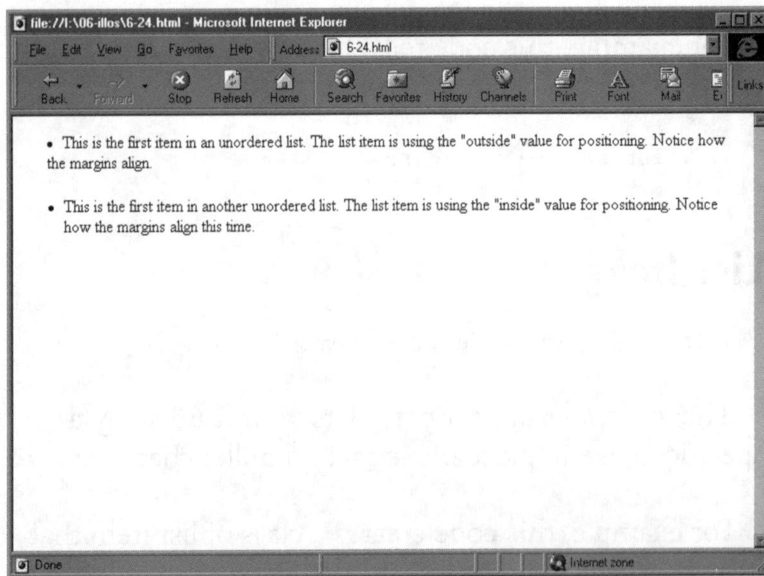

Figure 6.20
Your list can have a hanging indent or be flush to the margin.

flexible—make it worth the time you spend learning about it. Even if you end up using styles in a very basic way, they will still enhance your site and you'll benefit from them.

As time goes by, styles will become more common and more widely accepted. Editing programs will take away some of the hand-coding pain. And you'll be glad you took the time to learn to incorporate them into your site.

7

USING DYNAMIC HTML

Dynamic HTML is, as of this writing, either the latest and greatest technology to enter the web market or a gigantic compatibility headache that can only be sorted out by a full-time programmer and product testing team. The truth, as always, lies somewhere in between.

In a nutshell, Dynamic HTML—DHTML for short—lets you control individual page elements through various types of scripting or programming. Think of DHTML as a being a little like "Cascading Style Sheets Meets JavaScript." Not only can you specify how an element appears, but you can also change that specification on-the-fly, as the page is downloaded or as a reader interacts with the page.

It's a little hard to show the full effect of a dynamic event on a static page, but the series of screenshots in Figures 7.1 through 7.4 show the progression of action on two different web pages. All the effects were created with DHTML. [To see the page "live" you need a 4.0 or better browser. If you have one of these browsers, go to the companion website to this book (http://www.projectcool.com/guide/enhancing).]

All the information about the page loaded when the page loaded. Some of it was hidden until the user did something that made it appear. There was no extra server time required to produce the effect, there was no loading of other HTML pages; everything was created by the commands programmed with DHTML.

The first page is the Project Cool homepage. Saturn emerges from the upper-left corner and smoothly rolls down the screen. This effect was done using DHMTL and CSS positioning. There is no GIF animation loop or animation plug-in involved.

The second page is the Project Cool Future Focus page. We used DHTML to access the letterspacing value to make the logo "expand." Again, this is all done with

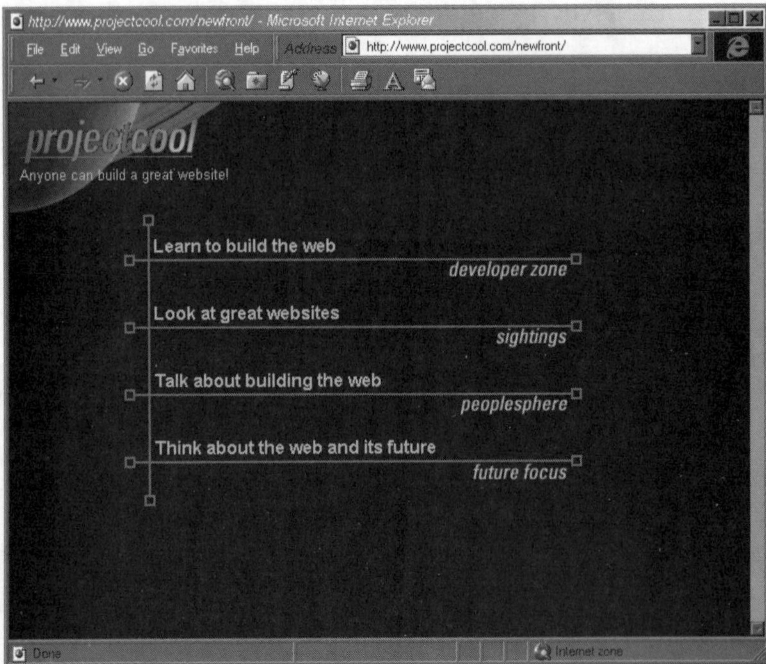

Figure 7.1
This is the page as it begins to load.

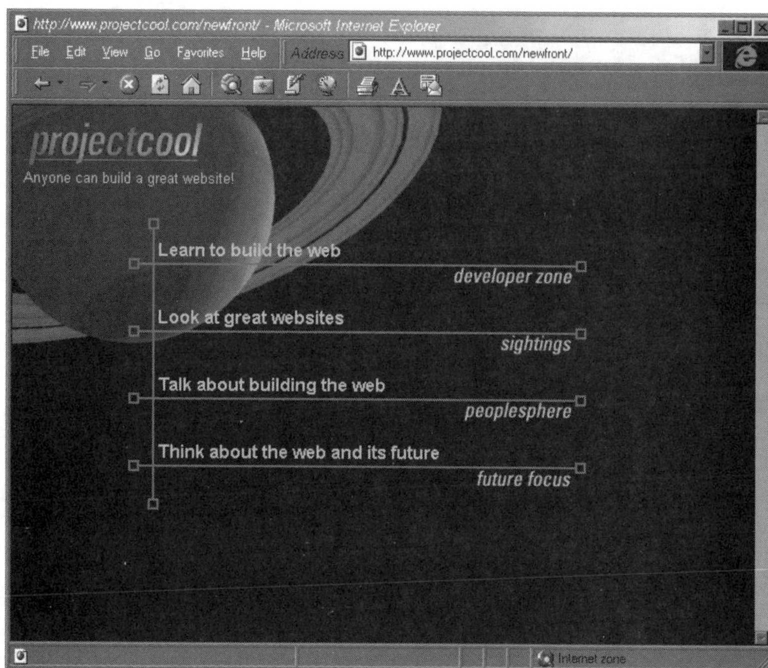

Figure 7.2
This is the page as the load ends. The animated effect was created with DHTML.

HTML text, CSS, and DHTML. Except for the background images, there are no graphics and no prestructured animation.

As with CSS, Netscape and Microsoft have taken some different approaches and support somewhat different features of DHTML. This is not an insurmountable barrier; it is just one that you need to be aware of as you create pages using DHTML features. The support is likely to change as time goes on, with a wider set of features being commonly supported across browsers. In this chapter, the examples we show work with IE 4.0, which, as of this writing, comes the closest to the W3C DHTML specifications.

This chapter is an overview of the potential of DHMTL. It should get you started thinking about nonstatic presentation possibilities and how you might want

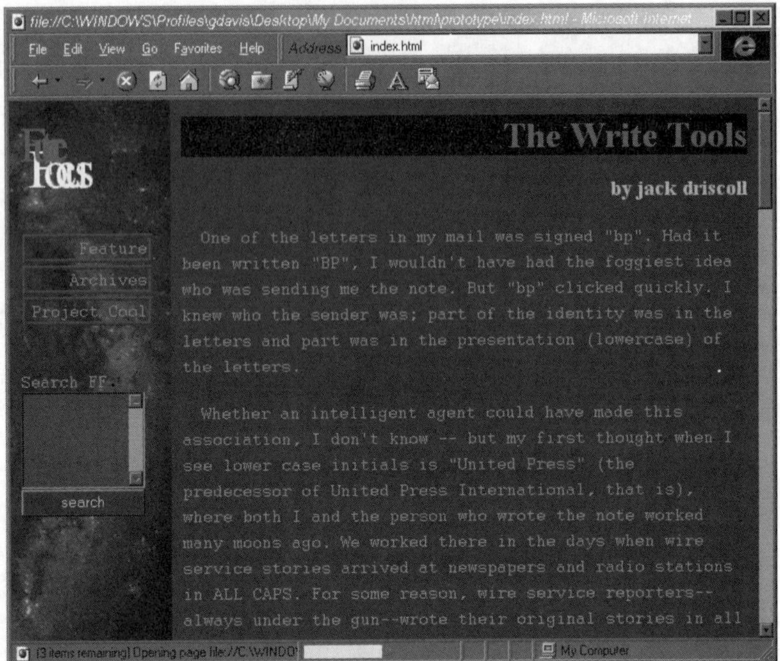

Figure 7.3
This is the page as the reader first sees it.

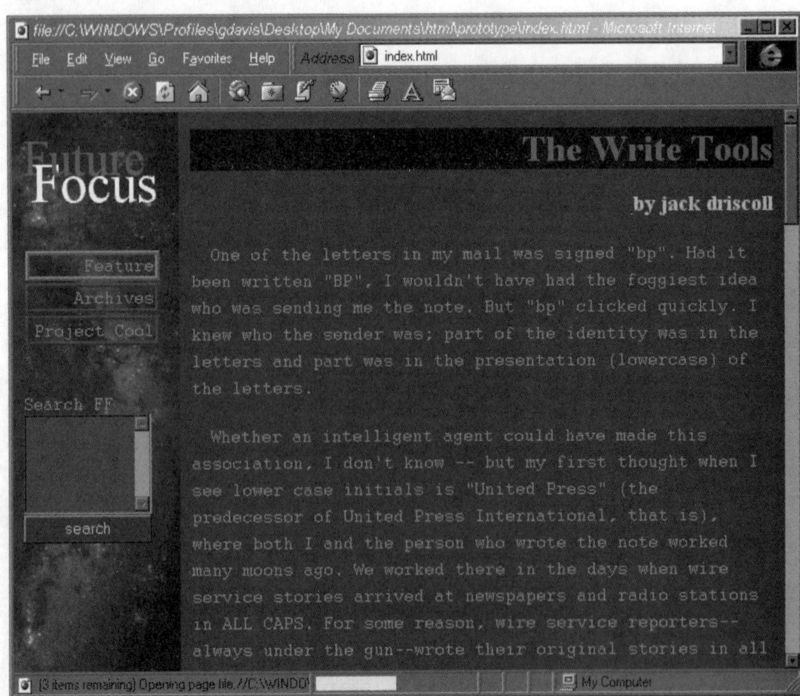

Figure 7.4
This is the page after the letterspacing value was changed on-the-fly.

to incorporate new ways of thinking about the web. It is not a detailed tutorial or a full description of the technology. If you like the idea of what DHTML can do and want to learn some hands-on techniques, try visiting http:www.projectcool.com/developer and checking out the DHTML area, which is being updated as this emerging technology continues to develop.

DHTML adds exciting possibilities for enhancing your website. It lets you add meaning and interaction, it trims bandwidth requirements, and it helps you present information in new ways that are only possible in the web medium. However, it also gives you new ways to add odd, ugly, pointless features to your website, or to create a page that can be seen only by a small set of people using a particular platform or browser version.

The bottom line with using DHTML is exactly the same as it is with other enhancement features: The most important thing to learn when using DHTML is to understand what real value the technology brings to your site and to use it in a way that is appropriate for your readers and your content.

DOCUMENT OBJECT MODEL

At the heart of the concept of DHTML is something called the Document Object Model, or DOM. The phrase Document Object Model just means that the technology looks at the document as being a collection of individual objects instead of one single unit.

Under the DOM model, the document isn't one monolithic beast; it is instead a set of components. Each component can be addressed and changed on its own, without bothering the rest of the document. For example, you can change the color of a headline without

Document Object Model (DOM): A philosophy that treats the page as a series of individual components rather than as one monolithic whole.

downloading a whole new page; you just tell the headline object to display in red instead of in green.

In addition, the document object model works on three axes: x, y, and z. Because you can work on the z, or depth, axis, you can place objects in front of or in back of other objects.

Here's how the W3C consortium defines the concept:

The Document Object Model is a platform- and language-neutral interface that will allow programs and scripts to dynamically access and update the content, structure, and style of documents. The document can be further processed and the results of that processing can be incorporated back into the presented page.

You might think of a web page as being a little like a pizza. Right now, you can pick up the pizza, you can take a bite of a slice. You can see that it has pepperoni and olives and mozzarella cheese. The pizza is one single unit. If you want sausage instead of pepperoni, you need to order a whole new pizza. If you want your cheese below the sauce, order another pizza.

The Document Object Model lets you change components of that pizza individually. If you want sausage, you just tell the pizza to display sausage instead of pepperoni. No need to send the whole thing back. If you want green olives instead of black olives, you just make the change on-the-fly. If you want to put the cheese underneath the sauce and the olives on top of the pepperoni, just change each item's z value.

By changing the underlying philosophy of the pizza—or the web page—you suddenly open up whole new possibilities for customer-specified combinations, created on demand, without kitchen—or server—overhead.

PRACTICAL APPLICATIONS

Dynamic HTML is an emerging technology. This section shows some practical applications that you can do with it today, which should be generally supported across the 4.0 browsers from both Microsoft and Netscape. However, as of this writing, we can only confirm that they work with Microsoft 4.0, so we recommend that you download the free Microsoft browser when working with the TRY IT examples in this section.

The applications fall into four categories:

- Mouseover-driven events
- Hiding and showing content
- Positioning and moving objects
- Special effects

Mouseover Events

Mouseover events are one of the most useful ways to combine CSS and DHTML to provide user feedback to your readers. You first met the mouseover event in JavaScript—it is the action of and response to a user putting his or her mouse on a specific element or location in the HTML page. With DHTML you can create mouseover events that provide feedback through changing an element's style attributes, without adding additional scripting.

Here's how it works:

- Through Cascading Style Sheets (CSS), you learned to define the stylistic look of most HTML elements on a page.

Mouseover Event: A feedback action that happens in response to a reader placing his or her cursor over a specific element or location on the page.

▶ Through DHTML you can change the CSS values automatically, when certain events happen.

The combined power of the two gives you a powerful tool for creating responses to a reader's action. You can create mouseover events that change a stylistic feature of an element without additional scripting or calling in additional graphics.

For example, to make a menu choice turn green when your reader puts the mouse over it, you'll just insert a tag that says "when there's a mouse over this piece of text, change the text color value from normal to green." That code snippet looks like this:

```
<h3 onmouseover="this.style.color  = 'green';"
onmouseout="this.style.color = 'black';">Mouse over
this text</h3>
```

TRY IT

The best way to understand what DHTML can do is to actually see it in action. With IE 4.0 or higher, go to the TRY IT section of this book's website.

Then, type this into the window:

```
<p>
When Froggy saw Miss Mouse flirting with
the handsome fox ... <h3
onmouseover="this.style.color  = 'green';"
onmouseout="this.style.color = 'black';">he
turned green with envy.</h3>
```

Then, click on TRY IT. Move your mouse over the phrase "he turned green with envy" and watch what happens.

Cool! And very, very simple to create.

Mouseover events are a great way to provide user feedback, but they can also be a trap. Just because you can change elements easily doesn't mean you should. Become your user and picture what your proposed feedback will feel like.

Here's a few things to think about when you are playing around with mouseover events under DHTML.

- **Don't make your readers motion sick.** If you make text grow larger on a mouseover, the entire page will ripple around the new size. Make your reader experience this several times in a row and you'll see some eyeballs having a hard time focusing, and people will feel like they're on a rocking boat. A heaving stomach probably isn't the sort of reader feedback you want to supply.
- **Pick a meaningful style attribute change to use for your feedback.** Don't just randomly change some attribute to show that you can. Be sure that changing the attribute signals some information to your reader. Yes, you can make the word blink, but what does that blinking signify?
- **Be consistent in your feedback.** If you are changing color to indicate that the cursor is over a linked piece of text, use the same color change throughout. Remember, feedback is part of the user interface of your site. Readers will quickly expect that certain types of feedback have certain types of meaning. Don't confuse them just to be clever.
- **Make the feedback noticeable enough to be meaningful.** You're not going to be sitting there to explain why the subtle change in color from light blue to barely blue reflects your philosophy of gentle perception. Your reader might not notice your feedback. That probably won't cause any harm, but you won't have gained anything for your effort either.

Hiding and Showing Content

With CSS and DHTML you can chose to hide or show page elements based on the reader's actions. This effect provides you with an additional tool for presenting information in a way that adds value for your reader. You can also use this effect playfully as well, making parts of your page spring out alive at certain times.

Here's how it works:

- Through Cascading Style Sheets (CSS) and the display attribute, you can define a page element or division as being hidden or visible.
- Through DHTML you can change the display value automatically, when certain events happen.

The combined power of the two gives you a powerful tool for hiding or displaying elements or entire divisions of the page.

For example, you might want to create a dynamic outline that expands when the reader clicks on an outline heading. Figure 7.5 shows the page before the reader clicks on the headline. Figure 7.6 shows the page after the reader clicks on the headline. (You can see a live version of this page on the companion website to this book.) The code that creates this effect looks like this:

```
<h1>Soup 2 Nuts</h1>
```

Click on the headline to see links to our recipe options for today.

```
<ul>
<h3 onclick="showMe1.style.display='';">Soups</h3>
<div id="showMe1" style="display: none">
<ul>
```

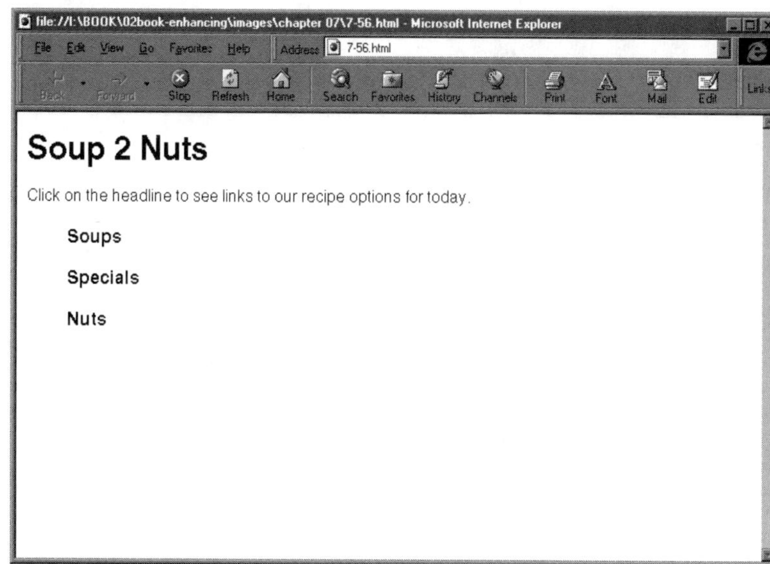

Figure 7.5
This is the page as it first loads.

```
<li>Carrot
<li>Chicken Noodle
<li>Alphabet
</ul>
</div>

<h3
onclick="showMe2.style.display='';">Specials</h3>
<div id="showMe2" style="display: none">
<ul>
<li>Chicken Stir Fry
<li>London Broil and Snow Peas
<li>Venison Stew
</ul>
</div>

<h3 onclick="showMe3.style.display='';">Nuts</h3>
<div id="showMe3" style="display: none">
<ul>
<li>Cashew
<li>Brazil
<li>Almond
</ul>
</div>
</ul>
```

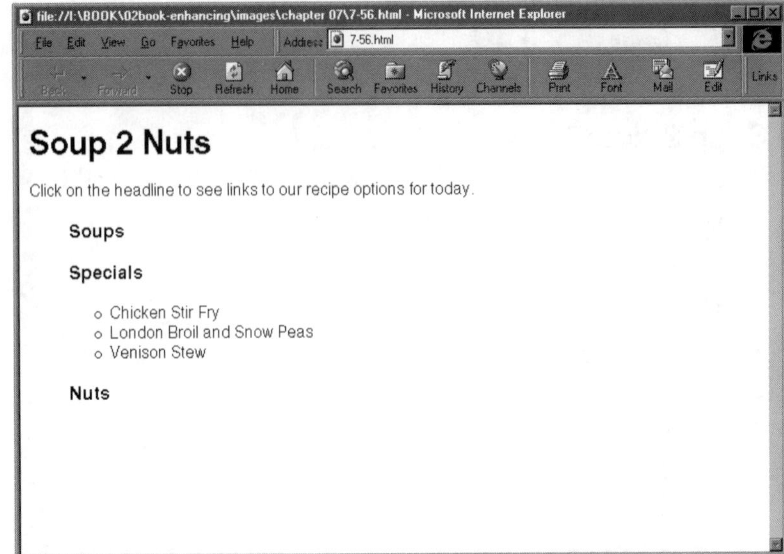

Figure 7.6
This is the page after the reader has clicked on an outline head.

TRY IT

The best way to understand what DHTML can do is to actually see it in action. With IE 4.0 or higher, go to the TRY IT section of this book's website.

Then, type this into the window:

```
<h3
onclick="showMe.style.display='';">Brochure
s</h3>
<div id="showMe" style="display: none">
<ul>
<li>Wool Wrap
<li>Children's Umbrella
<li>Hats for All
</ul>
</div>
```

Then, click on TRY IT. Move your mouse over the phrase "Brochures" and click on it. Watch what happens.

Click on "Brochures" again. Now the extra text disappears.

Hiding and showing part of a page can be a great way of breaking down content into manageable-sized pieces for readers to learn from and explore through. It lets you deliver a page within a page without additional server overhead time. It can also be used for special effects—imagine a Halloween page in which ghostly images appeared only at certain times.

Here are few things to think about when you are playing around with hiding and showing page elements under DHTML.

- **A little bit can go a long way.** Don't go overboard using this effect. If things are appearing and disappearing every time the user does something, the end result will be more confusing than clarifying.
- **Make sure reader cues are clear.** Create an obvious cause-and-effect relationship between the reader performing some action and the hiding or showing of information. Don't leave the reader wondering: "What did I just do? How do I make this go away?"
- **Be consistent.** If clicking on outline heads is going to display additional content, make all outline heads act the same way. Or visually differentiate between those that expand and those that don't. Readers quickly start to expect consistent results from actions.
- **Be explicit.** It's OK to literally say "Click here for more information." Readers are reading your page, not your mind.
- **The division tag (<div>) is your friend.** You can address entire divisions at one time, hiding or

showing them at will. Take advantage of this and use the <div> tag, along with the CSS ID attribute to create individually addressable segments within your page.

Positioning Objects Dynamically

With CSS and DHTML you can move page elements based on the reader's actions. You can bring elements to the foreground, send them to the background, or move them up, down, right, or left, based on an x, y, z positioning scheme.

x, y, z: Planes of positioning: x is horizontal, y is vertical, z is depth.

Here's how it works:

- Through Cascading Style Sheets (CSS) and the position attribute, you can tell the page element precisely where to appear.
- Through DHTML you can change the position value automatically, when certain events happen.

The combined power of the two gives you a powerful tool for positioning elements on the page.

For example, you have a content presentation that has data in two tables. Sometimes you want to focus reader attention on one, sometimes on the other. You could create an interface that, on a reader's command, moves the appropriate table center and front. Figures 7.7 and 7.8 illustrate how this example might work. The code that creates the effect looks like this:

```
<html>
<head>
<title>Menus</title>
</head>
<body bgcolor="#FFFFFF">
<div align=center onmouseover="Layer1.style.left=30"
```

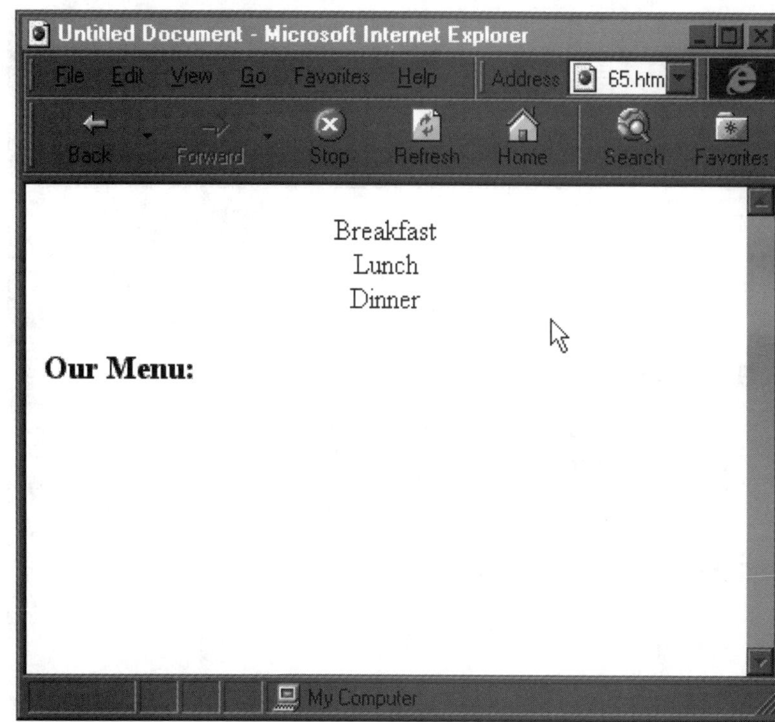

Figure 7.7
This is the page as it first loads.

```
onmouseout="Layer1.style.left=-200">Breakfast</div>
<div align=center onmouseover="Layer2.style.left=30"
onmouseout="Layer2.style.left=-200">Lunch</div>
<div align=center onmouseover="Layer3.style.left=30"
onmouseout="Layer3.style.left=-200">Dinner</div>
<h3>Our Menu:</h3>
<div id="Layer3" style="position:absolute; left:-
200; top:120; width:175;
height:113; z-index:3;">
  NY Strip Steak<br>
  Grilled Salmon<br>
  BBQ Babyback Ribs<br>
  Porcupine Pie<br>
  Fettucini Alfredo
</div>
<div id="Layer2" style="position:absolute; left:-
200; top:120; width:175;
height:116; z-index:2;">
  <p> Tuna Sandwich<br>
    Chicken Salad Sandwich<br>
    Cheeseburger<br>
```

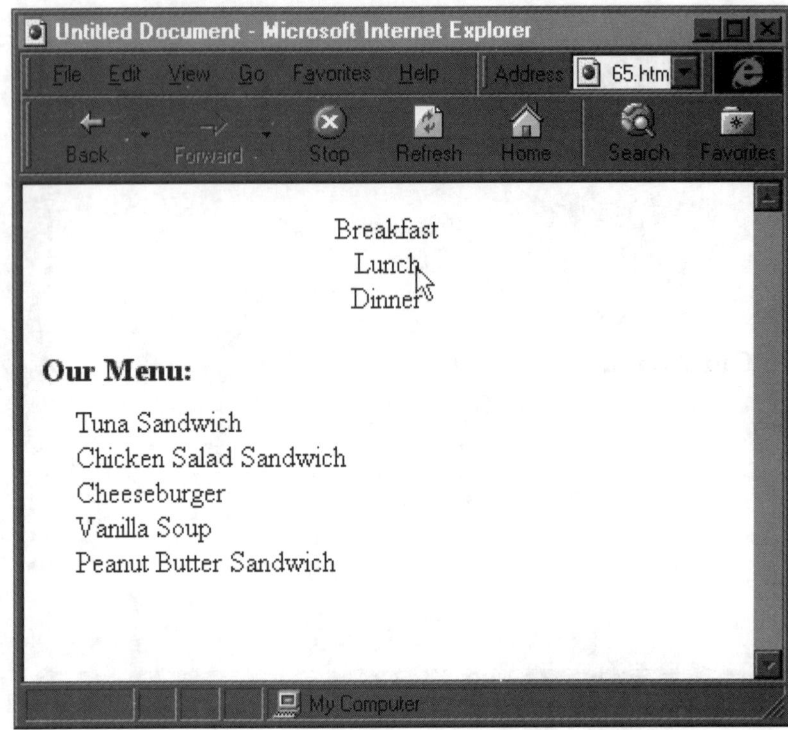

Figure 7.8
This is the page after the reader has clicked on a menu.

```
    Vanilla Soup<br>
    Peanut Butter Sandwich
</div>
<div id="Layer1" style="position:absolute; left:-
200; top:120; width:175;
height:101; z-index:1;">
  <p> Eggs: your way<br>
    Pancakes<br>
    French Toast<br>
    Snarf Fritters<br>
    Waffles<br>
</div>
</body>
</html>
```

TRY IT
The best way to understand what DHTML can do is to actually see it in action. With IE

4.0 or higher, go to the TRY IT section of this book's website.

Then, type this simple example in the window:

```
<div style="position: relative;"
onclick="this.style.left=100">
Click anywhere in this<br>
text to watch it move<br>
left 100 pixels.
</div>
```

Then, click on TRY IT. Click on the text and watch it move.

Moving components can make your page very active . . . and interactive. It can be a fun effect that your readers will want to play with. But it can also become a "why" and "so what" feature very easily, and it is not browser food-chain compatible. That is, when you use it, be careful to incorporate other ways of relaying your content to people with non-DHTML browsers because this effect is DHTML specific.

Here are a few things to think about when you are playing around with dynamic element placement under DHTML.

- **A little bit can go a long way.** This is just as true for dynamic placement as it is for showing and hiding elements. Don't overdo it. One well-placed feature may enhance your page; a dozen moving elements will drive your readers crazy unless your site is a pseudo-video game.
- **Know why you're adding the effect.** It's really cool to move elements around the page, but what value is it adding? Make sure you are adding dynamic positioning for a reason, and not just "because I can."

- **Make sure readers know why this is happening.** As with hiding and showing elements, make sure you have clear reader cues in place on your page. You don't want readers to feel frustrated because something changes position for no obvious reason. Or to have readers miss being able to move the element because they couldn't figure out your presentation.

Special Effects

With CSS and DHTML you can create many different special-effects features. For example, you can do a sort of pseudo-animation by using x, y positioning to move a sun across your page as the page loads. Or you can "unfold" a headline. Or change line-height attributes to make a paragraph stretch or shrink.

To get the most out of special effects, you'll want to become familiar with the CSS attributes and spend some time playing around, looking for ideas, and getting a sense of what they do and how they act.

One early crowd pleaser that shows the idea of special effects is the growing headline. The headline starts out all smushed together and then "magically" expands across the page. You can see this effect live at the companion website to this book. The code that creates this effect looks like this:

```
<body bgcolor=ffffff onload="expandText('expand',-
10,10,1,30);">
<h1>Expand <span id=expand>Your Mind</span></h1>
```

TRY IT

The best way to understand what DHTML can do is to actually see it in action. With IE

4.0 or higher, go to the TRY IT section of this book's website.

Then, type this simple example in the window:

```
<body onload="expandText('expand',-
10,10,1,30,45);">
<h1>Chewey Cheese <span id=expand>that
stretches and stretches</span></h1>
```

Then, click on TRY IT. Watch the headline grow and stretch.

Special effects do have the potential to add pizzazz to your page. They also have the potential to make it look like a three-ring circus, which is great if your site is about circuses but rather annoying for the 99.9 percent of sites that aren't about them. Use special effects with care.

Here are a few things to think about when you are playing around with special effects and DHTML.

- **Why did I create this effect?** There are many valid reasons to add a special effect. Maybe you want one nice eye-catching activity to draw in readers. Maybe the effect illustrates a point you are making in your content. Maybe the effect marks a certain type of content or an action a reader can perform. It matters less what the reason is than that you do indeed have one. Give some purpose to the effect.
- **Limit the number of special effects.** Don't create the mind-numbing, eye-crossing page where things are shrinking, growing, spinning, and vanishing willy-nilly. It doesn't do a thing to enhance your site.

- **Test, test, test.** Because CSS and DHTML are still standards in progress and still have mixed levels of support, test your effects on different browsers to be sure they don't create unpleasant or really odd results.

This chapter just touches the surface of DHTML. It is a technology that has the potential to not just enhance your own site but to change the face of the web, making it faster, more interactive, and more, well, dynamic.

It will take some time before the DHTML bugs get shaken out and the kinks massaged away, but that does not lessen its potential. The best way to explore DHTML is to start experimenting with both CSS and JavaScript and get an understanding of what each of these can do. Then, start to think about ways to combine them, to use scripting to change style attributes.

Another step in absorbing the potential of DHTML is to change the way you think about your page. It takes time to make the transition from a document to a document-object approach. Start to use the <div> tag to create regions within your pages. Start looking at elements as individual items and watch how they interact—or could interface—with other elements.

The web is not print. Early HTML tags lets us sort of mimic print presentations and add hyperlinks. DHTML and other new features give us the power to make the web a full medium of its own, one in which we create web-specific interfaces to information, and one in which the elements of time, space, and interaction will play increasingly vital roles. The best way to take advantage of DHTML features is to change our mind sets and to see web information as live, flowing, and active, and to prepare ourselves for designing and presenting within that environment.

Adopting new underlying approaches is more important than memorizing the nuts and bolts of any given implementation of DHTML code. The implementation will be changing as the standard and its support grows more solid, but our use of the technology is driven by our vision of what can be and by our "playing around" to make it so. This is the time to play and imagine the potential.

8
ADDING ANIMATION

One way of enhancing your web page is to add a sense of motion to it. Enter *animation*.

Animation is the process in which a still image moves. Well, actually, the image itself doesn't move—animation is, more accurately, the process in which several still images are displayed one after the other to give the illusion of motion. The motion can tell a story, set a mood and tone, deliver a message, or create a character.

In this chapter, you will learn how to add several different types of animation to your own pages and get a little background about how animation works. It will show you how to create different types of animated effects using:

- HTML tricks
- JavaScript
- Animated GIFs
- Plug-ins, including Macromedia's Flash and Shockwave technologies, and Microsoft's NetShow

The chapter approaches animation from the perspective of someone with a background in creating HTML pages. It does not assume that you are an artist or an illustrator and it won't go into the details of the multimedia programs one uses to create the original art.

Using this chapter, you can create simple effects and incorporate existing animated files into your HTML page. But if you want to create elaborate effects that look highly professional and you aren't an animator, spend some time with a book specifically dedicated to the *art* of animation. You see, technology is the easy part. The challenge in animation is creating the visual flow, the artistry, and the effect that builds a desired mood, a tone, or character.

That's not to scare you off using animated effects. Start simple. See what works. Don't be afraid to play around. Play around with pen and paper and sketch out some of your ideas to help you think them through. Then pick a technique and try it out on your site. The more you play, the more your eyes and brain will learn to see the possibilities of images in motion.

THINKING ABOUT ANIMATION

Animation is displaying two or more still images in fairly rapid succession to create the illusion of motion or action. When most people think "animation," they think about Saturday morning cartoons or Disney characters. But animation takes many forms.

Some animations are displays of unrelated images which, when taken together, create a mood, tone, or message.

- Quickly pulsing pictures of different foods might tell a story about how someone loves to eat and make the reader feel hungry. (Think about those movie theater short advertisements that flash the pictures of popcorn, soda, and candy bars to a thumping buy-buy-buy music soundtrack!)

- Chronological photos appearing one after the other could tell about baby's first year.
- Six squares of alternating reds and purples appearing one after the next might create a mood of alarm or discomfort.
- A series of words can be a form of animation. Think about flashing neon signs—"Eat at Joe's" or "Buy Tickets Here"—that use a series of individual words, each appearing after the other, to send a message. Clever typography can make text an interesting part of an animation.

Other animations are the same image with a slight variation which, when taken together, create the sense that the object is moving.

- Will Vinton used clay as his medium to create his California raisins dancing to "I Heard It Through the Grapevine."
- Warner Brothers used a series of painted film cells to make Wiley E. Coyote chase the Roadrunner across the desert.
- Flip books you might have seen as a child use an image per page to create a little scene of a bat flying or a cow dancing.

Some animations are designed not to create mood or develop character, but to instruct or illustrate.

- A 3-D rotating DNA chain that you see from three different angles can illustrate the idea of DNA better than a static drawing.

- Six screenshots strung together into an animated series might teach the steps in a computer program more visually than the same shots on six different pages.
- A rotating wire model spaceship and the moon could demonstrate the trajectory of the two and highlight their relative sizes.
- A pulsing dot might appear next to a selection in a menu, to draw the eye to it.

Understanding the Pieces

Creating animation involves a little technical skill and a larger amount of artistic sense. The end result is only as good as the components that you put into it.

As you build an animation, you'll need to be aware of several factors. Together, these factors will create your animated effect. You'll need to consider:

- A series of images that serve as your basic building blocks.
- A sense of timing and pacing to string the images together to create a rhythm.
- The technique for producing the animation and the effect your choice has on the end result.

Working with Images

Images are your animation's basic building blocks. The images can be almost anything you want them to be: text treatments, pictures, drawings, even a simple line.

The two most important things to remember about images are:

- Make the quality as good as you can.
- Make them as small as you can.

That old saying "garbage in/garbage out" is as true for animation as it is for data entry. You won't get stunning animations from poorly crafted images. Just because the images are moving doesn't mean you can skimp on their quality. Remember, a cheesy animation doesn't just sit there quietly—it draws attention to itself by jumping up and down or spinning around. Create your component illustrations with care and thought.

But using care and thought doesn't mean your images need to be fancy. A clean simple spinning line might be exactly the effect you want. In fact, simpler is often better. The readers won't have time to stare at a single image—they'll be receiving a visual packet of multiple images. No one will notice the subtle brushstroke above the eyelid—when the image is moving, that subtle stroke might even end up looking like a speck of dust.

Because the animation will be made of a series of images, it is important to consider the amount of download time each individual image requires. Optimize each image as much as possible. Because the images will be moving, you can often sacrifice a little more to the side of file size than you might with a single still image. The amount of time your reader will be waiting for the animation is the sum of all its component images. Is it really worth your readers' time for them to wait for an animation comprised of 10 30K images? That's 300 seconds—or nearly five minutes—of modem wait time!

Thinking of the Visual Whole

The component images are going to be combined into one visual whole. Think about how each image relates to the next.

- What is the relationship between each image? Is it a progressive story? A related mood? A step of motion?
- Is there a jarring jump from one to the next? Is this the effect you want or should you soften the transition?
- If you are creating a single moving object, how smoothly do you want the object to move? The closer each component illustration is to the next, the smoother the motion will feel. The greater the difference from one to the next, the more jumpy the action will feel.
- How few images do you need to create the effect? Is there any way you can reduce the number of images without weakening your effect?

Trying a Flip Book

One way to get a sense of how images combine is to create a simple flip book. You might have made flip books in elementary school. You'd draw a series of illustrations at the corner of a notepad, and then, with your thumb, you'd rapidly flip through the edges of the page. The illustration would move! Well, it would seem to move anyway.

TRY IT

If you have a notepad handy, try this:

1. In the bottom corner of the first page, draw a simple stick figure, with its arms at its sides.
2. On the second page, draw the same figure, in the same spot, but make its arms a little bit higher.
3. On each successive page, draw the figure, raising its arms each time.

4. After the arms have reached the top, draw each figure, lowering its arms each time.
5. After you've created the full cycle, use your thumb to flip through pages and watch the character raise and lower its arms.

Working with Frames

Each component illustration in an animation is often called a frame. As you can begin to see with flip books, the number of frames and their relationship to each other have a big effect on the feeling of the final animation.

If you are creating a character animation, the more closely spaced frames you use, the more smoothly the character feels. The fewer, more loosely spaced frames you use, the more jerky the character feels.

TIP: *Balance the number of frames you use with the reality of the web's download time.*

But, as with all things on the web, balance is important. Lots of frames can create a nicely moving animation, but lots of frames also create a very large block of data to download. When you are building a web animation, try to use as few frames as possible to give you the quality or the message you want.

Also, remember both the effect you want and the visual whole you are creating.

Does the style of transition match the style of the images? A child-like crayon stick figure could wave in a jumpy motion and it would look natural. A swirling pastel cloud will feel odd if it swirls jerkily around the screen.

Does the motion match the mood or tone you are evoking? A "Click here NOW" message would work with three pulsing frames. But, if you have a smooth rivulet of water dripping down the page, you might want more frames to create the smoothly flowing effect that matches the mood you're setting.

Working with Timing

Timing is another important consideration in animation. Try picking up that flip book again. Flip your thumb through it quickly. Then, flip your thumb through it slowly. The end results are very different.

TIP: *Try playing with the intra-frame timing; you can create different effects by simply changing the time between frames.*

With several of the web animation techniques, you can control the time that elapses between each frame in the animation sequence. Don't be afraid to adjust the element of time.

Does the timing match the effect you want? A little character raising and lowering its arms with very little time between each frame ends up looking a bit spastic, and feels really annoying. It's sort of like using the blink tag for a graphic. The same little character raising and lowering its arms more slowly might feel very calming and pleasant.

Do you have a balance between timing and the number of frames? Cramming a lot of frames in a fast sequence produces a different result from flipping quickly through one or two frames.

When thinking about timing, also consider the realities of data transmission on the web. If you're using a meta tag-created effect, be sure to factor in potential connection sluggishness.

Don't Overdo It!

Before you create your first animation, chant this phrase three times:

I won't overuse it!

I won't overuse it!

I won't overuse it!

It is very easy to annoy readers with your "clever" animation. We can think of one music festival site in which every item on the page was animated, leaving the poor unsuspecting reader feeling a little seasick and unable to focus on any one item. The result? A quick search for the Back button and a rapid exit from the site.

TIP: *A small dollop of animation goes a very long way.*

A horse-racing site made the reader wait for what felt like an eternity (well over a minute at least) for a plug-in animation of a not very cute, not very well-drawn, cartoon-like horse raising and lowering its head and whinnying. The annoying animation added no value to the site and the long wait set up an expectation of something really good to come. The result? Again, a quick search for the Back button and exit from the site.

Remember, a small dollop of animation goes a very long way!

Ask yourself these questions when you are considering using an animated effect:

- Will the readers see this effect once or will it be running continuously as they work with the site? If it is running continuously, will it distract from the rest of the content?
- If the site draws repeat visitors, how charming will the animation seem the fiftieth time someone sees it? Will it grow old, stale, and wear out its welcome?
- What is the animation adding that a smaller still image can't? Is it adding meaning? Is it adding eye candy?
- Is the animation worth the wait? If you were the reader rather than the creator, how would you feel about the animation after waiting the 20, 30, 50, or more seconds for it to download?

Animation can truly enhance a site. It can show content in a way that static images can't. It can deliver a message. It can attract and draw in readers. It can set a mood, a tone, and a pace. Use it well and your readers will love you. Use it badly and your readers will snicker.

CREATING ANIMATION WITH HTML

You can create the most basic type of animated effect with simple HTML tags. The HTML tags won't let you create character animation or smooth 3-D models, but they let you string together a series of images for message, mood, or effect.

There are two tags you can use to create animated effects:

- The image tag <img>
- The meta tag <meta>

Using the Image Tag

The most simple, basic way to add a little bit of animated feel is by using the Low-source switch in the image tag.

The Low-source switch lets you load one image first, followed by a second. A common use of this is to load a small, Low-bandwidth image as a placeholder, and then load a larger image on top of the first fast-loading image.

TRY IT

If you want to see how this effect works "live," go to this book's companion website at http://www.projectcool.com/guide/enhancing and look at A to Z construction.

This online example is also illustrated here. Figure 8.1 shows the first image that loads; Figure 8.2 shows the second. This one-two combination lets you add a little extra message about AtoZ Construction.

AtoZ Constuction

Figure 8.1
The first image that loads is a small GIF that loads quickly—and also provides the start of a message.

AtoZ Constuction
for more
[i m p a c t]

Figure 8.2
The second image is larger and more memorable—and adds the punchline of the message.

Low/High Source Considerations

The low/high source trick is a very rudimentary form of animation. It uses only two steps, it can't loop, and there are no time-lapse controls. It happens only once, when the page first loads. But it can display on any browser, it requires no time to create, and it uses very little overhead.

And just because it is simple doesn't mean it can't be used to good effect. Sometimes a simple trick is just the extra touch your page needs. Here are a few things to think about when considering a low/high source effect.

- Do you have two images, graphics, or textual messages that naturally follow one another?
- Are the two images the same size?
- Is one image small and fast-loading?
- Will the message be lost if the reader isn't watching the page load?

Creating the Effect

Using a low/high source effect is a very quick and easy matter of inserting one additional switch into the image tag.

To use low/high sources:

1. Start an image tag.

```
<img
```

2. Instead of typing "src=", type "lowsrc=".

```
<img lowsrc=
```

3. Type the URL of the first image, surrounded by quotes.

```
<img lowsrc="images/start.gif"
```

4. Type src= and the URL of the second image.

```
<img lowsrc="images/start.gif" src="images/
end.gif"
```

5. Finish the image tag as usual.

```
<img lowsrc="images/start.gif"
src="images/end.gif" width=150 height=250>
```

That's all there is to it! When the browser encounters this image tag, it loads the low-source image first. Then, once the entire page loads, it returns to the image tag and loads the high-source image.

Using Meta tags

You've probably encountered pages that appear in your browser window and, a few seconds later, disappear only to be replaced by another page. Use one of these effects and you have a splash page. Use several of these and you create a slideshow or animated presentation. The effect is created with meta tags.

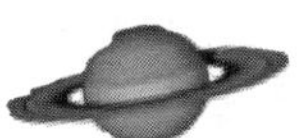

TRY IT

If you want to see how this effect works "live," go to this book's companion website at http://www.projectcool.com/guide/enhancing and look at the A to Z slide show.

This online example is also illustrated here (although, of course, you don't quite get the full effect on a static page.) Figures 8.3 through 8.6 show a series of three images and a logo that cycle through to create a slideshow effect for a page about a building under construction. The slideshow happens in a separate framed area of the page.

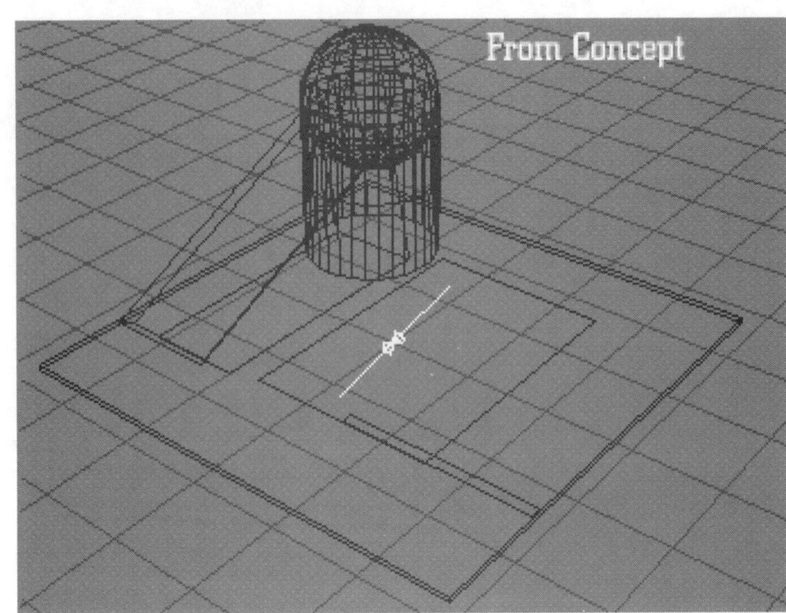

Figure 8.3
This first image shows a wire frame conceptualization of the project.

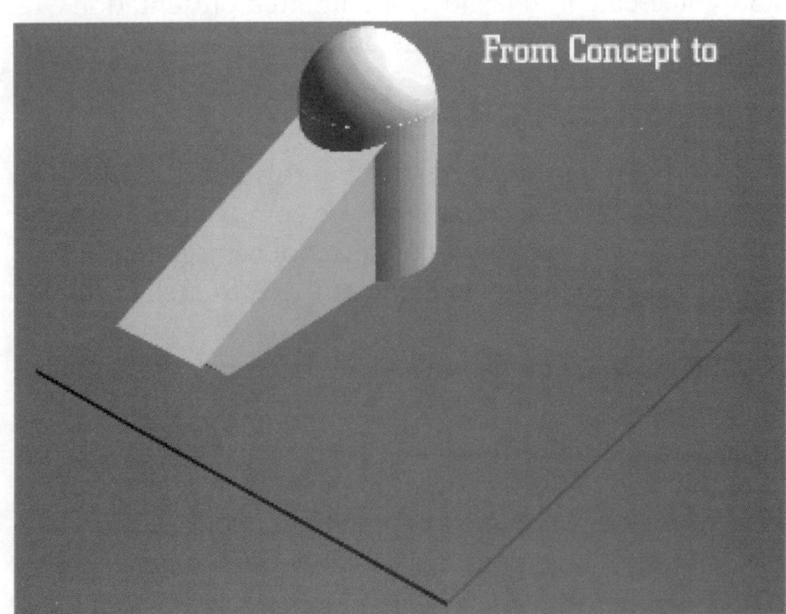

Figure 8.4
The second image in the sequence shows the construction at its next stage, with more components filled and colored.

Figure 8.5
The third image in the sequence shows the building as it will look when completed, with texture and landscaping.

Figure 8.6
The final image in the sequence shows the construction company's logo, as a message to the reader.

Meta Tag Considerations

Using meta tags to automatically load a series of pages is a cross-browser solution for creating an animated effect. It's quite easy to do—all you need are the images you want to use and some basic HTML knowledge to make it work. Your readers don't need anything special either.

The effect works best when you want a series of images to fill a certain portion of the screen. It is not the best solution for creating an animated object.

Remember that each of the images will take time to load into the reader's page. Try to keep each image as small as possible so that you don't send your reader off browsing someplace else because your clever effect takes so long to download! A good rule of thumb is that on a 14.4-speed modem it takes one second for every 1K of information transferred.

Additionally, when you are setting up this effect, you will need to specify the amount of time between when one image starts loading and the next starts loading. Make sure you specify enough time between pages. If you don't leave enough time, a partially loaded page will just disappear to be replaced with another—and you'll have a reader shaking his or her head in frustration. Again, that 1K/1 second rule comes in handy. If you have a series of 15K images, wait at least 15 seconds between loading each one.

For best use of this effect, you'll want to create a framed page and place the automatically loading image into one of the frames. If you have the whole page refresh over and over it won't feel very comfortable to the reader—unless, of course, you want to create the effect of a pulsing, blinking screen.

As with all effects, think about how this presentation

will add value to your content or grab the reader's attention—without becoming annoying or overbearing. Here are a few things to think about when creating a meta tag-driven slideshow.

- Which images do you want to use?
- Are the images optimized for download time?
- How many times do you want the series of images to cycle through?
- How much time should elapse between each?
- Will readers have the bandwidth to handle the images you want to cycle through?
- What information will the series of images convey?
- What is the relationship between the images and the rest of the page?

Notice how in the example, the text portion of the screen stays static and in the control of the reader. Only the image frame changes. The animation adds value by showing a project before and after and making the building seem more "alive," but the static text portion gives the reader something concrete on which to focus. The two parts are in balance.

Creating the Effect

It's quite simple to create a series of automatically loading pages. You simply use a meta tag named "refresh" to force the browser to pull in something else automatically from the server.

There's one very important item to remember, however. To automatically refresh a page, *the meta tag must be the very first item in the HTML file,* even before the opening HTML or header tags. If it is not the first item, some server/browser combinations will not display the correct page after the refresh. If you are trying to create this effect and it just won't work right, make sure the meta tag is the absolute, first line in the HTML text file.

TIP: *To work correctly, the refresh metatag must be the very first line in your HTML text file.*

To create a slideshow:

1. Create your images.
2. Create a separate HTML page for each image. Make the very first line in each HTML file be this meta tag:

   ```
   <META HTTP-EQUIV=refresh CONTENT="#seconds; URLof
   the page">
   ```

   The first value after the Content switch is the number of seconds to wait between loading this page and beginning the load of the next.

   The second value in the Content switch is the URL of the next HTML page that should automatically load.
3. If you want the slideshow to continuously cycle through, include the meta tag in each HTML page. If you want the slideshow to cycle through once, then stop, do not include the meta tag in the final HTML page.

For example, this series of code creates the example effect of the construction site in progress. The first page is the frameset. It calls the page that contains the first image. The first image page calls the second image page. The second image page calls the third image page. The third image page calls the logo page. The logo page calls the first image page . . . and the cycle continues.

This is the frameset page, which loads first.

```
<html>
<head>
<title>
A to Z Construction
</title>
<frameset rows=300,100>
<frame src="../image01.html" name=slides margin-
width=0 marginheight=0>
<frame src="intro.html" name=text>
</frameset>
</html>
The first image page:
<meta http-equiv=refresh content="15; ../images/im-
age2.html"
<html>
<body>
<div align=center>
<img src="../images/image1.html width=220
height=300>
</div>
</body>
</html>
The second image page:
<meta http-equiv=refresh content="15; ../images/im-
age3.html"
<html>
<body>
<div align=center>
<img src="../images/image2.html width=220
height=300>
</div>
</body>
</html>
The third image page:
<meta http-equiv=refresh content="15;
../images/logo.html"
<html>
<body>
<div align=center>
<img src="../images/image3.html width=220
height=300>
</div>
</body>
</html>
The fourth image page:
<meta http-equiv=refresh content="45; ../images/im-
age1.html"
<html>
```

```
<body>
<div align=center>
<img src="../images/logo.gif width=220 height=300>
</div>
</body>
</html>
```

Following is the first image page, which loads immediately after the frameset.

```
<META HTTP-EQUIV=refresh CONTENT="15; http://www.
AtoZ/images/image2.html">

<html>

<head>
<title>
</title>
</head>

<body>
<img scr="http://www.AtoZ/images/image1.jpg"
width=220 height=300 border=0>
</body>

</html>
```

This is the page that contains the second image; it loads automatically and is called by the first image page.

```
<META HTTP-EQUIV=refresh CONTENT="15;
http://www.AtoZ/images/image3.html">

<html>

<head>
<title>
</title>
</head>

<body>
<img scr="http://www.AtoZ/images/image2.gif"
width=220 height=300 border=0>
</body>

</html>
```

This is the third image page, which loads automatically from the second image page.

```
<META HTTP-EQUIV=refresh CONTENT="15;
http://www.AtoZ/images/logo.html">

<html>

<head>
<title>
</title>
</head>

<body>
<img scr="http://www.AtoZ/images/image3.jpg"
width=220 height=300 border=0>
</body>

</html>
```

Finally, this is the fourth image page, which contains the logo and loads automatically from the third image page. In turn, it calls for the first image file again, restarting the loop. It also has a 45-second interval before calling the first image and starting the loop again. This design decision leaves the logo on the reader's screen for a longer period of time and changes the rhythm of the animation.

```
<META HTTP-EQUIV=refresh CONTENT="45;
http://www.AtoZ/images/image1.html">

<html>

<head>
<title>
</title>
</head>

<body>
<img scr="http://www.AtoZ/images/logo.gif" width=220
height=300 border=0>
</body>

</html>
```

CREATING ANIMATION WITH JAVASCRIPT

If you want your animated effect to have some correlation with the actions of your reader, consider using a JavaScript to create the effect.

TRY IT

If you want to see how this effect works "live," go to the Try It section in the companion website.

1. Move your mouse over the menu options. Watch the planet rotate.
2. Move your move off the menu options. The planet stops rotating.

In this effect, the planet spins when the reader is moving the mouse over the menu options. The planet stops spinning when the reader leaves the menu options. Figures 8.7 through 8.9 show a segment of the animated series.

JavaScript Considerations

JavaScript animation works with Navigator 3.0 and IE 4.0 and newer browsers, so think about your readers' technical environment when you consider using it. If most of your readers are using Navigator 2.0 or earlier,

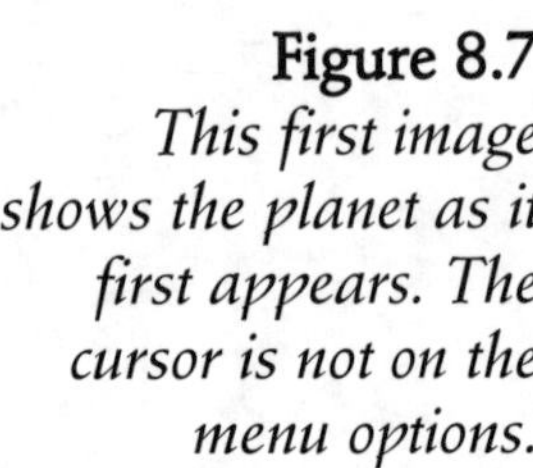

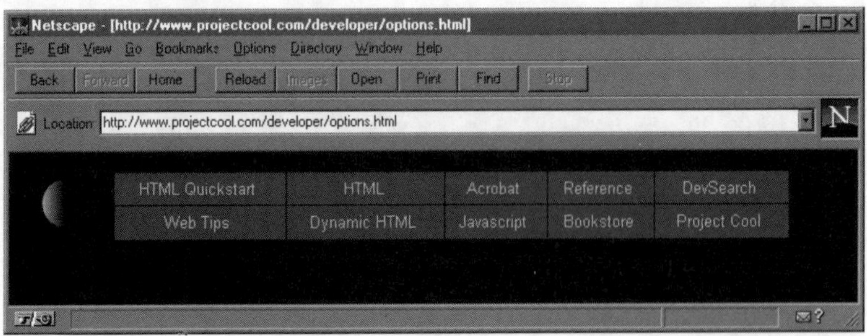

Figure 8.7 *This first image shows the planet as it first appears. The cursor is not on the menu options.*

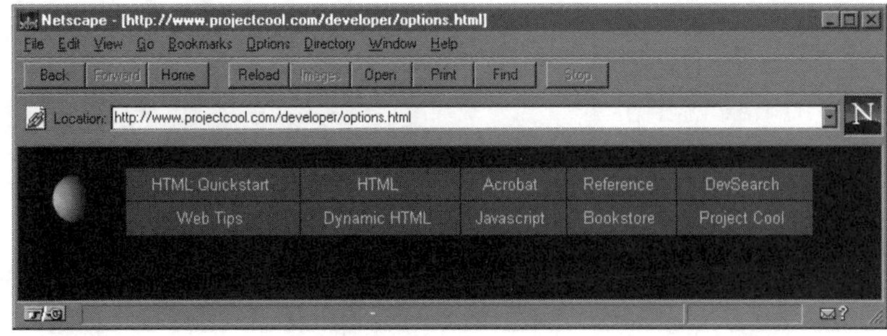

Figure 8.8
Notice how the planet made one rotatation step. The effect is subtle when broken into a one-step phase but the small steps create a smooth rotation when watched in sequence. The rotation occurred because the reader moved the cursor into the menu options

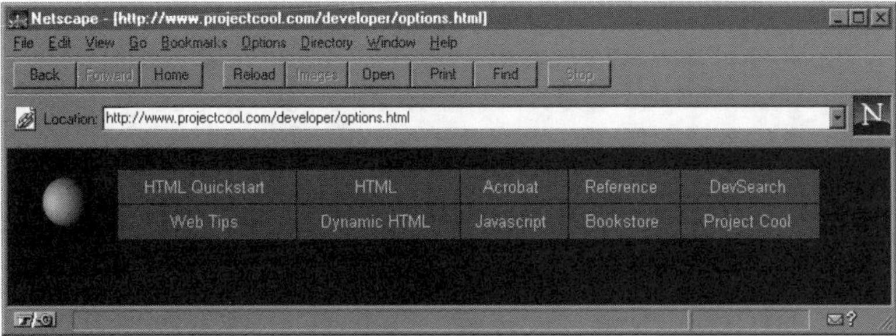

Figure 8.9
The reader is still moving around the menu options. Notice how the planet has made another rotation step and is now nearly a full circle.

you might want to select another method of creating a similar animated effect.

JavaScript is also best used when there is some correlation between reader action and the action of the animation. If there is no correlation, you might want to consider using an animated GIF instead.

As with all animations, remember to keep the file size of the component illustrations as tight as possible to minimize download time for your reader.

This section doesn't explain how to create JavaScript.

If you are not familiar with JavaScript and how to insert it into your page, look at Chapter 5, "Adding Interactivity with JavaScript."

Creating the Effect

Creating a JavaScript animation is quite similar to creating any other mouseover effect with an array of changing graphics. The only difference is that you add a counter to track where the reader is in the rotation sequence.

Here is the script that creates the animation of the planet Venus rotating. It does four things:

- Names and creates an array of the 22 separate images that make up the animation sequence.
- Sets a variable named "counter" that will track which image in the sequence has been used last.
- Sets up a test sequence to increment the counter and determine which image to display next.
- Sets up a mouseover event that triggers the display of the next image in the array.

You can substitute any series of you own images for the images in the example. If you change the number of images you use in your animation, make sure you also change the number value in the rotate array (the second line of this sample code). The number in the array is always the number of images, plus one.

```
if (browser) {
     rotate = new MakeImageArray(23)
     var count = 1

     rotate[1].src = "venus/venu0026.gif"
     rotate[2].src = "venus/venu0025.gif"
```

```
    rotate[3].src = "venus/venu0024.gif"
    rotate[4].src = "venus/venu0023.gif"
    rotate[5].src = "venus/venu0022.gif"
    rotate[6].src = "venus/venu0021.gif"
    rotate[7].src = "venus/venu0020.gif"
    rotate[8].src = "venus/venu0019.gif"
    rotate[9].src = "venus/venu0018.gif"
    rotate[10].src = "venus/venu0017.gif"
    rotate[11].src = "venus/venu0016.gif"
    rotate[12].src = "venus/venu0015.gif"
    rotate[13].src = "venus/venu0014.gif"
    rotate[14].src = "venus/venu0013.gif"
    rotate[15].src = "venus/venu0012.gif"
    rotate[16].src = "venus/venu0006.gif"
    rotate[17].src = "venus/venu0005.gif"
    rotate[18].src = "venus/venu0004.gif"
    rotate[19].src = "venus/venu0003.gif"
    rotate[20].src = "venus/venu0002.gif"
    rotate[21].src = "venus/venu0001.gif"
    rotate[22].src = "venus/venu0000.gif"

    }

     function MakeImageArray(n) {
            this.length = n
            for (var i = 1; i<=n; i++) {
                    this[i] = new Image()
                    }
            return this
     }
      function MakeStringArray(n) {
            this.length = n
            for (var i = 1; i<=n; i++) {
                    this[i] = new String()
                    }
            return this
     }

function msover() {
           if ( browser) {
                  count++
                  if (count >= 21 ){
                         count = 1
                  }
                  document.images[0].src =
rotate[count].src
           }
    }
```

```
function msout(num) {
          if ( browser) {

document.images[num].src = normal[num].src
                              window.status =
blurb[7]
          }
    }
```

CREATING ANIMATED GIFS

Animated GIFs are little gems that emerged on the web in late 1996. It seems the ability to store multiple images within one GIF file had been there all along in the GIF 89A spec. And, unknown to anyone, the GIF 89A spec had been fully implemented in Navigator browser. Suddenly, there was a way to create compact, downloaded animations into a web page—with no special plug-ins required.

GIF animations can loop or stop after one iteration. They have an element of time control between each frame. And they can be created easily, with both shareware and shrink-wrapped products.

People have used GIF animations for a series of "mood" images, to build sequencing textual messages, to add animated sizzle to an otherwise still image, or to create very simple character animations. The GIF animation is very flexible and very popular—the majority of animation on the web is probably an animated GIF.

Best of all, GIF animation requires no effort on the part of the reader. No plug-ins, no special software. All the current browsers support GIF animations.

Animated GIF Considerations

To create an animated GIF, you'll need to create a series of images. Then you'll use a program to link the images together, set the time interval, and save the whole package under one name.

Here are a few things to consider if you are thinking about using GIF animations.

Will your page really benefit from the addition of an animated GIF? Since they are so easy to create, there are a great many pages out there that seem to include animated GIFs because "they can." Why is your animated GIF on the page?

How will your readers be accessing your site? If they are mostly on dial-in connections, you'll want to really concentrate on keeping those GIFs small and tight. If they are mostly on ISDN or T1 speed connections, you have a little more leeway in creating the effect.

What color palette will you be using? Unless you are sticking within the same palette you can easily create some strange color-shifting effects.

If you are creating a moving character, make sure the image is the same pixel size throughout. As small as a one- or two-pixel difference can create jumpy or wavey animations.

Creating Animated GIFs

Before you create an animated GIF, you'll have to create a series of illustrations that make up the animated GIF. You'll do this with any drawing or paint program.

Then you'll need to use a special program for creating an animated GIF. This program makes it easy to combine several frames under one filename, and then play the frames in a specified manner.

Finally, you'll insert the animated GIF into your HTML file. You'll do this exactly the same way you insert a normal GIF image.

Animated GIF Programs

The best-known program for creating GIF animations on the Macintosh is called GIF Builder. It is a freeware program. You can download it from the web page that goes with this book, http://www.projectcool.com/guide/enhancing.

With the program, you use basic drag-and-drop techniques to import the individual images into GIF Builder. You arrange them the way you want. Then you set the time interval between each frame. You can make parts be slower and other parts be faster. You can also use the program to optimize the frames, dropping out redundant segments and tightening up the overall size of the final animation. Finally, you specify the number of times you want the animation to loop, or to play through.

GIF Builder is fairly simple and straightforward to use. It comes with a documentation file and tutorial that present the program and its options.

The Frames screen, through which you assemble your animated GIF pieces into one animation, resembles the one in Figure 8.10.

As you can see, GIF Builder tracks the number of frames in an animation, the playing length of the animation, the size the image fills on the screen, and the number of times the image loops. It also displays each frame and information about its size and timing.

A popular program for creating GIF animations in a Windows environment is called GIF Construction Set. It,

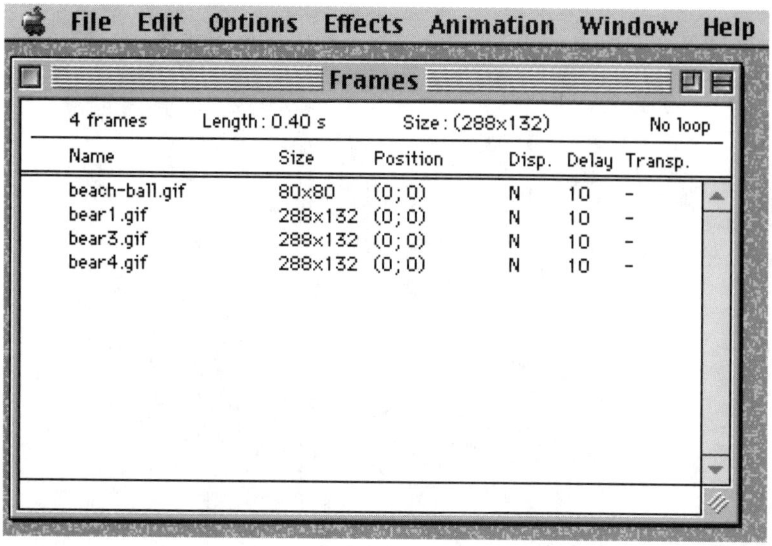

Figure 8.10
The Frames screen in GIF Builder lets you assemble individual GIF images into an animated GIF file.

too, is a shareware program. You can download it from the web page that goes with this book, http://www.projectcool.com/guide/enhancing.

With the program, use the Insert function to import individual images into the animated GIF sequence in the order in which you want them to play. You can use the Manage function to arrange images and the Control function to set the time interval between each frame. You can make parts be slower and other parts be faster. As with GIF Builder, you can also specify the number of times you want the animation to loop.

The main working screen resembles the one in Figure 8.11.

As you can see, GIF Construction Set offers similar functions to GIF Builder. Both programs are good choices; your choice will depend on which platform you use.

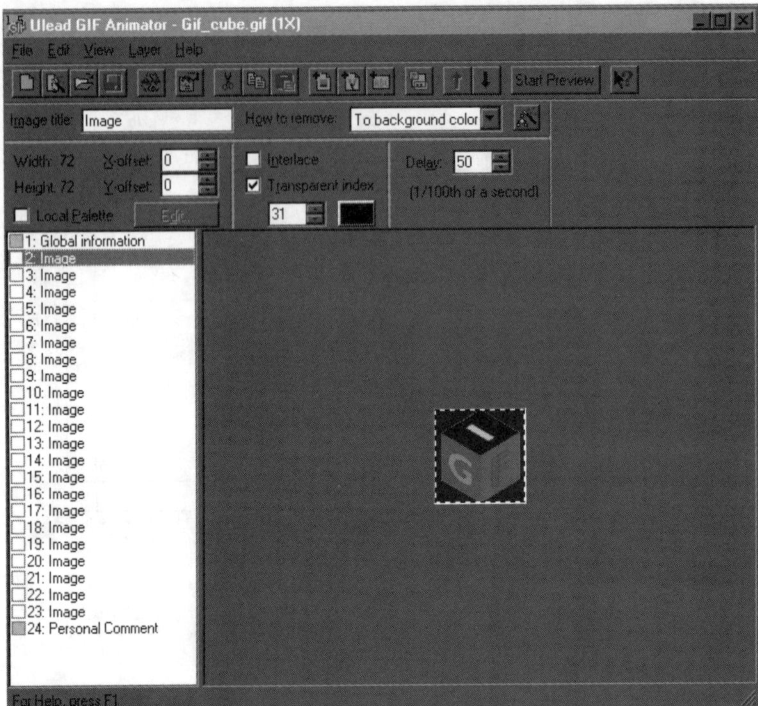

Figure 8.11
The main control of the GIF Construction Set program.

In addition, programs such as Adobe's Premiere offer plug-in options for building GIFs. If you use Premiere, you may want to visit Adobe's website (http://www.adobe.com) and download the plug-in. And major vendors, such as Microsoft, offer their own animated GIF tools. Full details are available on the vendor's websites.

Building an Animated GIF

This example walks through the process of building a simple, five-frame animated GIF of two little bears on an online birth announcement. The purpose of the GIF was to amuse and entertain, and to add a whimsical mood to a personal page. The artist of this piece is Lyn Bishop (http://www.zama.com), an online artist and web designer.

TRY IT
If you want to see how this effect works "live," go to this book's companion website at http://www.projectcool.com/guide/enhancing and look at Animated Bears.

The animated GIF resembles Figures 8.12 through 8.16.

Figure 8.12
In the first frame, both bears move across the screen, facing left.

Figure 8.13
In the second frame, Little Bear turns to look at the reader.

Figure 8.14
In the third frame, both bears move across the screen, facing left again.

Figure 8.15
In the fourth frame, Big Bear turns to look at the reader.

Figure 8.16
In the fifth frame, both bears are looking left again. It is the same artwork as the first frame.

To build this animated GIF:

1. Create the artwork using a program like PhotoShop or Illustrator. In this example, the characters will be moving, so be sure to make the character in each exactly the same size and shape, except for the part that is moving.

   In this case, there are three different images.

   - The first, has the little bears looking to the left.
   - The second has the bear in front looking at the reader.
   - The third has the bear in the cart looking at the reader.

2. Optimize the images, making each one's file size as small as possible, and save each as a GIF file.
3. Open up your animated GIF program.
4. Drag the first image into the program. The animation starts out with the bears looking to the left. This is the first frame in the sequence.
5. Drag the second image into the program. The bear in front has turned his head to look at you. This is the second frame in the sequence.
6. Drag the first image into the program again. Now the bear has looked back to the left. This is the third frame in the sequence.
7. Drag the third image into the program. The bear in the cart has turned his head to look at you. This is the fourth frame in the sequence.
8. Drag the first image into the program again. The bear in the cart looks back to the left. This is the fifth frame in the sequence.
9. Use the program controls to set the time delay between each frame. If you aren't sure where to start, try 20 seconds and see how the result looks, then tweak up or down, depending on the effect you want. In this example, the bears nod at a leisurely, relaxed pace.
10. Use the program controls to set the number of times the animation loops.
11. Preview the animation to see the effect. Try changing the timing or reorder the frames to get a different effect.
12. When you are happy with the result, save the file. The animated GIF program will store each frame and the display information under a sin-

gle name. You'll insert the image into your page just as if you were inserting a normal, unanimated GIF.

CREATING ANIMATION WITH PLUG-INS

Several different plug-in programs can be used to format and view animated effects. Among the most common are:

- Flash
- Shockwave
- Java
- NetShow

In each of these cases, using the animation on your web page is a several-part process. First, you need to create the audio and visual content. Then you need to use an editing program to format the content in the appropriate file format for the player you are using. Finally, you need to place the animation object into your web page. Oh, and in several cases your readers will need specific plug-in players installed on their computers in order for them to view the animation.

The steps and tools for creating the audio and visuals are the same steps and tools you use when working with that type of content for other purposes—there are dozens of different audio recording and editing programs, as well as dozens of illustration and paint programs. The one factor to remember is that for content that will be viewed on the web, there is still a bandwidth issue, so you should try to minimize file sizes wherever possible.

In some cases, such as Flash formatted files, your creation and editing/formatting tool may be the same. In others, you have many choices for the tool that formats the content. For example, if you are creating a Java applet for your animation you'll create your artwork in one program and write your Java code in another. If you are using a Shockwave animation you may create your animation in any of the several programs that save data in the Shockwave format, including Macromedia's Director.

The way you place the animation object into your HTML page will depend on whether you are preparing the page for Netscape Navigator or Internet Explorer. One uses the <embed> tag to place objects; the other uses the <object> tag. Both these tags are explained in the next section.

All of the players for the animated files are free and downloadable from their respective vendors. Your readers just need to take the time to retrieve them. Often, when people are incorporating a particular technology in their pages, they will warn reader that a certain plug-in is required and place a link on their page to the plug-in vendor's download page to make it easy for people who do not have the player to find and download it.

Placing an Animated Object in Your HTML File

Creating and saving the animation is only the first step of the process. In order to actually use the files you need to place them in your HTML file using a specific tag. In Navigator, this tag is named <embed>. In IE, this tag is named <object>.

The <embed> Tag

The <embed> tag tells the browser that what follows is a type of data that may require a plug-in to view it. Older browsers that do not support plug-ins and the embed tag will just skip the tag—no harm done. Your readers won't see the effect, but their systems won't get confused either.

If your readers may be using either Navigator or IE, be sure to include both <embed> and <object> tags in your HTML file. The browser will use the one it recognizes and ignore the other.

To use the embed tag:

1. At the location where you want the animation to appear, type:

   ```
   <embed
   ```

2. Add the source URL of the animation. Make sure you enclose the filename in quotation marks.

   ```
   <embed src="pathname/filename"
   ```

3. Add optional Width and Height switches, as you would in an image tag. The height and width can be a percentage of the current window or a fixed pixel size.

   ```
   <embed src="pathname/filename" height=90%
   width=90%
   ```

4. Add the Quality switch. The values for quality can be high, medium, or low. Generally, you'll use the value "high."

   ```
   <embed src="pathname/filename" height=90%
   width=90% quality="high"
   ```

5. End the tag as usual.

```
<embed src="pathname/filename" height=90%
width=90% quality="high">
```

The <object> Tag

The *object* tag and *end object* tag create a self-contained area that describes the object you are placing in your web page.

Each type of plug-in—and each version of plug-in—may have different values. If you are building a page for IE users, it is a good idea to look at the documentation for the object type you are using for the most recent information, and if you aren't sure how to insert it, contact the specific vendor directly, as any printed information is likely to change between the time we write it and you attempt to use it.

To use the object tag:

1. At the location where you want the animation to appear, type:

   ```
   <object
   ```

2. The object tag has a number of switches. The only required switch is the one that tells IE what program or class object you are inserting. The program or class information is specific to the type of plug-in you are using, and you can find it at the appropriate vendor's site.

   The switch to specify program is called *progid* and its value looks something like this: vendorname.component.version. The switch to specify class is called *classid* and its value is typically a long string of numbers beginning with the letters clsid:. For example:

```
<object progid="ADODB.Connection">
```

or

```
<object classid="clsid: D27CDB6E-AE6D-11cf-96B8-
444553540000>
```

3. There are also a number of other switches and parameters that may be added. This is the code that adds a Flash animation to an HTML page, as of this writing.

```
<object classid="clsid:D27CDB6E-AE6D-11cf-96B8-
444553540000"
codebase="http://www.projectcool.com/plugins/fs-
plash.cab"
width=95% height=95%>
<param name="movie"
value="flash/macromedia.spl">
<param name="quality" value="high">
<param name="salign"  value="t">
</object>
```

- The Height and Width switches specify the percentage of the window or size in pixels that the object will fill.
- <param name="movie" value="flash/macromedia.spl"> calls out the type of object and the name of the file.
- <param name="quality" value="high"> specifies the quality of the movie.
- <param name="salign" value="t"> says to align the placement of the object to the top of the area.

4. Finally, be sure to end the object area with an end object tag.

```
</object>
```

Flash

If animated GIFs don't pack quite enough oomph for your animations, try looking at *Flash* technology. Flash, formerly called Future Splash, is now owned by Macromedia. It lets you easily create strong visual animations. And, because it creates vector-based rather than bitmapped art, its resulting files are reasonably bandwidth friendly.

Flash is both a creation tool, which you purchase from Macromedia, and a display format, which is played by the Flash plug-in, available free from Macromedia's website (http://www.macromedia.com).

The Flash format is ideal for animations that are more complex than those created with an animated GIF, but do not require audio or a great deal of user interactivity. If you want audio or user interactivity, you'll probably be looking at either a Java or Shockwave solution. (The next release of Flash is scheduled to include audio support, so Flash may become even more broadly useful in the near future.)

Flash is also a good choice to explore if your readers are going to use your pages via a modem; Flash animation technology creates compact files that feel fast and zippy playing over 28.8 dial-in speeds.

The Flash creation tool is quite easy to work with and has a relatively quick learning curve. You don't need to be a professional animator or experienced illustrator to create Flash animations.

To see some additional sites that showcase Flash animations, visit the web page that goes with this book and click on the Flash links.

After you have created the Flash animation, you'll need to use the <embed> or <object> tag to place it into your HTML file.

Shockwave

Shockwave is the most popular format for highly complex animations that include user interactivity or sound. It is commonly used for high-quality, rich, and complex animations, presentations, and interactive games. To see it, a reader needs to install the Shockwave plug-in, which is available for free, for all platforms, at Macromedia's website, http://www.macromedia.com.

In the near future, the need for a separate plug-in may disappear. The ability to play Shockwave files is rumored to be incorporated into 4.0 and later releases of Netscape Navigator, eliminating the need for a separate Shockwave plug-in by early 1998.

Several creation tools let you save a file in Shockwave format. They include Director, Freehand, Authorware, and Flash. Ideally, to create good Shockwave animations, one should be familiar with a powerful multimedia program like Macromedia's Director and with the process of building multimedia presentations. Some experience in scripting is also handy, as programs such as Director and Authorware allow you to script user interaction options as part of the file.

If you want to incorporate Shockwave into your site, it is worth your time to pick up a good Shockwave book, learn about building effective multimedia presentations, and explore some of the "Shocked" sites featured in Macromedia's special "Shocked" section of its website.

If you've never built a multimedia presentation, be aware that Director is a professional-level tool, and that incorporating Shockwave requires a serious investment in learning and production time. Many people hire specialty multimedia firms to produce high-quality Shockwave presentations. Don't let this scare you off the technology, but do think through carefully what it is that you want your animated effect to produce and, if Shockwave is the best match, plan on going forward and doing it well.

Be aware also that, because its content is so rich, Shockwave files can be rather large to download, although recent releases of the product are incorporating some streaming features.

Streaming: Audio, video, or other multimedia content that begins to "play" as it reaches the reader's browser. Readers don't have to wait for the entire file to download before experiencing the content.

If many readers will be accessing the page via a modem, make sure the presentation is worth the wait. Also, it is good etiquette to warn your reader about the file size and the amount of time it may take to download. Readers tend to wait more patiently if they know what they are waiting for and approximately how long they will be waiting. This sort of information puts them in control of the process.

To incorporate a Shockwave file into your site, you'll use the <embed> or <object> tag.

Java

Java was not created specially for animations, but Java applets are sometimes used to run and present them. This can be an effective use of technology, requiring no outside plug-ins.

However, remember that some corporate IS departments (fearing security problems) have set up their firewalls to screen out Java applets. Also, some individuals choose to turn Java off in their browsers. The rule here again is to know your user base as you consider using Java as your animation tool.

Java programming is well beyond the scope of this book. If you are considering using a Java applet to present animation, work on the task with a knowledgeable Java programmer.

To use a Java applet, you'll insert it into your HTML page with the <embed> or <object> tag.

NetShow

Starting with IE 4.0, Microsoft is supporting a plug-in called *NetShow*, which can play streaming audio. It is also ideal for creating "illustrated audio," that is, slideshow-like presentations that incorporate GIF or JPEG images along with sound. It saves files in a format called "active streaming format," or ASF.

The NetShow player is available for free from Microsoft's website, http://www.microsoft.com. A variety of editing tools allow you to create ASF files, including Microsoft's ASF Editor and Publish to ASF, a PowerPoint add-on tool that is part of Office 97. A number of third-party tool vendors are also beginning to release tools for creating ASF files.

To insert a NetShow animation in your page, you'll use the <embed> or <object> tag.

As you can see, there are many different methods of adding animation to your site, and there are many different types of animation you can add, from the simple two-frame image source replacement to the complex Shockwave presentation. The features they all share are that they can be used to enhance your site, enliven your content, and make a visit to your pages more fun, informative, or interesting for your readers. Just be careful to use them with thought and restraint, and you'll be able to add a new dimension to your work.

9
ADDING SOUND AND VIDEO

The web gives you the power to enhance your message with the dimensions of sound and motion.

On one hand, adding these capabilities is very exciting. It opens up the door to new content and new types of presentation. Many kinds of information are best presented with sound or video—think how thin a musician's site feels without any music samples, or how a movie clip meshes with a movie promotion site. For sites where the content is about sound or video, adding sound and video isn't an enhancement; it is a necessity.

On the other hand, using sound and video can be rather frightening. Both audio and video require large amounts of bandwidth to be used well. It also takes experience and some degree of technical skill and knowledge of A/V tools to create well-crafted sound and motion content. Poorly used, bandwidth-rich content can slow a site's performance to a crawl, without adding any value.

This chapter will not teach you everything you need to know about either sound or video. It will give you an understanding of what is involved in incorporating these features into your website, but if you plan to use them beyond their simplest forms, it is worth your while to invest in training or partner with an audio or video expert.

It isn't that difficult to incorporate sound or video into a web page. It is difficult, however, to create well-edited, well-assembled sound and video files that match content, compression, and delivery to create a compelling package.

ADDING SOUND

There are three stages in the process of adding sound to your site:

1. Authoring
2. Distribution
3. Playback

Along the way you'll also need to consider how the sound integrates into your site, how it works with your design, and if it adds value for your readers.

Authoring Sound

Sounds don't create themselves. Somehow, somewhere, you need to record or generate the sounds, edit them, compress them, and package them into a file. These steps make up the sound authoring process.

At one end of the spectrum, the authoring process can be fairly simple. If you have a microphone and sound editing program on your computer (many computers come with these features built in), you can speak into the microphone and create a very simple sound file. The file is minimal in size and when played back probably sounds a little fuzzy. If your site is about your new baby and the sound file is your little precious saying "mama-mama," this may be all the sound power you need. It may be exactly the snippet you want to enhance your personal web page.

This is a great use of sound—as a way to share something with others. It's hard to put your baby's first words into an envelope and send them around to the family (well, you could duplicate tapes, but then you couldn't integrate them with images or make the sound play when your mother-in-law clicks on the baby's face), but the web is well suited for integrating these different types of content.

But often people have much more in mind when they think about adding sound to their site. They want a "sound track" behind their content. Or they want to showcase their garage band's work. Or they want readers to hear their commentary about a trip down the Red River.

The authoring for these types of sounds can be considerably more complex and requires knowledge of sound mixing, compression techniques, and many other features. If you're an audio engineer, you're all set—you have the tools, you have the knowledge, and you can create an effective digital sound experience for your readers. But if you aren't an audio engineer, be honest with yourself about it. You'll want to study techniques for using digital sound, understand the different compression options and how some are best matched for certain types of sounds over others, and have a basic familiarity with sound editing.

The ear is probably the least-forgiving organ and sound is the most demanding sense. People will tolerate and interpolate information from poor-quality video, but poor-quality sound is annoying, distracting, and a total waste of bandwidth. The average human ear requires a reasonable sound fidelity to turn the sound into meaningful information.

Distribution

Once you have your sound files, you'll need to consider how they get from you and your server to your readers and their browsers. You have two basic options:

- You can embed the files into your web page and your readers must download them in order to hear them.
- You can make use of a streaming technology, which plays the file as the reader accesses it.

For smaller files, like the baby saying "mama" or the sample of the tree frog chirping, an embedded file may be just the solution. The web page thinks of the audio file as being just one more file type placed on the page with an HTML tag.

For longer files, streaming technology is the way to go. With streaming technology, you'll need a special program on your server to serve the audio data. Progressive Network's Real Audio is probably the best-known streaming audio server on the market today.

When your readers click on a file that is designed to stream, a little bit of the file downloads into the browser. As soon as there is enough data, the sound begins to play and continues to transfer. There is no "wait for download" process. The browser just seems to "play" the sound.

However, you cannot use a streaming technology without server support. If you are running your own site, you may have already invested in Real Audio or another audio server. If you are relying on an ISP to host your site, streaming audio may not be an option for you; you should check with your ISP to see what sound options they offer their hosted sites.

Playback

So, you've embedded a file or are ready to send streaming data, but how will your reader hear your sounds?

Playback is the third leg of the audio stool. Newer browsers include some built-in sound players that launch automatically. These players handle most of the basic audio file types. Other sounds may require external plug-ins that your readers must download.

For example, readers can't hear streaming audio from Real Audio unless they have a Real Audio player. Real Audio players are one of the most commonly installed plug-ins. They come in flavors for different user bandwidths and maximize performance for the data over the bandwidth.

Be careful about making sound deliver critical information unless you know your audience parameters very well. You can never assume that your readers will be able to play your sound or be in an environment where they can easily hear them.

Sound File Formats

Sound is delivered in a digital file. There are many variations in how the sound is recorded, mixed, and compressed; this part of the process is controlled by the authoring and editing tools.

Once the sound is prepared, it is placed into a file. There are several common types of sound files, as well as a number of proprietary ones. The file format has more to do with the playback platform than with the creation of the sound itself.

Recorded Sound

Much of the sound you hear has been recorded. Maybe it is a voice speaking, music playing, an animal yowling, or the environment crackling; but in all cases something produced actual sound waves and a recording device captured those sound waves. An editing program turned the analog waves into digital form, where they were manipulated and output into a format that a computer can play and turn back again into analog sound waves that the human ear can hear.

There are three common file formats that are recordings of actual sounds.

- The au format (sound.au) originated on the Unix platform.
- The wav format (sound.wav) originated on the MS-DOS platform.
- The aiff format (sound.aiff) originated on the Macintosh platform.

All three formats do essentially the same thing: contain digital sound data. Most platforms can now play all three formats, and you are likely to see downloadable files in all three formats.

Sound Mapping

The other type of file you are likely to encounter is a *midi* file. Unlike au, wav, and aiff files, midi files are not actual recordings of sound. Instead, they contain information about how sound—specifically, music—should be played.

A midi file is a little like the musical equivalent of a graphics vector file. Instead of storing a whole bunch of bits, the midi file stores directions for pitch, tone, duration, volume, and so forth. A midi player interprets the file and turns the information about the music back into actual music. Midi sound is only as good as the midi player that plays it.

Design Considerations

When you are considering adding sound to your site, think carefully about how it works with your other content, how your readers will use the sound, and what sort of environment the readers will be working in.

For some types of content, sound is a natural. For example, if you have a site about music, it would feel barren without music clips. The sound *is* the content.

In cases like these, content considerations come first. If a reader is using the site, they expect sound and will be willing to accommodate it. They may well be in an environment that feels comfortable for sound and certainly won't be surprised when it comes playing out of your site.

When sound is content, your major design considerations are deciding which compression and file types will best present your sound, and how you can visually integrate your sound options into your web page.

Are you matching a voice format with voice data? Voice and music have different requirements. The better you match compression and other editing techniques to your exact type of sound, the better the final result will be.

Will the compression method you choose give you the depth you want your readers to hear?

Much as you do when you are optimizing graphics, be sure your sound compression choice gives you the best balance of quality and file size. Different types of sound compress best with different compression techniques; make the best match between the two that you can.

When readers enter your page, is it clear what they need to do to hear the sound? If the sound isn't going to play automatically, or if there are many different sound clips, be sure readers can find them easily and identify them as sounds. Give them directions for what they should do to hear or download the sounds.

If sound is playing automatically, is it clear what readers can do to stop it, replay it, or change its volume? Don't hide sound controls. Sound is something that most people like to control; and remember, one person's comfortable volume is another's "too soft" and a third's "blaringly loud."

If you are using streaming audio, do you have a link for downloading the audio player? Unless you are working with an audience in which you are also controlling their environment, don't assume that they have the plug-in you want them to use. If they don't have it, give them a means for getting it.

If you are embedding sound files, will their size be reasonable for download over a modem? Like graphics, sound can easily become too much of a good thing. If readers will be downloading the files, keep them reasonable in size—in reality, very few people are willing to wait 20 minutes to hear your dramatic narration of last summer's vacation. Would you?

If you are downloading sound files, have you warned readers how long it may take? Someone who is willing to wait 45 seconds may not want to start a download process that will take five minutes and 45 seconds. It's polite to let people know what they are in for with a download.

In cases where the sound is an ancillary part of your site, think not only about the points just given, but think also about what the sound is adding. Don't add sound just to show that you can. As with large graphics or other bandwidth-eating components, you'd better be sure the result really enhances the message if you're asking your readers to hang around and wait for something to download.

Figures 9.1 through 9.4 are a series of screenshots from Carnegie Hall's website. One part of the site is a guided tour through its well-known building. It does a nice job of incorporating sound into the overall page design.

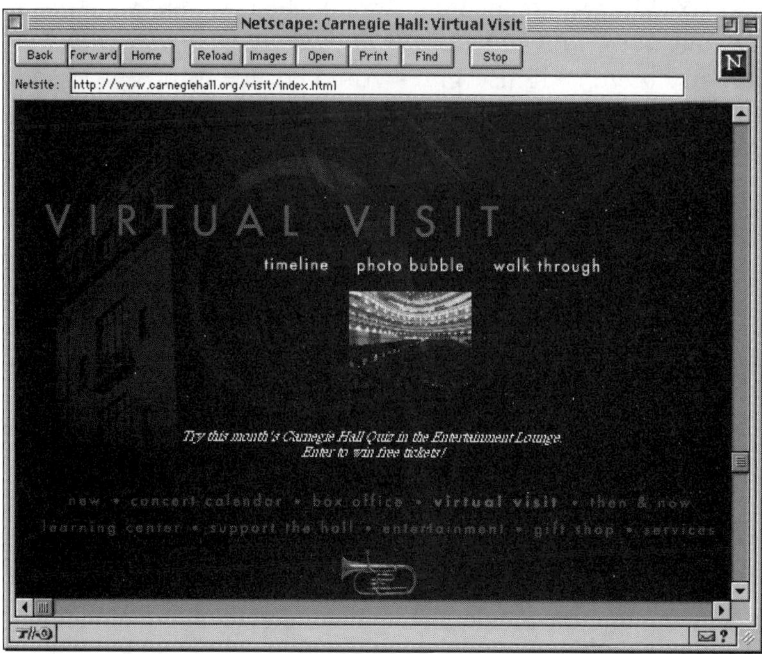

Figure 9.1
The entry to Carnegie Hall's Virtual Visit.

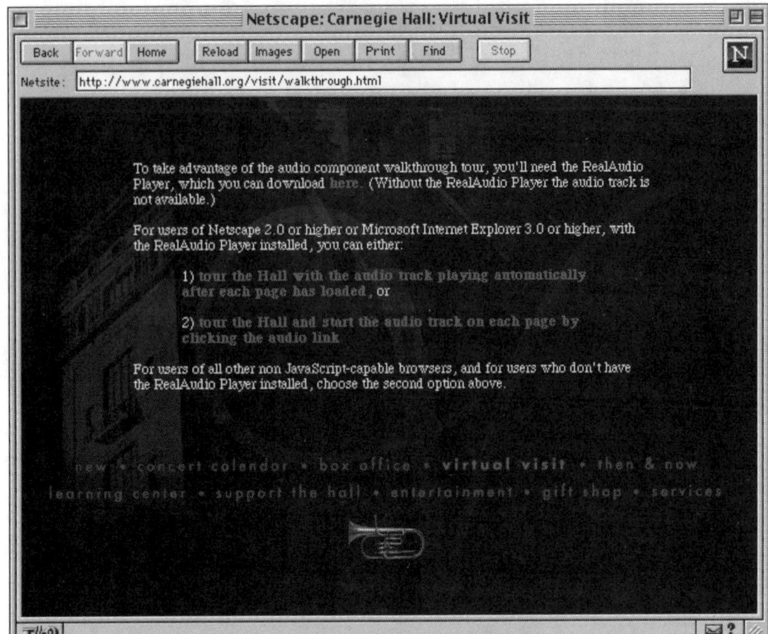

Figure 9.2
An example of clear directions, a link to the sound player, and a statement of what to expect from the sound element.

Figure 9.1 is the starting point for the Virtual Visit. After you select the Virtual Visit, you'll see Figure 9.2. It clearly tells you what you need to fully experience the visit. It has a link to the audio player in case you don't already have it. It also gives you a choice in how to use the audio: as an automatically playing sound track or one that you control by clicking on the audio link as you enter each page. If you don't want the player, it tells you what happens: The audio isn't available and you should choose the second option for the tour.

Now that you, the reader, know what to expect, the tour begins. Figures 9.3 and 9.4 show the start of the tour. Again, there are clear statements about what to expect (Isaac Stern's introduction, narrated by Gino Francesconi, Carnegie Hall archivist).

Figures 9.5 and 9.6 show two pages from a band's website. The band is called the Penetrators and music is

Figure 9.3
The beginning of the tour. Again, the page states what to expect from the sound and includes directions for what to do next.

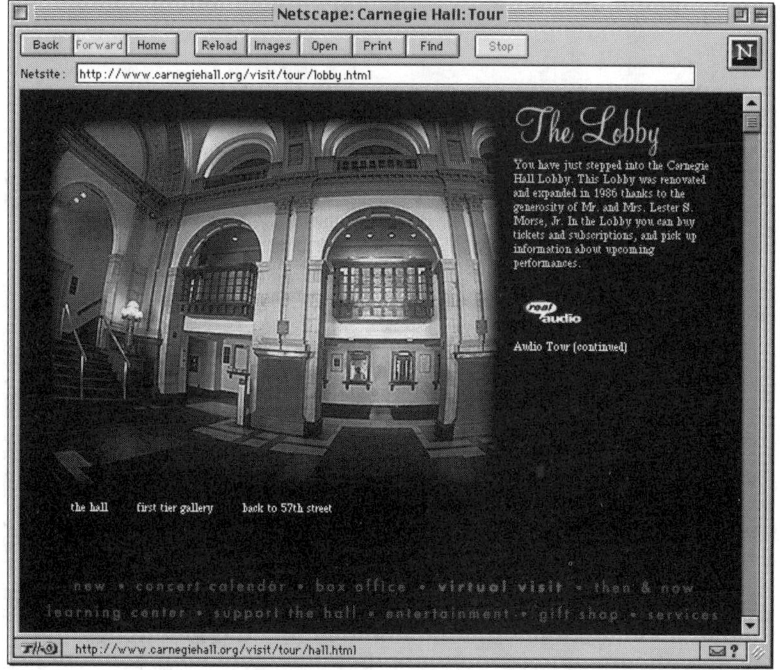

Figure 9.4
Another stop on the tour.

Figure 9.5
The band's front page. It's quite clear that the site includes audio and where that audio is located.

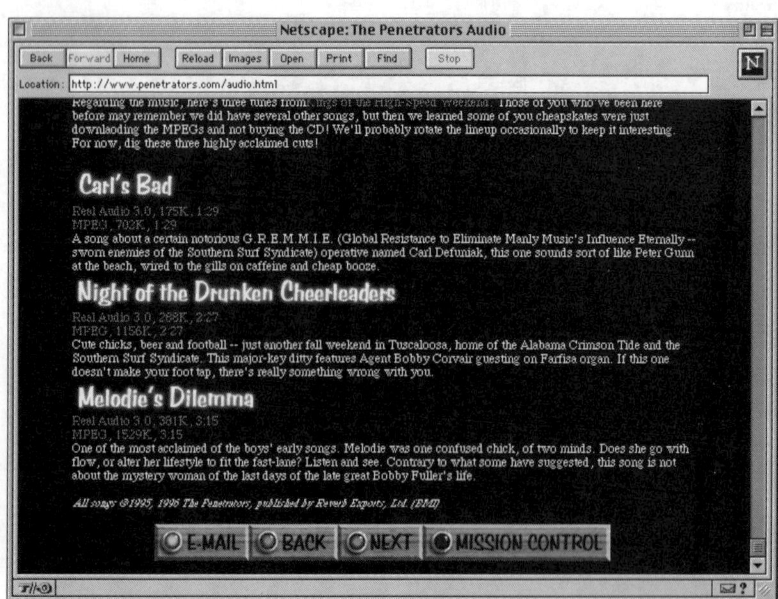

Figure 9.6
How the audio clips are presented, with enough detail that readers can judge whether and through what playback method they want to experience the music.

obviously an important part of the site. From the front page, shown in Figure 9.5, it is quite obvious where the audio clips are located. In Figure 9.6, the actual audio clip options appear. The reader has two choices: downloading an MPEG version (MPEG is another file format often used for high-quality video as well as sound), or listening to the streaming file through Real Audio. In both cases, the band lets you know what to expect from the sound element and tells you how large each file is.

In both the examples, the way in which the sound is integrated into the site is consistent with the site's overall tone and style. Sound isn't some appendage stuck into a page; it is a well-thought-out, integrated component, both in its visual presentation and in the value it brings.

To see either site "live," visit http://www.carnegiehall.org for Carnegie Hall or http://www.penetrators.com for The Penetrators site. Or, visit the companion website to this book (http://www.projectcool.com/guide/enhancing) and click on the Carnegie Hall or Penetrators links.

User Considerations

In addition to the content and design of the site, you need to consider the environment in which your reader is working. Unlike almost any other component, sound has a way of reaching out and interacting with the world around it. While most web pages site quietly on the reader's screen, the sound-enhanced page screams out "I'm here!"

If the reader is sitting alone in his or her own home, that sound might startle him or her but it won't be a big deal. However, if the reader is sitting in the office, a whole group of people might get an unpleasant surprise when the computer announces loudly: "Welcome to surfers world. Surrrrrrfs Up!"—especially the web surfer who hoped to check out the waves quietly (and invisibly) during a lull in the work day.

The first user variable to consider is where, physically, people might be using your site.

- Will they be working at home?
- Will they be in a cybercafe?
- Will they be in the office or cube?

Think about the effect sound has in those different environments and give your readers as much control over the playing of the sound as possible.

Another user variable to consider is the platform on which your reader is browsing. Different platforms have different technical capabilities. When you think about adding sound, try to hear what that sound will be like coming from your typical reader's browser platform. For example, if you are including MIDI files, what sort of MIDI interpreter is your reader likely to have, and how will that impact the end playing result?

A second platform issue is that different platforms create different expectations. For example, most people working on a computer don't expect sound. But someone browsing on WebTV does expect sound. The display platform—the television set—implies sound, and a silent website feels as if it is missing something. Sound that could be annoying in one user environment could feel completely natural in another.

If you know your readers will be working on very different platforms, such as WebTV and a corporate PC, you may want to consider incorporating a JavaScripted browser detection routine to deliver a sound-enhanced version that takes advantage of WebTV's excellent sound playback capabilities and the WebTV browsers' expectations, and another that delivers a version more appropriate for the PC in a group setting.

One more user variable to be aware of is bandwidth. Bandwidth impacts both the time a reader has to wait for your sound and the quality at which that sound can be delivered. Streaming technology Real Audio offers different players for different connect speeds; these different players try to balance speed and quality to create the best possible result at different bandwidth. In reality, any connect speed lower than 28.8 can feel painful for any but very, very small sound files.

Again, think about your user's environment. If your target audience is corporate users on T-1 connections your sound decisions may be different than if your target audience is dial-up users on 14.4 modems.

Linking to Sound Files <a href="file">

The process of inserting a sound file into your HTML page is quite simple. One way you can add a downloadable sound file is through the *anchor tag*. You simply use the anchor tag to link the sound file. If the reader wants to hear the sound, he or she just clicks on the link. For example, this code inserts a link to a sound file called "dance.wav." To download and then hear the file play, the reader just clicks on the link. After the browser downloads the sound, it launches a player and the reader clicks on the Play button to hear the sound.

```
<a href="../sounds/dance.wav"> <b>"Waltzing Bear:
Papa Bear Dances"</b>
```

```
<br>
250K/.wav file.
<br>
This sound clip is 30 seconds long, but it captures
the essence of the entire movement. Click on this
paragraph to download it.</a>
```

The result resembles the HTML page shown in Figure 9.7.

TRY IT

Try creating a small page with an embedded sound.

1. Go to the Try It page of the companion website.
2. Type this code:

```
<h2>Music and Sound</h2>
<p>
```

There's nothing like a sound to catch a reader's ear.

Click on one of the following headlines to hear some sound files.

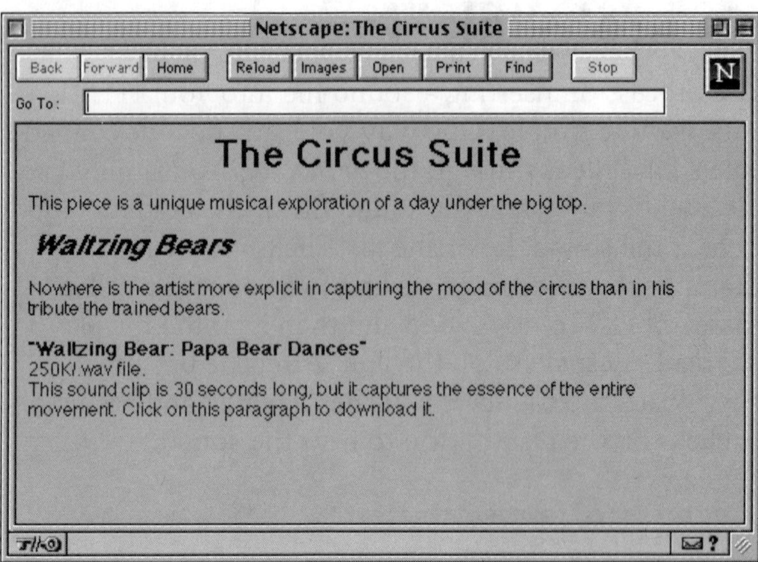

Figure 9.7 *Clicking on the linked paragraph will download and play the audio file. This is the easiest way to place an audio file in your HTML page.*

```
<h3><a
href="http://www.projectcol.com/guide/en
hancing/sounds/sound1.wav">Click here
for the sound behind headline number
one!</a></h3>
<h3><a
href="http://www.projectcool.com/guide/e
nhancing/sonds/sound2.wav">Click here
for the sound behind headline number
two!</a></h3>
```

3. Click on the Try It button to see the results, then click on the different headlines to hear the different sounds.

Autoplaying Sound Files <meta>

You've probably encountered pages in which the sound plays automatically. One way to do this is through the use of a *meta tag*. As you may remember, meta tags are either a storage bin for data or a way of passing information to the server. In this case, you'll use them as a way of passing information to the server.

It's quite simple to create an automatically playing sound. You simply use a meta tag named "refresh" to force the browser to pull in something else (a sound file) automatically from the server after a certain amount of time has elapsed.

There's one very important item to remember, however. To automatically play a sound, *the meta tag must be the very first item in the HTML file*, even before the opening HTML or header tags. If it is not the first item, some server/browser combinations will not play the sound. If you are trying to create this effect and it just won't work right, make sure the meta tag is the absolute, first line in the HTML text file.

TIP: *To work correctly, the refresh meta tag must be the very first line in your HTML text file.*

To add an automatically playing sound:

1. Create your sound files.
2. Create your HTML page. Make the very first line in the HTML file be this meta tag:

```
<META HTTP-EQUIV=refresh CONTENT="#seconds; URLof
the sound file">
```

   - The first value in the Content switch is the number of seconds to wait between loading the sound file.
   - The second value in the Content switch is the URL of the sound file that you want to play automatically.

   For example, this series of code plays a file called "dance.wav" 10 seconds after the page begins to load:

```
<META HTTP-EQUIV=refresh CONTENT="10;
http://www.mysite.com/sound/dance.wav">

<html>

<head>
<title>
</title>
</head>

<body>
```

That's all there is to it. Just one simple HTML tag will play a file automatically. But remember, your readers won't necessarily be expecting the sound, so consider the effect the sound will have on your reader when you are selecting this method of adding audio to your site.

Embedding Sound Files <embed>

Another way to insert a sound file is with the <embed> tag. The newer versions of both Netscape and IE support the embed tag. This tag is the same tag you use to insert other plug-in components.

The embed tag displays the plug-in—a sound file, in this case—within a rectangular block. When the reader clicks on the embedded sound it either downloads, then launches and plays, or begins to stream and play.

The embed tag has several switches. These pertain to embedding a sound:

src=URLname is the source file, the name of your sound file.

hidden=true hides the sound file. Your readers won't be able to see any visual sign of the file. When people are embedding sounds for background music, they will typically hide the file.

autostart=true starts the sound playing automatically.

loop=true plays the sound continuously.

You may also want to know about these additional embed switches:

height=XX defines the depth of the block, in pixels, in which you want your sound file to appear.

width=XX defines the width of the block, in pixels, in which you want your sound file to appear.

frameborder=no removes the block's border.

border=XX sets a width for the block's border.

This code embeds a file called "dance.wav" into the page, hides it, and starts it playing automatically as soon as the browser parses the embed tag.

```
<embed src="dance.midi" hidden=true autostart=true>
```

These are a few other tips to keep in mind when you use the embed tag to add sound:

- If you place the tag at the beginning of the HTML file, the sound will start playing first, and then the rest of the page will load.
- If you place the tag in the middle of the HTML file, the page will start loading, then the sound will begin playing, and then the page will finish loading.
- If you place the tag at the end of the HTML file, the page will load and then the sound will play.

Adding Background Sound <bgsound>

If much of your audience is using Microsoft's Internet Explorer, you can insert a background sound with the <bgsound> tag.

The bgsound tag has two switches:

src=URLname gives the name of the sound file you want to play in the background.

loop=X/infinite lets you replay the sound a specified number of times or continually.

For example, this code plays the sound file named "dance.wav":

```
<bgsound src="dance.wav">
```

This one plays the same file five times in a row:

```
<bgsound src="dance.wav" loop=5>
```

And this one plays it over and over and over as long as the page is in the browser window:

```
< bgsound src="dance.wav" Loop=infinite>
```

Adding Sound via Scripting

Yet another way to add a sound is to include a snippet of JavaScript in your page. For example, if you want to start the sound automatically when the page loads, you'd add this as a switch in your body tag:

```
onLoad="window.location='url of sound file'"
```

This body tag code sets a black background for the page and, when the page loads, tells the browser to start playing a file called dance.au:

```
<body bgcolor="#000000" onLoad="window.loca-
tion='../sounds/dance.au'">
```

You can treat a sound file as you would any other page element in a script. For example, you could use a sound file instead of or in addition to a graphic during a mouseover array for user feedback—maybe you want the computer to "bing" when the reader selects a certain menu option. Or, you could have a voice say "thank you" when someone submits a form. The applications are entirely up to you.

If you aren't familiar with Java Script, Chapter 5 provides an introduction and solid overview to scripting.

ADDING VIDEO

Unless your site's content is about video, or unless your target readers are sitting on nice wide Internet connections, think carefully before you add video to your site.

Video sounds very sexy. It makes us think "film" and "television." But when it comes to actually delivering video, the web is a poor cousin to these other media. It won't always be this way, but for now there are severe limitations on both the quality and speed of the video your site can deliver in the real world.

As with sound, there are three stages in the process of adding video to your site.

1. Authoring
2. Distribution
3. Playback

And, like sound, you'll also need to consider carefully how the video integrates into your site, how it works with your design, and if it adds value for your readers.

Authoring Video

Creating video requires a way to capture video images and edit them into a coherent story. To create your own video from scratch you'll need a video camera. The quality of your video starts here; the end result on your site is only as good as the technical quality of the original recording.

You'll also need a video editing program to turn your raw footage into the clip you want to show the world, and a computer capable of running the program and working with the video data. Although these programs are much easier to use than in the past, before using them it is still helpful to have some background in working with video or to have an ample amount of time to explore and experiment with both the program and the concept of video editing.

Distribution

Once you have your video files, you'll need to consider how they get from you and your server to your readers and their browsers. You have two basic options:

- You can embed the files into your web page and your readers must download them in order to view them.
- You can make use of a streaming technology, which plays the file as the reader accesses it.

Most video is currently placed in the page, downloaded, and viewed.

Companies such as Progressive Networks, VDO, and others are developing streaming video technologies. Some of these technologies are designed for streaming video files while others are being adapted for "broadcasting" live video. In all cases, they require a substantial investment in both time and money in server software and setup. If you are considering one of these options, study the different vendors and their options (which seem to change monthly) and pick the best match for your type of video application and your core reader's environment.

Playback

So, you've gone ahead and added that video file to your page. Now, how will your readers be able to see it?

Video requires a special player plug-in. The most common player is probably QuickTime, but other options for other video formats are emerging. Be sure to include a link for downloading the video player of your choice and never assume that your reader will be immediately able to watch your video.

Video File Formats

Video is delivered in a digital file. Once the video is prepared and, if necessary, converted into digital form, it is saved in a file in a particular format. The two most common video formats are QuickTime and MPEG.

QuickTime, which was created by Apple Computer, is the most accessible video format on the market today. A good number of computers have QuickTime players and the technology has been in play for several years, long enough for many users to feel comfortable. The QuickTime format lets you make tradeoffs between file size and quality of video.

MPEG (and its newer sibling MPEG2) are "professional" standards for video. The files are larger, both audio and video tracks are of better quality, and the playback is smoother than that of QuickTime.

Design Considerations

When you are considering adding video to your site, think carefully about how it works with your other content, how your readers will use it, and what sort of environment the readers will be working in.

Video is a bandwidth hog. There are compression techniques and these techniques are improving, but the bottom line is still that video packs a lot of data, and that data requires a substantial pipe through which to move.

Unless your readers are in a corporate environment scooting about on T-1- and T-3-level connections, think carefully about what you're asking when you incorporate video: Is the content you're adding worth a 3- or 5- or 10-minute wait?

This isn't to say that there aren't places where video can't enhance your site. Just be sure there is a value and that you aren't using video because you grew up with TV and just assume "film at 11" is the best way to demonstrate your message.

That said, the design considerations for video are similar to those for sound. Remember, most video also includes a sound element.

Is the quality of your video clip acceptable in your reader's environment? The size of the video window will be small, probably less than 2 × 2 inches. The images may be grainy. The movement may feel jerky. And the sound may break. The degree to which this happens depends in large part on the processing power of your reader's viewing platform. If most of your readers have MMX-boosted machines or super-multimedia charged Macs, this is less of an issue than if the majority have 486 PCs. Give some thought to the viewing environment of your reader and the environment's ability to support video well.

When readers enter your page, is it clear what they need to do to see the clip? Be sure readers can find the video elements easily and identify them as video. Give readers directions for what they should do to watch the clips.

Is it clear what readers can do to stop the video, replay it, or change its volume? Don't hide controls. Video is something that most people like to control. In fact, one of the benefits of delivering video via the web versus a broadcast medium is that readers can better control, rewatch, rewind, and use the information within it.

If you are using streaming video, do you have a link for downloading the video player? Streaming video is still fairly uncommon and it is likely that your readers will need to download a player in order to experience yours. Make that get-the-player process as direct and easy as possible.

How large are your video files and how long will it take to download them? Like graphics and sound, video can quickly become too much of a good thing. Try to keep your video clips reasonable in size, and calculate what the download time will be. Then ask yourself, "Would I wait five minutes for this clip?"

Have you told your readers what to expect from the clip and how long it will take to download it? Set expectations as clearly as you can. It will help your readers make an intelligent choice about whether to view or pass on your video. And, it will prevent frustrated readers who either get impatient with waiting or, after waiting, end up with a clip that isn't what they expected.

Adding Video to Your Web Page

The most common way to add video to your page is with a simple link. Typically, you'll place one frame of your video into your page as an image. When the reader clicks on the image, the video will download and, if the reader has it installed, the correct player will launch and play the video.

As you can see, both sound and video can add new depth and enhance the content richness of your site; but both come with a large amount of overhead. The trick in using these elements is to balance what they add with what they detract. The right balance produces an effective page that really reaches out to your readership. The wrong balance produces a slug page that no one wants to visit.

Use your common sense when adding sound and video. Don't let your ego demand that every page needs video just because you've gone out and created special video. Pretend that you are the reader and judge your own willingness to wait versus the enhancement the sound and video components add.

Don't avoid sound and video if it makes sense for your site, but don't embrace sound and video just because it seems like something you "should" do. Remember, enhancement is about making your site more effective and a better place to visit. As long as you keep that in mind, you're bound to use sound and video wisely.

10
CROSS BROWSER, CROSS PLATFORM, CROSS DESIGN

If there's one thing that people who build for the web agree on, it's this: Browser wars are driving us all crazy!

Every week seems to bring a new feature or enhancement. The web is an evolving medium; we can live with that. But it often seems that each new feature is supported differently—and sometimes not at all—on different browsers. This makes it difficult to decide which features to incorporate into a site and when it is safe to do so. Cascading Style Sheets are great, but if your readers are a typical cross-section of the general web public, they may be using any of the following common browsers:

- Internet Explorer 4.0 for Windows
- Internet Explorer 3.0 for Windows
- Internet Explorer 3.0 for the Mac
- Netscape Communicator 4.0
- Netscape Navigator 3.0
- AOL (and who knows what version of what browser)

- ▶ WebTV

And there are probably some stragglers out there still using Navigator 2.0 or other older browsers. By the time you read these words, there will likely be even newer versions of each of the aforementioned browsers waiting in the wings . . . each offering its own definition of "support."

SEEKING THE STANDARD

To give you a sense of the variation among browsers, the sample page in Figure 10.1 uses all "standard" code, including Cascading Style Sheet tags that meet the W3C specifications. This page shows the columns that ran in the Future Focus editorial section (used with special thanks to Jack Driscoll, editor-in-residence at the MIT Media Lab).

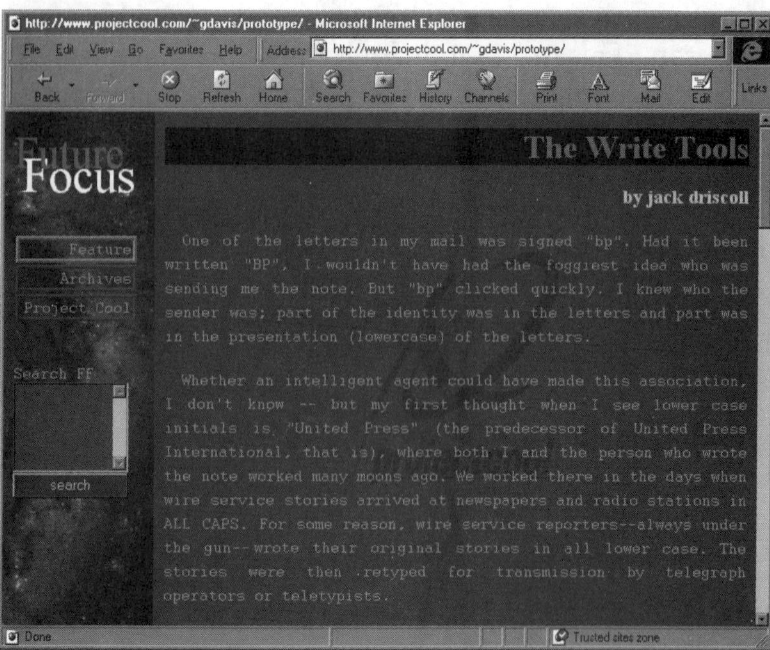

Figure 10.1
The Future Focus page looks and acts very nicely under IE 4.0 for Windows, but the next series of screenshots shows why testing is important.

There are two frames. The *control* frame uses a JavaScript script and DHTML to create an interactive reader environment—under the IE 4.0 browser. The right three-fourths of the page is a frame with the article itself.

This is the code for the control frame:

```
<html>
<head>
<title>Future Focus</title>
<style type="text/css">
<!--

BODY{font-family: courier;
          font-size: 12pt;
          color: limegreen;
          background: URL(images/arm.jpg)}

h1{font-family: Times New Roman;
   font-size: 36pt;
   color: ffffff;
   font-weight: 100}

h2{font-family: Times New Roman;
   font-size: 32pt;
   color: 9966cc;
   font-weight: 100}

TD{border-style: ridge;
   border-color: 9966cc}

TD.out{border-style: none}

#focus{position: relative; width: 100%;
       top: -49;
       left: 8;
       z-index: -1}

#controls{position: relative;
          top: -40;
          width: 125}
-->
</style>
<script language=javascript>

<!--
```

```
function overItem(){
  event.srcElement.style.borderColor = "gold";
}
function offItem(){
  event.srcElement.style.borderColor = "9966cc";
}

function openText(){
        if (null==document.counter){
                document.counter = -15;
        }
        document.counter++;
        future.style.letterSpacing =
document.counter + 'pt';
        document.all.focus.style.letterSpacing =
document.counter + 'pt';
        if (document.counter<0){
                        setTimeout("openText()",30)
        }else{
                        document.counter = null
   }
}
//-->

</script>

</head>
<body bgcolor=000000 background="images/arm.jpg" on-
load="openText();" link=gold vlink=gold alink=red>
<div id=FadeMe style="width: 100%" height: 100px>
<div id="future"><h2>Future</h2></div>
<div id="focus"><h1>Focus</h1></div>
</div>
<div id="controls">
<table width=100%>
<tr>
<td id="choice1" align=right
onmouseover="overItem();"
onmouseout="offItem();">Feature</td>
</tr>
<tr>
<td id="choice2" align=right
onmouseover="overItem();"
onmouseout="offItem();">Archives</td>
</tr>
<tr>
<td id="choice4" align=right
```

```
onmouseover="overItem();"
onmouseout="offItem();">Project Cool</td>
</tr>
</table>
</div>
<div id="search" style="width: 100%;">
<base target="contents">
<form
ACTION="http://io.projectcool.com/search97cgi/vtopic
.exe">
<INPUT TYPE="hidden" NAME="action" VALUE="Fil-
terSearch">
<INPUT TYPE=HIDDEN NAME="ServerKey" VALUE="Primary">
<INPUT TYPE="hidden" NAME="resulttemplate"
VALUE="results.hts">
<INPUT TYPE="hidden" NAME="maxDocs" VALUE="100">
<INPUT TYPE="hidden" NAME="filter"
VALUE="srchflt.hts">
<INPUT TYPE="hidden" NAME="command" VALUE="GetMenu">
<INPUT TYPE="hidden" NAME="collname" VALUE="Coll3">
Search FF<br>
<textarea name=QueryText cols=12 rows=5 wrap=virtual
style="background-color: 505050; color:
ffffff"></textarea><br>
<input type=submit value=search style="color: gold;
background-color: 404040; width: 115px;">
</form></div>
</body>
</html>
```

And this is the code for the content window:

```
<html>

<head>

<TITLE>Future Focus: The Write Tools</title>

<META name="description" content="Daily Sighting,
Developer Zone and Future Focus. Explore and build
your own effective websites with Project Cool.">

<style type="text/css">

<!--

BODY{ background-image:
URL(http://www.projectcool.com/~gdavis/logo.gif);
```

```
        background-position: center center;
        background-repeat: no-repeat;
        background-attachment: fixed;
        background-color: 404040;
        font-family: Courier;
        color: limegreen;
        text-align: justify}

H1{font-family: Times New Roman;
    font-size: 24pt;
    color: 9966cc;
    background-color: 000000;
    letter-spacing: 0pt;
    text-align: right}

H2{font-family: courier;
     font-size: 18pt;
     font-weight: 400;
     text-align: center;
     background-color: black;
     color: 9966cc;
     letter-spacing: 1em}

H3{font-family: Times New Roman;
    font-size: 14pt;
    color: cccccc;
```

```
   text-align: right}

P{font-family: Courier;

   font-size: 13pt;

   line-height: 17pt;

   font-weight: 10;

   text-indent: 1em;

   text-align: justify}

PRE{font-family: Courier;

      font-size=12pt;

      color: orangered;

      lineheight: 10pt;

      margin-left: 4em}

BLOCKQUOTE{font-family: Times New Roman, Times,
Serif;

                    font-size:14}

A{color: gold}

A:link{color: gold}

A:vlink{color: gold}

-->

</style>

</head>

<h1>The Write Tools</h1>

<h3>by jack driscoll</h3>
<p>
```

One of the letters in my mail was signed "bp". Had it been written "BP", I wouldn't have had the foggiest idea who was sending me the note. But "bp" clicked quickly. I knew who the sender was; part of the identity was in the letters and part was in the presentation (lowercase) of the letters.
<p>
Whether an intelligent agent could have made this association, I don't know – but my first thought when I see lower case initials is "United Press" (the predecessor of United Press International, that is), where both I and the person who wrote the note worked many moons ago. We worked there in the days when wire service stories arrived at newspapers and radio stations in ALL CAPS. For some reason, wire service reporters—always under the gun—wrote their original stories in all lower case. The stories were then retyped for transmission by telegraph operators or teletypists.
<p>
So, it was a natural extension of this habit to write memoes in lower case. Even though I haven't worked for UP for 42 years, I still type my name in all lower case at the bottom of letters. So does "bp."
<p>
That is, until Office 97 came along! It contains the latest version of Microsoft Word, called Office Word. When writing with Office Word, it doesn't want to let me – or bp – use all lowercase characters. It wants to "correct" us. It wants to be sure we write the "right" way.
<p>
In addition to spell checking, my newest tool engages in grammar checking. Now we could argue about a lot of grammar issues. For instance, should it be:

<pre>Red, white, and blue...</pre>

Or:

<pre>Red, white and blue...</pre>

<p>
Either one could be correct, according which style guide book you follow. A computer doing grammar checking doesn't allow for this debate on the issue.

```
Its way is the only way and it strongly suggests
that you conform.
<p>
But Style A vs. Style B issues bother me less than
matters of what I would call "personal style."  With
Office 97, (damn, just now as I type this it changed
my margin settings without prompting!!), if you type
your name in lower case at the bottom of a letter,
the software goes back and capitalizes.  Properly.
Well, dammit, there are times I don't want to be
proper. Or when being "proper" removes some of the
meaning: Who is this person BP anyway?
<p>
To make matters worse, if you happen to have your
name as part of your company title, it adds words
when you try to type your name at the end of a let-
ter and you can't stop it.  My company's name is
Jack Driscoll & Associates.  If I type "jack
driscoll" and hit return, it not only turns "j" and
"d" into capitals but it adds "& Associates."  Sud-
denly I'm no longer a person!
<p>
Now there's probably a fix somewhere in the system,
but it ain't a quick fix. (Gosh, I'm surprised I got
away with typing "ain't" without getting a squiggly
red line of disapproval under it.) I'm a writer and
editor and not a software expert. I use the writing
tools to write; I want to spend my time creating
with them, not digging through books and manuals and
help files to learn to use them.  I often wish more
effort were put into making software easier to use
than making a perfect grammarian out of those of us
who like to have occasional fun with language.
<p>
Fun is part of creativity. All of which makes me
wonder...
<p>
Will "Shadowland"  ever sound the same if...

<pre>

singer k.d. lang

becomes K.D. Lang?

</pre>

<p>
```

```
Hmmm...
<p>
And what of e.e. cummings?  Somehow his words don't
have the same ring:

<pre>

i was sitting in mcsorleys... by e.e. cummings

I was sitting in McSorley's... By E.E. Cummings.

</pre>

<p>
If you think the latest version of Word does a num-
ber on mcsorleys, what will it make of the following
verse from a cummings' poem:

<pre>next to of course god america i

love you land of the pilgrims' and so forth oh

say can you see by the dawn's early my

country tis of centuries come and go

and are no more what of it we should worry

in every language even deafanddumb

</pre>

<h2>-XXX-</h2>

Do computer tools shape our creativity? Do they
change how we think and what we build? Check out our
<a href="http://www.projectcool.com/cgi-
bin/fpoint.pl">discussion area</a> to see what oth-
ers are saying and to share your thoughts.

<h2>---</h2>

<a HREF="mailto:driscoll@media.mit.edu">jack
driscoll</a> is Editor-in-Residence of the MIT Media
Lab and former Editor of the Boston Globe.
</body>
</html>
```

The following series of screenshots (Figures 10.2 to 10.6) show how the page displays on different—but commonly used—browsers and platforms. In this series of examples, we did not compensate for the different browsers; we just took the code that looked good on the most recent version of IE 4.0, which as of this writing supports the largest segment of the W3C spec, and displayed it as is.

In Figure 10.2, you can see that some—but not all—of the CSS commands are supported by Netscape Communicator 4.0. Notice how the words "Future" or "Focus" are no longer correctly positioned and how the size of the body text displays differently than it did under IE 4.0. (Of course, by the time you read this, there may be a later release of 4.0 that supports or even surpasses IE 4.0; that's the nature of browser wars.)

In Figure 10.3, you can see that some—but not all—of the CSS commands are supported by IE 3.0 on the Mac-

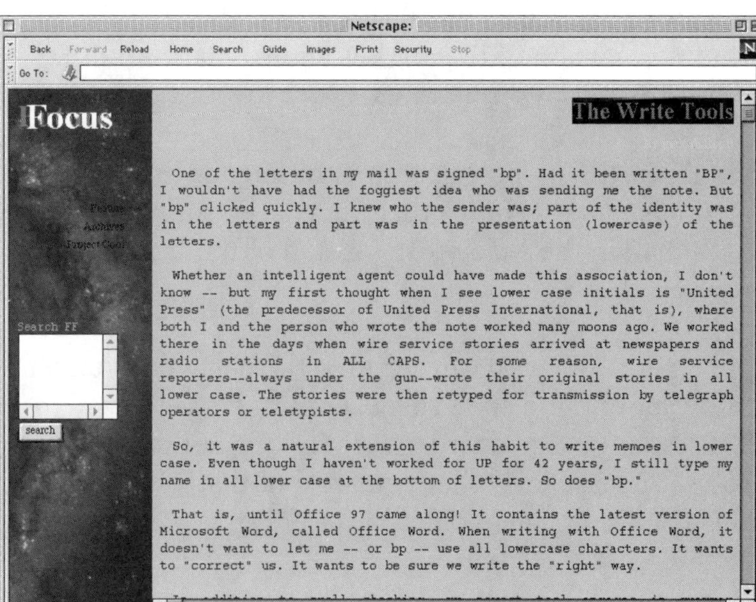

Figure 10.2
The Future Focus page as displayed by Netscape Communicator 4.0. Some CSS features are supported. Others, especially CSS placement, work differently than the W3C spec recommends.

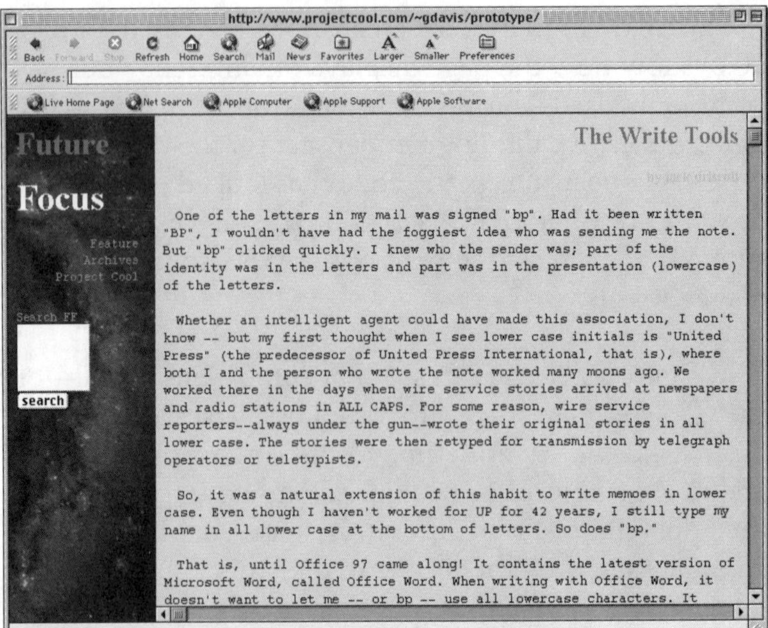

Figure 10.3
The Future Focus page as displayed by IE 3.0 for the Macintosh, which includes some, but not complete, style sheet support.

intosh. Notice yet another variation on the placement of the words "Future" and "Focus" and a lack of support for the size and background style tags for the headline. The Macintosh version of IE 3.0 is one step ahead of the Windows version of IE 3.0, thus adding platform differences to the browser war mix.

In Figure 10.4, you can see the difference IE 3.0 for Windows makes. Notice that there is less support for styles than in the Macintosh version of the "same" browser.

In Figure 10.5, you can see how the page looks under a browser with no style sheet support. It's very easy to start assuming that everyone is working at the same browser release level that you are, but that's seldom true. The results in an older browser can be somewhat dismaying.

Many industry observers are predicting that con-

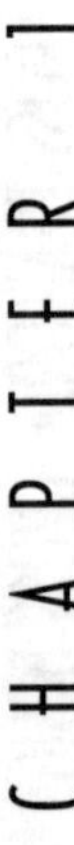

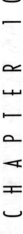

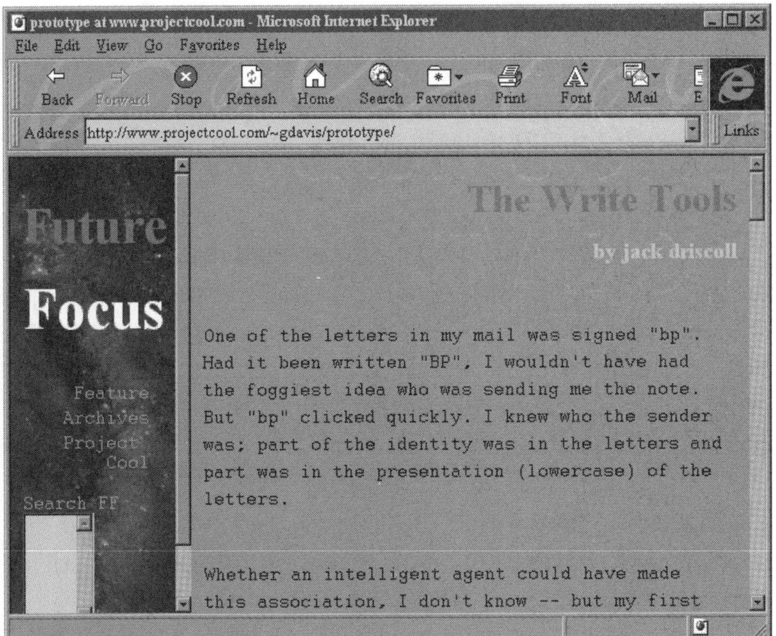

Figure 10.4
The Future Focus page as displayed by IE 3.0 for Windows, which offers less style sheet support.

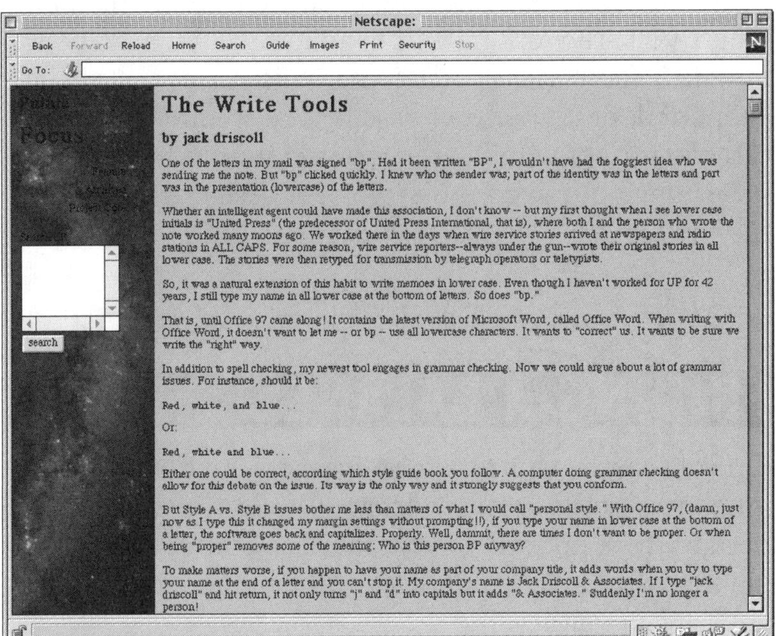

Figure 10.5
The Future Focus page as displayed by Netscape Navigator 3.0 on a Macintosh, with no support for style sheets.

sumer-focused devices like WebTV will become more and more common; being aware of the way a page displays on these types of devices may be important if your audience is the general consumer.

Now add to this the variation a user gets based on modem speed, monitor size, monitor calibration, monitor color support, computer platform, and processor speed. Many web builders are quite surprised to see how the page they loved so much on their own computer looks barely recognizable on one of their reader's computers.

No matter how much of a professional you are, no matter how many pages you design and build, it is still very easy to fall into the trap of designing for your own viewing experience. (We know we've been guilty of it!) Designing for your own environment also leaves you with fewer gray hairs—and fewer handfuls of hair between your frustrated fingertips!

Yes, designing for cross-browser use is frustrating. But unless you are working within an intranet environment in which someone is proscribing which browser will be supported, or if your user base is very specific and you can comfortably predict the browser with which it will be visiting your page, cross-browser design is a necessary evil.

So what's a web designer to do?

FINDING A BALANCE

One of the first things is to stay sane. Don't be overwhelmed by the browser debate. While cross-browser design and support is a very real issue that you shouldn't ignore, you can't support every possible browser on the entire planet either.

A few years ago, we knew someone who contracted to test a set of pages with all possible browsers upon which the pages might be displayed. The matrix yielded something like 36 different combinations of browsers and computer platforms with an estimated three-month test period. The page owners felt compelled to support any and every combination. Development ground to a halt when faced with the seemingly insurmountable challenge the browser issue created. Eventually, someone just threw up his or her hands and said "Enough is enough. We've not supporting everything!" That was a wise person.

Balance is important when thinking about browser support. On one hand, you need to be aware of the different ways your pages might be viewed. On the other, you don't want to spend your entire production cycle doing nothing but creating endless variations on the same page. There's a middle ground that each web builder needs to find.

TIP: ***Apply a sense of balance. Balance the need for browser support and the number of browsers you'll worry about with the reality of the web and its possibilities. Dont' let browser support issues drive you crazy.***

No matter what you do, someone out there in cyberspace will complain that they can't read your page, that your page loads "funny," that the colors of your links don't look "right" on the screen, that the page is too dark, too light, or too graphic heavy. Someone will complain that he or she is color blind and why didn't you think of that when you built your page? Yet another person will tell you that he or she has been using a version of Lynx since 1995 and can't see graphics/frames/tables—why didn't you think about them when building your page?!?! Listen to your readers' feedback, but temper it with reality. Is this a one-time complaint or is the complaint raising an issue that impacts a slice of your readership?

Don't let yourself fall into the trap of the "least common denominator" web page. If you limit yourself to the original HTML tags, you'll have a very basic page of text and links. Period. Today, most readers don't find the gray background and long scrolling areas very exciting. You may be safe for every possible permutation of browser, but you'll also be boring and rather ineffective.

Balance browser support with the needs of your content and with the reality of your web publishing world and your core readers.

FINDING THE READERS

We don't mean to sound like a broken record repeating itself over and over, but your audience defines what makes sense for your site. Don't forget to ask:

- What platforms are my readers using?
- What browsers are they using?

TIP: *Remember thine readers. It can't be said often enough—understand your readers' environment and make it the prime consideration for browser support.*

If you are working in an intranet environment, go ahead and design specifically for your supported browser. If you are designing for Windows programmers whom you know download the latest of everything, design for the latest version of IE. If you are designing for a family market, think about 14.4 modem access and AOL browsers.

There are several ways to get a sense of which browsers your readers are using.

Common Sense

Don't overlook this basic tool. If you have some understanding of who you want to visit your site, you can probably interpolate some information about their viewing environment.

This means that the answer to "who is my audience?" cannot be "everyone on the web." Reality check! Nothing in any medium can attract "everyone." Be more selective and think about your ideal user; try to absorb and understand as many details about this person as you can. If you have market research tools at your command, take common sense one step further and learn all you can about your market and how it uses technology.

When you design, you have someone in your mind. That's a good place to start. And start by doing what seems logical for them.

TIP: *Apply some common sense. Sometime doing the logical thing is the logical thing.*

Log Files

Once your site is up and running, look at your log files, specifically the access log or the user agent log. Both these logs record which browser made each call to the server.

TIP: *Look to the logs. Your log files can supply you with valuable hard data about who is using your site, with what browser and what platform. Take a look at this information from time to time.*

This code shows one entry from a typical access log. This log is presented in standard NCSA format and typically appears in your log file in one long line. Depending on how busy your site is, you may have hundreds or thousands of these entries.

```
dialin65.oanet.com - - [31/Jul/1997:12:45:48 -0700]
"GET
/developer/venus/venu0017.gif HTTP/1.1" 304 -
"http://www.projectcool.com/developer/options.html"
"Mozilla/4.0
(compatible; MSIE 4.0b2; Windows 95)"
```

- The first item in the log describes where the user is coming from. If it is a dial-in connection, you'll see the text "dialin." You might also see that the location is a proxy server or a particular domain name.
- The next item is the date and time stamp that notes when this user accessed your server.
- The third item is what the user did. Typically, this is what URL or page item the user's browser was requesting.
- After that is the "referring page," or the place from which the reader is making the request. In this example, the user is within the "options.html" page when his or her browser requests the image "venu0017.gif."
- Next is something called the "user agent." This describes the type of device your reader is using. Anything with the phrase "Mozilla" is a web browser.
- Last is the item you've been waiting for. In parentheses, at the end of the log entry, is the browser name, version, and computer platform your reader was using when he or she accessed your site. If you don't see a specific web browser named, the browser is Netscape Navigator, of the version specified in the user agent.
- In this example, the reader was using MSIE 4.0b2—

Microsoft Internet Explorer, version 4.0b2. The platform was a Windows 95 machine.

The access log easily becomes quite large in size. If you are running and storing one, you'll probably want to purge it routinely or it will quickly eat up your disk space. For many people, taking a peek at the access log once a month or so is enough to give you a sense of who and what is accessing your site.

Following is a sample entry from the user access log. This log records less information than the full access log; it focuses specifically on user agent, browser, and platform.

```
Mozilla/2.02E-KIT  (Win95; U)
Mozilla/2.02E-KIT  (Win95; U)
Mozilla/2.02E-KIT  (Win95; U)
Mozilla/2.02E-KIT  (Win95; U)
Mozilla/2.0 (compatible; MSIE 3.0; Update a; SK;
Windows 95)
Mozilla/2.02E-KIT  (Win95; U)
Mozilla/2.0 (compatible; MSIE 3.0; Update a; SK;
Windows 95)
Mozilla/2.0 (compatible; MSIE 3.0; Update a; SK;
Windows 95)
Mozilla/3.0Gold (WinNT; I)
Mozilla/3.0Gold (Win95; I)
Mozilla/4.0 (compatible; MSIE 4.0b2; Windows 95)
Mozilla/4.0 (compatible; MSIE 4.0b2; Windows 95)
Mozilla/4.0 (compatible; MSIE 4.0b2; Windows 95)
Mozilla/2.0 (compatible; MSIE 3.02; Windows NT)
Mozilla/3.0Gold (Win95; I)
Mozilla/3.0Gold (Win95; I)
Mozilla/3.0Gold (Win95; I)
Mozilla/3.0Gold (Win95; I)
Mozilla/2.0 (compatible; MSIE 3.02; Windows NT)
Mozilla/3.0Gold (Win95; I)
Mozilla/3.0Gold (Win95; I)
Mozilla/2.0 (compatible; MSIE 3.02; Windows NT)
Mozilla/2.0 (compatible; MSIE 3.02; Windows NT)
```

- First is the user agent. Anything with the word "Mozilla" is a web browser.

- Next, in parentheses, is the browser type and computer platform. If you don't see a specific web browser named, the browser is Netscape Navigator, of the version specified in the user agent.

  In this snippet of log file, you'll see that few users are coming in with Navigator 2.0 on Windows 95 machines. A few users in the middle are accessing the site with IE 3.0, update 1, on Windows 95 machines. Near the bottom are a cluster of users working with Navigator 3.0 on Windows machines. At the very bottom are a couple of users working on NT boxes, with IE 3.02.

There are also commercial programs that analyze your log files and compile reports about their content. These programs make the log files more accessible and understandable and, if tracking reader use and access mode is important, may be a worthwhile investment for you.

User Surveys

There is also the time-tested method of actually asking your readers what they are using. You can set up a simple form that automatically records your reader's responses as to which computer and which browser they are using. A survey isn't as accurate as seeing actual log files, but it can give you a sense of what your readers' environment is like.

TIP: *If you aren't sure, ask. Ask your readers about what they use to view your site and what they do and don't like about the results. Then, listen to them.*

Let your readership be your guide. None will serve you better.

FINDING THE SCOPE

The most common "disease" on the web might be called "because you can." There are people who use every new feature for no other reason than the features are available—at least on that person's machine. Don't fall into this trap.

But don't fall into the trap of avoiding every new feature, either. A lack of support or a different style of support doesn't necessarily mean the end of your page to the noncompliant browser. If you are interested in a particular feature, understand how it acts under different conditions—the support difference may be smaller than you think and not really worth worrying about.

TIP: ***Don't "just do it." Just because you can doesn't mean you should. Don't fall into the trap of using technology for the sole reason that your browser and computer let you.***

As you examine the cross-browser issue, look at your content and the newest feature sets.

- Where are there logical matches?
- Where are there likely to be problems with browser compatibility?
- Is the benefit of the feature worth the possible incompatibility?
- How severe is the incompatibility? Will it crash a noncompliant browser or will the text just appear black instead of goldenrod?
- What percentage of your readership (yup, remember those readers!) will see the feature versus what percentage will miss it?
- How quickly is this feature spreading on the web?

The more you understand the scope of the compatibility issue for the features you want to use, the better judgment you'll be able to make on using or not using them.

TIP: *Understand the scope of the browser issue. Are you looking at a browser-crashing incompatibility or a minor difference in text display? The level of incompatibility helps define how—and if—you design around it.*

Tables and frames are good examples of features that caused big problems for designers when they were first introduced. But they offered obvious benefits and within a matter of months, the latest versions of most browsers offered reasonable (and reasonably similar) support. Within a year, the browsers that offered this support had saturated the market. Today it is rare for anyone to wonder if they dare use tables or not.

JavaScript and Cascading Style Sheets (CSS) are the latest example of the features that are causing the most hand wringing. JavaScript support (although still varied) is becoming increasingly common because the feature offers so many benefits for sites, their creators, and their readers. Many web builders are scripting their sites on the belief that in a very short time most readers will have browsers that support a reasonable version of JavaScript.

CSS is a slightly different story. Although there are obvious benefits to using styles, the support for styles is spotty and uneven, and the results are quite different from browser to browser. It doesn't add the same interactive aspect that JavaScript does and so may be a less-compelling feature; the jury is still out on how much pressure there will be on the different vendors to adopt a consistent implementation of CSS. We suspect that in a year or so CSS will become commonly, and more or less consistently, supported, but it hasn't taken off with the same speed as JavaScript. But then again, tables took off faster than frames and both are in common use today.

FINDING THE FOOD CHAIN

One way to think about design for multiple browsers is to see the different browsers in a sort of food chain. At the top of the food chain are the latest releases with the largest set of supported features. At the bottom of the food chain are the oldest browsers with the least level of support.

When you think about the design of a cross-browser page, think about the features that last throughout the food chain and use them as a base. That way, the littlest fish will still see a page that is understandable and usable, even if it doesn't have JavaScripted mouseovers and fancy styles.

Each step up the food chain, add a layer of features. At the very top, go all out. Do your dream page, but choose the features and implement them in a way that doesn't "break" the browsers that are lower on the food chain.

TIP: *Think of browsers as a food chain. Create a scaleable page by keeping a basic core and adding elements to it.*

Think about the food chain, and you'll have an approach that creates a scaleable page—one that functions (albeit very basically) at one level and performs to its best at another.

Here are some things to think about as you work your way up and down the browser food chain. These are by no means hard and fast rules; rather, they are some suggestions that may help you work through some of the browser compatibility issues. Some of these ideas will also make your pages accessible for groups of people who are using the web in untraditional ways, such as through voice synthesizers or Braille readers.

- First and most importantly, be sure that if you are doing something fancy for the "bigger fish," the smaller fish can use some part of it.

  Don't fall so in love with certain features that the bottom half of the food chain falls off your map. For example, when Netscape was promoting its "layer" approach, it was very easy to create pages that looked great under the latest and greatest Netscape browser, but which displayed blank pages when viewed under an older browser. This was not a scaleable page, and it wasn't a page that was friendly to anyone but those with the newest Netscape browser.

- Include useful "alt" text in your graphics. There are still readers who turn off graphics or who can't see them; including useful alt text ensures they don't lose important information that may be embedded in the graphic.

  For example, if all your menu options are in buttons and you don't specify alt text, there will be no navigation options for people who aren't seeing the graphics.

- Include text links at the bottom of your page, in addition to graphical menu buttons or imagemaps. That way, you'll be sure readers can always access the options on your page.

- Consider having a <noframes> version of your framed pages. This lets people with older browsers use your site comfortably.

- Don't assume that readers will be seeing your display choices. Some readers set up their systems to their own preferences; for example, they set custom font sizes in their browser options menu.

- If you are using style sheets, make sure the style information is commented out so that your pages are still usable with non-CSS browsers. And take a look at how the page displays without styles—make sure the pages are still functional.
- If you are specifying fonts, make sure your font selection will work across platforms and include a generic alternative for readers who don't have the font.
- If you are using JavaScripting, comment out the scripts so that your pages are still usable with non-JavaScript browsers. As long as the script is commented out, the browser will happily display the rest of the HTML page.
- Make sure that your design is not script dependent and that it will still function even if your reader's browser doesn't support scripting—or if the reader has scripting turned off.
- A common use of scripting is to create mouseover effects. If your site uses mouseovers, make sure the page is still functional without the mouseover effects and that you are not using the technology to hide crucial information.
- If you are using Dynamic HTML, make sure that critical parts of your page aren't hidden from browsers that don't support DHTML.

  For example, if you are using DHTML to create fold-out lists or outlines, be sure your design allows the full outline to be visible to non-DHTML browsers so that your readers don't lose content.
- Plug-ins can add value, but don't require that a read-

er have them in order to access the page. Or provide some alternate means of presenting or noting the information so that the reader knows what is going on.

For example, if you are relying on a Shockwave presentation, don't leave your non-Shocked readers with a large gray box, a broken icon, and no information about what they might be seeing.

FINDING THE BROWSER

Sometimes you will need to—or want to—create different versions of your page for readers using different browsers. You can implement these different browsers by incorporating a JavaScripted browser detection routine at the top of your default page. The browser detection routine identifies the type of browser that is accessing your page and tells the server to deliver the appropriate page.

TIP: *Browser detection is a good use of JavaScripting. An intelligently used browser detection script can automatically route your readers to the pages that match their particular browser types.*

You'll find an example of a browser detection script in the JavaScript section of this book. A downloadable script is also available at the companion website to this book. In addition, the Project Cool JavaScript Developer Zone and Reference sections (http://www.projectcool.com/devsearch) contain browser detection routines and information on the latest browsers and their identification names.

The browser detection routine is nearly invisible to your readers; they just see the page that works for them. You'll need to decide how many browsers to test for and whether the effort of testing, creating, and delivering different pages is worth the effort.

Many people use browser detection routines when they want to be sure a JavaScript effect works—JavaScript is one of those feature sets that is supported slightly differently in different browser versions. Often, the interactivity which is added by a script is indeed worth the effort of maintaining separate pages.

Another way to route people with different browsers is to create an entry page that offers different links. You'll sometimes see this approach when there is a "low graphic" and "high graphic" version of a site. This involves no scripting at all; simply create an entry page that will work on any browser. On the page, give the reader the option of clicking on the path they want to follow through your site.

Be careful, however, of creating too many different paths. You'll need to maintain them all, and few people have the time, energy, or interest in maintaining multiple versions of the same site. After a while, you'll probably see that readers are using one option more than another. (Look to your WHAT NAME log for information about what pages are most-often accessed on your site and compare the access numbers of your different paths.) This is the time to take this information as valuable feedback and focus your development efforts on the more popular path.

FINDING THE TEST

Testing isn't sexy. It isn't exciting. And it is easily forgotten.

However, testing is critical to understanding how your site reacts under different viewing conditions—don't underestimate the power of the test.

TIP: *Don't forget to test.*

Try looking at your pages under two different browsers on two different computer platforms.

If possible, it is a good idea to look at your pages on both a PC and a Macintosh, and with at least two different browsers. You don't need to do a detailed functionality test, but do take 5 or 10 minutes to scan through the site and spot-check different areas. It's a valuable sanity pitstop, and it may open your eyes to the various ways your readers may be seeing your site.

There is no magic bullet for the issue of browser compatibility. The best way to deal with it is to apply some simple common sense. Remember your readers and design for them. Create a scaleable page that provides at least basic functionality for the small end of the food chain. And most importantly, test your solutions to be sure that they really do work.

Browser compatibility doesn't need to drag you down, quash your creativity, drain the life from your great ideas, or force the world to accept lowest-common-denominator websites. With a little thought, you can create pages that dazzle—but don't deny access.

Someday we may be able to design one set of pages that work universally, but that day is still a ways off. Standards are, for now, sort of general guidelines. Multiple browsers, and the occasional flaring up of vendor-to-vendor browser wars, are the reality. We can't change it; we can just find the best ways to live within it.

When we finally implemented the Future Focus design you saw in Figure 10.1, we used some combination of all the different approaches to create a version that works, in one way or another, on different platforms and browsers. Because of what we know about our reader base—from both logs and user surveys—we set Navigator 3.0 as our lowest-level browser. (We found very few readers were using anything earlier than that and trends were showing an ongoing upgrade motion.) We used the latest technology that made sense for our content, and also used a browser detection routine to provide alternative versions of the page. Over time, the set of browsers supported will change, as will the alternative pages and browser detection routines. Like everything else on the web, cross-browser compatibility is an ever-moving target.

And these browser battles, as frustrating as they may feel when we are designing pages, are actually beneficial to the industry as a whole. If Netscape didn't feel it had to leapfrog Microsoft which feels it has to leapfrog Netscape, we'd probably still be creating text-and-link pages and wondering what all the fuss over the web is about.

APPENDIX A
CASCADING STYLE SHEETS STYLE PROPERTIES

This appendix summaries the style properties supported by Cascading Style Sheets.

There are five categories of properties:

- **Text**, which lets you control basic text formatting. Some of these can also be applied to nontext elements.
- **Font**, which lets you control basic font characteristics.
- **Color and Background**, which lets you control the color and background of elements.
- **Placement**, which lets you specify where an element gets placed within its "box."
- **Classification**, which lets you classify elements by object type and assign characteristics based on those object types.

Remember: Not all implementations of style sheets support all these attributes. When in doubt, test the attributes with your browser or browsers of choice.

Remember also that CSS is still evolving and these new styles will likely appear as time goes by.

TEXT PROPERTIES

Property	Description	Values	Example
word-spacing	Lets you control the space between words.	normal XX units	p {word-spacing: 10px} Puts 10px of space between the start of one word and the start of the next.
letter-spacing	Lets you control the space between letters.	normal XX units	p {letter-spacing: 5px} Prevents 5px of space between the left edge of one letter and the left edge of the next..
text-decoration	Sets underlining, overlining, strike-through, or blink attributes for the element. Vendors may be adding their own text decoration formats as well.	underline overline line-through blink none	H1 {text-decoration: underline} Make all level-one headlines underlined .
text-transform	Sets the case of the text.	capitalize uppercase lowercase none	p {text-transform: capitalize} Capitalizes the first character of each word in the paragraph. H2 {text-transform: uppercase} Displays all level-two heads in all uppercase characters.
vertical-align	Aligns the element vertically to the baseline. Can be very useful with images.	baseline sub super top text-top middle bottom text-bottom	img {vertical-align: middle} Places the image in the middle of the baseline.

Property	Description	Values	Example

`text-align`	Aligns the element horizontally across the page or within the division.	`left`
		`right`
		`center`
		`justify`
			`H3 {text-align: center}`
			
			Centers all level-three heads.

`text-indent`	Sets the amount of indent for the first line of a text block.	XX units %	`p {text-indent: 2em}` Indents the first line of the paragraph 2 em spaces.
`line-height`	Also referred to as "leading" or "linespace"in desktop publishing or typesetting. Specifies the distance between baselines of consecutive lines of text.	normal XX units %	`p {line-height: 12pt}` Sets 12 points of space from baseline to baseline in the paragraph.

FONT PROPERTIES

Property	Description	Values	Example

`font-family`	Specifies the font family, or typeface, to use for the element. You can specify a series of names and the first available font is used.	`family name`
		
		`generic name: serif, sans-serif, cursive, fantasy, monospace`
			`p {font-family: futura, helvetica, arial, \sans-serif}`
			
			Displays the paragraph in Futura, if available. If not, try Helvetica, Arial, and finally, any sans-serif display.

`font-style`	Specifies the style of type to use for the element.	`normal`
		`italic`
		`oblique`
			`H2 { font-family: futura, helvetica, arial; font-style: italic}`
			
			Uses the italic variation of the typeface for all H2s.

`font-variant`	Lets you select the small caps style of the typeface.	`normal` `small-caps`	`H2 { font-family: futura, helvetica, arial; font-variant: small-caps}`

Property	Description	Values	Example
			Uses the small caps variation of the typeface for all H2s.

`font-weight`	Lets you select the weight or boldness of the font.	`lighter`
		`normal`
		`bold`
		`bolder`
		`100`
		`200`
		`300`
		`400`
		`500`
		`600`
		`700`
		`800`
		`900`
			`blockquote {font-weight: bold}`
			
			Makes the block quote bold.

`font-size`	Lets you select the size of the type in the element. Font size may be specified in absolute units or larger relative to the "current" size.	`XX units`
		`XX %`
		—
		`smaller`
		`xx-small`
		`x-small`
		`small`
		`medium`
		`large`
		`x-large`
		`xx-large`
			`p {font-size: 12pt}`
			
			Displays the paragraph in 12-point type.
			
			`H1 {font-size: 150%}`
			
			Displays all level-one heads at 150 percent of their normal size.

COLOR AND BACKGROUND PROPERTIES

Property	Description	Values	Example

`color`	Sets the color of the element.	`color name`
		`hex value`
		`RGB (R%, G%, B%)`
		`RGB (R, G, B)`
			`p {color: red}`
			
			Displays the paragrah text in red.

`background-color`	Sets the color for the background of the element.	`color name`
		`hex value`
		`RGB %`
			`H1 {background-color: green}`
			Displays the background area of all H1s as green. (The effect is like having a green bar behind the headline.)

Property	Description	Values	Example
`background-image`	Specifies an image to use for the background of an element.	`URL(URL Name)`	`blockquote {background-image: url(../images/sand.gif)}` Displays the image "sand.gif" in the background area of the block quote.

`background-repeat`	Specifies how and if a background image is repeated.	`repeat`
		`repeat-x`
		`repeat-y`
		`no-repeat`
			`blockquote {background-image: url(../images/sand.gif); background-repeat: repeat}`
			
			Displays the image "sand.gif" in the background area of the block quote and repeats the image both vertically and horizontally to fill the entire background area.

`background-attachment`	Lets you attach the background image so that it doesn't scroll.	`scroll` `fixed`	`blockquote {background-image: url(../images/sand.gif); background-attachment: fixed}` Displays the image "sand.gif" in the background area of the block quote and prevents the background image from scrolling.

`background-position`	Sets the initial position of the background image.	`% (for vertical)`
		`% (for horizontal)`
		`top`
		`center`
		`bottom`
		`left`
		`center`
		`right`
			`body {background-image: url(../images/sand.gif); background-position: center center}`
			
			Centers the background image vertically and horizontally on the initial body screen.

PLACEMENT PROPERTIES

Property	Description	Values	Example
`margin-top`	Places the top margin of the element; you can use negative values.	XX unit XX % auto	`div {margin-top: 2em}` Displays the top margin of the division 2 em spaces down from the last vertical element.
`margin-bottom`	Places the bottom margin of the element; you can use negative values.	XX unit XX % auto	`div {margin-bottom: 10%}` Places the bottom margin of the div element 10 percent down the page and displays the element from the bottom up.
`margin-left`	Places the left margin of the element; you can use negative values.	XX unit XX % auto	`div {margin-left: 6em}` Displays the left margin of the div 6 em spaces from the left edge of the page.
`margin-right`	Places the right margin of the element; you can use negative values.	XX unit XX % auto	`div {margin-right: 1em}` Displays the right margin of the div 1 em space from the right edge of the table.
`padding-top`	Inserts padding at the top of the element. auto	XX unit XX %	`table {padding-top: 12pt}` Inserts 12 points of space at the top of the table.
`padding-bottom`	Inserts padding at the bottom of the element.	XX unit XX % auto	`table {padding-bottom: 12pt}` Inserts 12 points of space at the bottom of the table.
`padding-left`	Inserts padding at the left of the element.	XX unit XX %	`table {padding-left: 2 em}`

Property	Description	Values	Example
		auto	Inserts 2 em spaces at the left margin of the table.
padding-right	Inserts padding at the right of the element.	XX unit XX % auto	table {padding-right: 2 em} Inserts 2 em spaces at the right margin of the table.
border-width	Sets the width of the element's border.	thin medium thick none	div {border-width: thin} Displays a thin border around the table.
border-style	Sets the style of the element's border.	none dotted double solid double groove ridge inset outset	table {border-style: double} Displays a double border around the table.
border-color	Sets the color of the element's border.	color name hex value RGB (R%, G%, B%) RGB (R, G, B)	table {border-color: red} Displays a red border around the table.
border border-top border-bottom border-left border-right	Sets the width, color, and style of a border simultaneously.	width value style value color value	table {border thick double red} Displays a thick, double, red border around the table. table {border-top thin double red} Displays a thin, double, red border at the top of the table.

Property	Description	Values	Example
`height`	Sets the height of the element.	`XX units`	`img.button {height: 70px}` Sets all the button class im ages to be 70 pixels high.
`width`	Sets the width of the element.	`XX units`	`img.button {width: 100px}` Sets all the button class images to be 100 pixels wide.
`float`	Places the element to the left or right and flows text around it.	`right/ left/none`	`img.button {float: left}` Places a button class image to the left margin and flows text around it.
`clear`	Prevents text from flowing around the element.	`right/ left/none`	`img.button {clear: left}` Places a button class image to the left margin and prevents any text or other elements from flowing beside it.

CLASSIFICATION ATTRIBUTES

Property	Description	Values	Example

`display`	Specifies the category of object an element belongs to: a block element, like a heading or paragraph; an in-line element, like emphasis or anchors; or a list-item element. If the category is `none`, the content of the element should not be displayed at all.	`none`
		`""`
		—
		`block`
		`inline`
		`list-item`
			`p {display: none}`
			
			Hide the contents of the paragraph.
			
			`p {display: ""}`
			
			Display the contents of the paragraph.
			
			`p {display: block}`
			
			Treats the paragraph as a block element, which can be positioned separately using the positioning attributes.

Property	Description	Values	Example

`white-space`	Describes how whitespace should be handled within the block elements.	`normal`
		`pre`
		`nowrap`
			`p {white-space: nowrap}`
			
			The paragraph lines will break only with a specific
			 tag.

`list-style-type`	Sets the type of symbol that appears in front of a list item.	`disc`
		`circle`
		`square`
		`decimal`
		`lower-roman`
		`upper-roman`
		`lower-alpha`
		`upper-alpha`
			`ul { list-style-type: square }`
			
			Unordered list items will use a square bullet.

`list-style-position`	Describes how the bullet marker and text in a list line up with each other.	`inside`
		`outside`
			`ul { list-style-position: outside }`
			
			Creates the effect of a hanging indent.
			
			`ul { list-style-position: inside }`
			
			The bullet and the second line of text are flush left.

`list-style-image`	Selects a specific image to serve as a bullet in front of list items.	`URL (URL Name)`	`ul {list-style-image:URL (../images.logo. gif)}` Unordered list items will use the image "logo.gif" as a bullet.

APPENDIX B COLOR NAMES AND HEX VALUES

Color	Hex Value
aliceblue	f0f8ff
antiquewhite	faebd7
aqua	00ffff
aquamarine	7fffd4
azure	f0ffff
beige	f5f5dc
bisque	ffe4c4
black	000000
blanchedalmond	ffebcd
blue	0000ff
blueviolet	8a2be2
brown	a52a2a
burlywood	deb887
cadetblue	5f9ea0
chartreuse	7fff00
chocolate	d2691e
coral	ff7f50
cornflowerblue	6495ed
cornsilk	fff8dc
crimson	dc143c
cyan	00ffff
darkblue	00008b

Color	Hex Value
darkcyan	008b8b
darkgoldenrod	b8b60b
darkgray	a9a9a9
darkgreen	006400
darkkhaki	bdb76b
darkmagenta	8b008b
darkolivegreen	556b2f
darkorange	ff8c00
darkorchid	9932cc
darkred	8b0000
darksalmon	e9967a
darkseagreen	8fbc8f
darkslateblue	483d8b
darkslategray	2f4f4f
darkturquoise	00ced1
darkviolet	9400d3
deeppink	ff1493
deepskyblue	00bfff
dimgray	696969
dodgerblue	1e90ff
firebrick	b22222
floralwhite	fffaf0
forestgreen	228b22
fuchsia	ff00ff
gainsboro	dcdcdc
ghostwhite	f8f8ff
gold	ffd700
goldenrod	daa520
gray	808080
green	008000
greenyellow	adff2f
honeydew	f0fff0
hotpink	ff69b4
indianred	cd5c5c
indigo	4b0082
ivory	fffff0
khaki	f0e68c

Color	Hex Value
lavender	e6e6fa
lavenderblush	fff0f5
lawngreen	7cfc00
lemonchiffon	fffacd
lightblue	add8e6
lightcoral	f08080
lightcyan	e0ffff
lightgoldenrodyellow	fafad2
lightgreen	90ee90
lightgrey	d3d3d3
lightpink	ffb6c1
lightsalmon	ffa07a
lightseagreen	20b2aa
lightskyblue	87cefa
lightslategray	778899
lightsteelblue	b0c4de
lightyellow	ffffe0
lime	00ff00
limegreen	32cd32
linen	faf0e6
magenta	ff00ff
maroon	800000
mediumaquamarine	66cdaa
mediumblue	0000cd
mediumorchid	ba55d3
mediumpurple	9370db
mediumseagreen	3cb371
mediumslateblue	7b68ee
mediumspringgreen	00fa9a
mediumturquoise	48d1cc
mediumvioletred	c71585
midnightblue	191970
mintcream	f5fffa
mistyrose	ffe4e1
moccasin	ffe4b5
navajowhite	ffdead
navy	000080

Color	Hex Value
oldlace	fdf5e6
olive	808000
olivedrab	6b8e23
orange	ffa500
orangered	ff4500
orchid	da70d6
palegoldenrod	eee8aa
palegreen	98fb98
paleturquoise	afeeee
palevioletred	db7093
papayawhip	ffefd5
peachpuff	ffdab9
peru	cd853f
pink	ffc0cd
plum	dda0dd
powderblue	b0e0e6
purple	800080
red	ff0000
rosybrown	bc8f8f
royalblue	4169e1
saddlebrown	8b4513
salmon	fa8072
sandybrown	f4a460
seagreen	2e8b57
seashell	fff5ee
sienna	a0522d
silver	c0c0c0
skyblue	87ceed
slateblue	6a5acd
slategray	708090
snow	fffafa
springgreen	00ff7f
steelblue	4682b4
tan	d2b48c
teal	008080
thistle	d8bfd8
tomato	ff6347

Color	Hex Value
turquoise	40e0d0
violet	ee82ee
wheat	f5deb3
white	ffffff
whitesmoke	f5f5f5
yellow	ffff00
yellowgreen	a9cd32

AFTERWORD

We hope that this book has given you some ideas for different ways that you can take your website to that next level, to enhance it with new (but useful!) features, and to add value for your readers.

We know that our own site is never done. By its very nature, the web makes everything a work in progress. Sometimes it might feel a bit overwhelming to try to keep up with the latest options, the latest technology, and the latest toys but that's part of the fun, too.

On the web, nothing is set in stone. Sure, there are times we all want to shout out "I'm done with my site!" and reach that sense of closure one gets when sending a print product off to the printers or the video off to be duplicated. In a way, though, working on the web is better than that. With each redesign, with each update, we can get a sense of accomplishment, a sense that something has been completed and is now presented to the world. And, we don't get penalized for making a mistake.

One of the best things about the web is that one can

play, one can try things and test things and see how it works . . . and if the approach doesn't work it's no big deal. Just undo it. Or do it a different way. Because the final product is never quite permanently printed, pressed, or recorded, there is always room for change. That means a freedom to experiment that we've never known before.

Experimentation is fun. It means we can start incorporating the things that we learn as we learn them. It means we can keep growing—and have our site reflect our growth. The two-way feedback cycle between us and our readers gives us useful input on what does—and doesn't—work. Not only are we creating a dynamic medium, but we are also working in one. And that is cool.

Whether you are building a personal page, a hobby page, a corporate site, a small business presentation, a publication, or anything else, this sense of the dynamic is something that all web builders share. It's what got so many of us hooked. It's the way the web is always offering up some tantalizing new possibilities, the way it makes us say "what if we tried this . . ."

The web is coming into its own as a medium. The tools that help make sites more interactive are starting to help us make that leap from printed-page-on-computer-screen or slimmed-down-CD-ROM to something that is carving its own place in the world. No longer limited to unmoving pages with links, the web is coming alive. That's exciting too.

The various new tools and technologies —from search functions to DHTML to multi-media applications—each plays a role in breaking the known paradigms of communication. Understanding how existing media work is helpful—but to take the next big leap we all have to embrace the web for what it is: it's own form, with rules that don't follow a pre-designated path.

The web isn't print.

Throw away the notion of complete control over the what the reader sees. On the web it just doesn't happen. The web is not a static page. There are variations you can't predict, some caused by technology and some caused by reader preference. The web responds to what readers do in a way that just isn't part of the print structure or the print mindset. Print is an ice-cube; the web is a moving fluid.

The web isn't television.

The web is non-linear and non-passive. The reader is engaged in directing his or her experience. He or she is not just sitting back and watching. There may be some moves afoot to make the web more television-like but if they succeed the web will no longer exist. We'll have only created another delivery band for the same old stuff we get over the air or over cable or via satellite today.

The web isn't CD-ROM.

This medium is not fixed on a disc. It changes, it updates, it is many packages all woven together. It hooks into the networked world and isn't a local experience. It doesn't sit on a retail shelf wrapped in pretty packaging. It is, by its nature, a real-time medium.

The web isn't computer applications.

Yes, lots of people watch the web with a browser on a computer, but the web is no spreadsheet or word processor. It has no clearly definable course of action, no specific outcome shared by its users. And the role of the personal computer as a viewing device for the web is in the process of changing—it remains the predominant viewing device but is no longer the *only* viewing device. And no one is quite certain where this trend is going.

"So what is the web?" you ask.

Well, the web is print. The web is television. The web is CD-ROM. The web is computer applications. The web is a little of all of these, but not equivalent to any of them. The web, as you build it and your friend builds it and your company builds it and your cousin builds it . . . as everyone in the web community tweaks and creates it is this: a giant work in progress.

All of us, by our work with various tools and various approaches, are answering that question day by day. Each time we find a new use for JavaScript or add a DHTML event, each time we figure out how sound can enhance our message or make the graphics perform faster and smoother we are answering a piece of the question.

So tell me again, what is the web? The web is what we make it. Good luck and happy site building!

INDEX